John Mc Loughlin (September 1981, London)
Mediaeval History. T— T— Dublin.

D0421717

University of London Historical Studies

XII

UNIVERSITY OF LONDON HISTORICAL STUDIES

TWELFTH-CENTURY DECRETAL COLLECTIONS

TO
MY MOTHER

AND TO
PATRICK DUGGAN
MILL HILL FATHER
UGANDA

Twelfth-century Decretal Collections

and their importance in English history

by

CHARLES DUGGAN

UNIVERSITY OF LONDON

THE ATHLONE PRESS

1963

Published by
THE ATHLONE PRESS
UNIVERSITY OF LONDON
at 2 *Gower Street, London* WC1

Distributed by Constable & Co. Ltd
12 *Orange Street, London* WC2

U.S.A.
Oxford University Press Inc
New York

© *Charles Duggan,* 1963

Printed in Great Britain by
WESTERN PRINTING SERVICES LTD
BRISTOL

PREFACE

Between the publication of Gratian's *Decretum* and the Counter-Reformation legislation of the Council of Trent, four centuries later, decretal letters or papal rescripts were the staple instruments of papal jurisdictional authority; and to this extent their importance has long been recognized. But at the beginning of that long period, and especially in the pontificate of Alexander III (1159–81), they are of exceptional interest not only to the historian of canon law in general, but in a particular way to the historian of the Church in England. As a result of the gradual expansion of decretal legislation during the twelfth century, canon lawyers were increasingly interested in decretal letters as a separate species of papal legislative authority, and attached a new importance to canonical collections composed predominantly of contemporary decretal decisions, considered at first merely as appendices to the *Decretum*. The present study is based primarily on the earliest of these collections, drawn up in the closing years of Alexander III's pontificate and shortly after, since their importance in preparing the way for later canonical developments and their general historical significance are still without a full or satisfactory treatment. But no attempt is made here to provide a complete or final analysis of the many unpublished manuscripts, since a definitive edition of twelfth-century decretal letters, based on all known decretal collections surviving from the period, is in an advanced state of preparation in the hands of Professor Holtzmann, to whom all historians at work in this field are much indebted. Nevertheless, in the chapters which follow, a striking English contribution to medieval canonical developments is discussed in some detail for the first time on the basis of all extant English manuscripts of primitive decretal collections. With very few exceptions, these manuscripts, though their existence is known to historians of canon law, have not been previously examined except very briefly.

The present investigation has been pursued, therefore, with three objectives: first, to fix both the decretals themselves and the decretal collections in their canonical and historical settings, to explore their place in canonistic theory and practice, and to trace in broad outlines the course of their technical evolution; second, to provide a general survey of all surviving manuscript resources for the earliest phases of decretal codification in England; and, third, to assess the historical importance of the English collections in English and European history, and in the history of canon law in general. The bulk of the source material used throughout the study is drawn from previously unpublished manuscripts, and in a few cases information has been added incidentally on the location of manuscripts not hitherto noticed. The discussion of distinct technical traditions in the evolution of decretal collections is developed with illustrative detail; and, in the final chapter, an attempt is made to relate these studies to the existing state of historical knowledge, modifying, where necessary, existing historical judgements. For clarity, the main interest of the investigation for English historians is stated briefly in the opening chapter.

In preparing this study through a period of several years, I have incurred a heavy debt of gratitude to many friends and scholars: to Professor C. H. Williams and Mr. I. P. Shaw, of King's College, London, under whose guidance my interest in this subject was first developed; in a special way to Dr. Walter Ullmann, of Trinity College, Cambridge, under whose stimulating and genial supervision the basic research was completed, as a doctoral thesis in the University of Cambridge; to the Delegacy of King's College for the award of the Inglis Studentship in History; to the University of London for the award of a Postgraduate Research Studentship; to the Master and Fellows of Trinity College for electing me to the Rouse Ball Research Studentship; to Professors R. R. Darlington and F. R. H. Du Boulay for many valuable suggestions in argument and presentation; to Dr. Eleanor Rathbone and Mrs. Mary Cheney for allowing me to read their unpublished dissertations; to the various scholars whose studies are acknowledged in bibliographical and footnote references, but particularly to Professors Walter Holtzmann and Stephan Kuttner and Dr. Ullmann; to

Professor Kuttner and to Fr. Edwin A. Quain, of Fordham University, for permission to reproduce passages from my articles recently published in *Traditio*; to Miss Anne Heslin for generous help with references and in reading the proofs; to the officials of the Manuscript Room in the British Museum, who have also given permission for the reproduction of several manuscript facsimiles; to the Librarian of Lambeth Palace; to the Librarians of Trinity College, Caius College, Pembroke College, St. John's College and Peterhouse, in the University of Cambridge; to the staff of the Anderson Room in the Cambridge University Library; to the Keeper of the Western Manuscripts in the Bodleian Library in Oxford; to the Reverend Librarians of the Cathedral Chapters at Durham and Lincoln, and of the Augustinian Priory at Klosterneuburg. For fear of misunderstanding, an obligation to two distinguished historians of the past must be recognized at the outset: if the major theme of this book involves a refutation of one aspect of the work of F. W. Maitland and Z. N. Brooke within the field of canonical history, it could not substantially reduce their great and permanent contribution to the history of the English Church, even within this context. Finally, since the present study is directed primarily to the primitive decretal collections of English provenance, wider problems relating to similar collections of continental origin, to systematic compilations, and to the formative influence of the Curia and the papal registers on the composition of decretal collections—all these are dealt with here in provisional terms only. The recent works by Professors Holtzmann, Kuttner, Cheney and Vetulani and by Dr. Deeters, listed below in the bibliography, record the latest state of knowledge on some aspects of these significant questions.

University of London   C.D.
King's College
September 1962

CONTENTS

ABBREVIATIONS

(i) PRINTED BOOKS

Abhandlungen	*Abhandlungen der Gesellschaft der Wissenschaften in Göttingen*
Canonessammlungen	E. Friedberg, *Die Canonessammlungen zwischen Gratian und Bernhard von Pavia*, Leipzig (1897)
CHJ	*Cambridge Historical Journal* Renamed: *The Historical Journal*
DDC	*Dictionnaire de droit canonique*
Deutsches Archiv	*Deutsches Archiv für Geschichte des Mittelalters*
EHR	*English Historical Review*
J-L	P. Jaffé and S. Löwenfeld, *Regesta Pontificum Romanorum*
LQR	*Law Quarterly Review*
Mansi	J. D. Mansi, *Sanctorum Conciliorum nova et amplissima collectio*
MGH	*Monumenta Germaniae Historica*
Mitteilungen	*Mitteilungen des österreichischen Instituts für Geschichtsforschung*
Nachrichten	*Nachrichten von der Akademie der Wissenschaften in Göttingen, Phil.-Hist.Kl.*
Neues Archiv	*Neues Archiv der Gesellschaft für ältere deutsche Geschichtskunde*
NRHD	*Nouvelle revue historique de droit français et étranger*
Pat.Lat.	J. P. Migne, *Patrologiae Cursus Completus: Series Latina*
PU	*Papsturkunden*
RHD	*Revue historique de droit français et étranger*
Sitz.KA.Wien	*Sitzungsberichte der kaiserlichen Akademie der Wissenschaften in Wien, Phil.-Hist.Kl.*
Studia Gratiana	J. Forchielli and A. M. Stickler, edd., *Studia Gratiana post octava Decreti saecularia auctore consilio commemorationi Gratianae instruendae edita*
ZRG., Kan.Abt.	*Zeitschrift der Savigny Stiftung für Rechtsgeschichte, Kanonistische Abteilung*

(ii) Decretal Collections

ENGLISH PRIMITIVE COLLECTIONS

Belver.	*Belverensis*	Belvoir
Bridl.	*Bridlingtonensis*	Bridlington
Cantuar.	*Cantuariensis*	Canterbury
Chelt.	*Cheltenhamensis*	Cheltenham
Claud.	*Claudiana*	Claudian
Claustr.	*Claustroneoburgensis*	Klosterneuburg
Cott.	*Cottoniana*	Cottonian
Dunelm.	*Dunelmensis*	Durham
Font.	*Fontanensis*	Fountains
Pet.	*Peterhusensis*	Peterhouse
Regal.	*Regalis*	Royal
Roff.	*Roffensis*	Rochester
Trin.	*Trinitatis*	Trinity
Wig.	*Wigorniensis*	Worcester
Wig.Altera	*Wigorniensis Altera*	Worcester II

CONTINENTAL PRIMITIVE COLLECTIONS

Aureaev.	*Aureaevallensis*	Luxemburg
Berol.	*Berolinensis*	Berlin
Cantab.	*Cantabrigiensis*	Cambridge
Dertus.	*Dertusensis*	Tortosa
Eberbac.	*Eberbacensis*	Eberbach
Paris. I	*Parisiensis I*	Paris I

SYSTEMATIC COLLECTIONS

Abrinc.	*Abrincensis*	Avranches
Appendix	*App.Conc.Lateranensis*	Appendix
Bamb.	*Bambergensis*	Bamberg
Brug.	*Brugensis*	Bruges
Cass.	*Casselana*	Cassel
Lips.	*Lipsiensis*	Leipzig
Sang.	*Sangermanensis*	St Germain

CHAPTER I

Canon Law and the Decretals

1. THE INTEREST OF THE INVESTIGATION FOR ENGLISH HISTORIANS

THE study of canon law in England has never quite recovered from the attack launched upon it in the sixteenth century, and a burden of suspicion has hindered not only the subject professionally, but even an interpretation of medieval ecclesiastical history in its necessary canonistic setting. The teaching of canon law in the universities was proscribed by Henry VIII's writ of prohibition, and, in addition to this frontal assault, encouragement was given at the same time to an interest in Roman Civil Law through the foundation of Regius Professorships at Oxford and Cambridge.[1] By these means English academic interest ceased in what had been the common law of western Christendom, entailing a sudden catastrophe in the history of the English Courts Christian.[2] For these reasons the story of canon law in the post-Reformation Church of England has no direct connexion with the law of the English Church in the twelfth century. Nor is it intended to attempt here a judgement on the decisions taken in the sixteenth century. But it was undoubtedly a misfortune, historically speaking, that with the eclipse of canon law as a branch of jurisprudence in England, an interest in its history became almost equally suspected. Today it is accepted axiomatically that a knowledge of the development of canon law is central to a true understanding of medieval history. From the eleventh century,

---

[1] F. W. Maitland, *English Law and the Renaissance* (Rede Lecture, Cambridge, 1901), pp. 8–9; 47, n.14: Injunctions of 1535, *Stat. Acad. Cantab.*, p. 134: 'Quare volumus ut deinceps nulla legatur palam et publice lectio per academiam vestram totam in iure canonico sive pontificio . . .' etc.

[2] Maitland, *Roman Canon Law in the Church of England*, London (1898), pp. 90–3.

at the latest, until the close of the middle ages, ecclesiastical law exerted a profound and far-reaching influence on European thought and civilization, both directly by its control of belief and practice, and indirectly by its provocation of a hostile or critical reaction.[1]

It is no longer possible to estimate the loss of canonical source material through the deliberate destruction of manuscripts, their supersession by more important works, and the lapse of so many centuries.[2] The evidence surviving suggests that such losses have been very great indeed. But the canonistic manuscripts surviving from the twelfth century (and they are still known for the most part in manuscript only) have a richness and variety far exceeding anything thought likely when Maitland restored the study of canon law to a place of central historical interest in England. Now by the exploitation of long neglected manuscripts and the publication of monographs on special aspects of English ecclesiastical history a more balanced interpretation is being gradually achieved. But the detailed research made in recent years (chiefly by continental scholars) on the work of the medieval canonists, strictly in their professional capacity, has not yet been linked satisfactorily with more general interpretations of ecclesiastical history in its social and political aspects. This is particularly true in English history, partly no doubt for the reasons already stated. The work of many scholars provides increasingly an ample basis for the reinvestigation of many familiar problems, and much has been achieved already. Among these scholars, to name only a few, Holtzmann, Kuttner, Ullmann, Le Bras, Plöchl, Stickler, Tierney, Vetulani and many others are both outstanding and characteristic; while, for English history more specifically, Barraclough, Mrs. Cheney, Professor Cheney, Morey, Christo-

---

[1] S. Kuttner, 'Scientific Investigation of Mediaeval Canon Law: the Need and the Opportunity', *Speculum*, xxiv (1949), pp. 493–501: even the critical comments of Roger Bacon, Dante and the satirists reflect 'the actual truth that in the mediaeval world canon law was an all-pervading social and cultural power'. For the development of canon law before Gratian, see P. Fournier and G. Le Bras, *Histoire des collections canoniques en Occident depuis les Fausses Décrétales jusqu'au Décret de Gratien*, 2 Vols., Paris (1931–2); and W. M. Plöchl, *Geschichte des Kirchenrechts*, I, Vienna (1954).

[2] Maitland, *Roman Canon Law*, p. 95: Gentili at Oxford: 'Flammis, flammis libros spurcissimos barbarorum. . . . Flammis omnes, flammis!'

pher Brooke, Kemp, Mlle. Foreville and others like them have already revealed the vital significance of these technical studies in the history of the English Church. But much remains to be done, to be undertaken afresh or brought to completion. There is still some lingering distrust of the subject-matter, and a disinclination to give the preliminary but necessary attention to the minutiae of textual criticism: necessary, not for its intrinsic interest, but so that, when the quarrying has been completed, valid bases may be provided for the broader historical conclusions. At the moment, in so far as these are based on reliable canonical authorities at all, they rest too frequently on a small number of well-known compilations, with little critical understanding of their value as historical, as distinct from legal, source material. Whenever the canon law is consulted to elucidate more general problems, it is misleading to refer simply to one or two of the most famous legal codices however great their professional importance.

It was a failure to realize this danger which misled first Maitland and then Zachary Brooke in their still-basic studies on the twelfth-century church in England, since they relied in their investigations on a small number of canonical codes drawn up somewhat later than the emergence of the problems in which they were interested, and were seemingly insufficiently aware of the nature of the sources on which the codices themselves depended.[1] Both were concerned to trace the course of papal decretal legislation in England, and more particularly the

---

[1] Maitland, *Roman Canon Law*, pp. 122–31; Z. N. Brooke, 'The Effect of Becket's Murder on Papal Authority in England', *CHJ*, II (1928), pp. 213–29; *idem*, *The English Church and the Papacy*, Cambridge (1931), pp. 211–14. With these the following should be read as a corrective: G. Barraclough, *EHR*, LIII (1938), pp. 492–5 (review of Kuttner, 'Repertorium der Kanonistik, 1140–1234', *Studi e Testi*, LXXI, Vatican City, 1937); Mrs. M. Cheney, 'The Compromise of Avranches of 1172 and the Spread of Canon Law in England', *EHR*, LVI (1941), pp. 177–97; Kuttner and E. Rathbone, 'Anglo-Norman Canonists of the Twelfth Century: An Introductory Study', *Traditio*, VII (1949–51), pp. 279–80. On the other hand, Brooke's arguments are accepted by R. Foreville, *L'Église et la Royauté en Angleterre sous Henri II Plantagenet*, Paris (1943), pp. 389 ff.; and Holtzmann has recently described Brooke's *CHJ* study as 'a short but very weighty paper': W. Holtzmann and E. W. Kemp, 'Papal Decretals relating to the Diocese of Lincoln in the Twelfth Century', *Lincoln Record Society*, XLVII (1954), p. xvi. The whole question is treated on the basis of fresh manuscript evidence in the chapters which follow. For simplicity, the canonists whose work is the basis of this study are described here as 'English', though it is realized that 'Anglo-Norman' is preferred by some historians.

influence of the Becket controversy on the rate of flow of decretals from the Roman Curia to English recipients. To illustrate their methods briefly: Maitland, in discussing the decretal letters which Alexander III sent to English bishops and judges delegate, relied exclusively on the authorized *Decretales*, published by Gregory IX and recommended by him to the canon lawyers at Paris and Bologna on 5 September 1234.[1] Brooke extended the basis of this discussion by examining also the *Quinque Compilationes Antiquae*: the five most important decretal collections made in the preceding half century.[2] Despite the apparent support provided more recently for Brooke's thesis by Holtzmann,[3] it will be shown later how seriously Maitland and Brooke erred in their reliance on these highly specialist productions, which were designed for essentially practical purposes and provide no real guidance in the problems which they were investigating. The fallacy underlying the arguments, which they advanced in consequence, has been noticed briefly by Barraclough and Mary Cheney. It is enough to remark here that the conclusions of general historical importance which were reached by Maitland and Brooke in this context have no necessary connexion with the materials on which they were founded.

Two major adjustments must be made to their method of historical enquiry. Firstly, it must be understood that the *Quinque Compilationes* and the Gregorian *Decretales* are simply the most well-known and highly favoured of a vast family of decretal collections whose genesis can be traced from the eighth decade of the twelfth century. They are the final issues of many generations which succeeded one another in the great schools of canon lawyers, most notably Italian, French and English. Each was not a novel and independent composition based on the papal registers or episcopal records, but rather (at least in most cases) an adaptation or amplification of already existing compilations.[4]

---

[1] A. van Hove, *Prolegomena ad Codicem Iuris Canonici*, Malines-Rome (1945), p. 358.

[2] *Ibid.*, pp. 355–7.   [3] Holtzmann and Kemp, *op. cit.*, pp. xvi–xvii.

[4] Van Hove, *Prolegomena*, pp. 348–63; but the papal registers left some traces in the decretal collections: cf. Holtzmann, 'Die Register Papst Alexanders III in den Händen der Kanonisten', *Quellen und Forschungen aus italienischen Archiven und Bibliotheken*, xxx (1940), pp. 13–87. See also A. Vetulani, 'L'Origine des collections primitives de décrétales à la fin du XIIe siècle', *Congrès de Droit Canonique Médiéval*, Louvain (1959), pp. 64–72.

From this it follows that the thirteenth-century collections, which provide the customary basis of reference in historical discussions, depend indirectly for their twelfth-century decretals on codices made shortly after the issue of the individual letters, which only very rarely survive in their true originals.[1] The historian's attention must be directed to these early collections rather than to their juridically more important descendants. If we are interested in the decretals which Alexander III issued, the most sensible course is to consult the collections made during his own pontificate. Until quite recently, these have been almost entirely neglected by the general historian.

But even with access secured to these sources more relevant in time to the wider historical problems, a second and equally vital question arises concerning their relevance in species. And it was in this respect above all others that both Maitland and Brooke were mistaken. The decretal collections, as stated already, were professional and specialist compositions. There can be no justification in accepting at its face value the evidence they seem to provide on general historical trends and problems, unless these are corroborated by independent testimony. Before the wider historical significance of a particular decretal collection can be established, many questions must first be settled: questions concerning its provenance and authorship, the motives prompting its composition, and the resources available to the collector. Only with such questions answered is it possible to gauge the value of a collection in reflecting the general policies of the legislator rather than the local or specialist predilections of the compiler.

The problems of interpretation are particularly acute for the

---

[1] For collections already edited or analysed, see E. Friedberg, *Corpus Iuris Canonici*, II, Leipzig (1881); *idem*, *Quinque Compilationes Antiquae necnon Compilatio Lipsiensis*, Leipzig (1882); *idem*, *Die Canonessammlungen zwischen Gratian und Bernhard von Pavia*, Leipzig (1897); the more recent survey by Holtzmann: 'Über eine Ausgabe der päpstlichen Dekretalen des 12. Jahrhunderts', *Nachrichten* (1945), pp. 15-36; *idem*, 'Die Dekretalen Gregors VIII', *Festschrift für Leo Santifaller: Mitteilungen*, LVIII (1950); *idem*, 'Die Dekretalensammlungen des 12. Jahrhunderts: 1. Die Sammlung *Tanner*', *Festschrift zur Feier des 200 jährigen Bestehens der Akademie der Wissenschaften in Göttingen, Phil.-Hist.Kl.* (1951), pp. 83-145; *idem*, 'La collection *Seguntina* et les décrétales de Clément III et de Célestin III', *Revue d'histoire ecclésiastique*, L (1955); *idem* and Kemp, *op. cit.*, pp. ix-xvii; Kuttner, 'Notes on a Projected Corpus of Twelfth-Century Decretal Letters', *Traditio*, VI (1948), pp. 345-51.

twelfth century, when the volume of decretals issuing from the papal chancery was swelling to previously unheard-of dimensions, but for which the papal registers survive no longer. The lost registers would doubtless have provided full and incontrovertible evidence of trends in papal policies; but their absence can scarcely justify the uncritical use made of the strictly partial and selective evidence surviving in the canon lawyers' collections. Both Maitland and Brooke tacitly assumed either that the Alexandrian letters in the extant decretal collections represent the total significant issue, or at least that they accurately reflect it in all essentials. Only on the basis of one or other of these propositions can their conclusions be sustained. In the event, in can be shown that neither is historically accurate.

Enough has been said, then, to indicate the value of a critical investigation of the earliest decretal collections available, and in them an unexpectedly promising field for historical revision is discovered. More than fifty manuscripts survive from the twenty years following the death of Becket. Less than half have been examined so far either for their technical or their political importance.[1] Many are of the utmost value in English history. Yet their value is by no means restricted to questions of historical method and enquiry. Setting aside this interest in an already well-known controversy, the mere numerical recovery of lost decretals is astonishing. Hundreds of papal letters, which had passed quite out of knowledge, have been recovered, though they have yet to be published.

All decretal collections before Peter of Benevento's *Compilatio Tertia* (1209–10) were private in character, their contents being subject entirely to the author's caprice and the materials available to him. In the course of a long process of selective development, many letters fell by the wayside, and were never received into the later, more widely-known, compilations. The Gregorian *Decretales*, itself a selection from the *Quinque Compilationes* and the most recent papal registers, superseded all earlier collections and drove them out of use and knowledge, though it

---

[1] Holtzmann, *Nachrichten*, pp. 21–4: Holtzmann lists forty collections as pre-*Compilatio Prima*, and a further fifteen as pre-*Compilatio Secunda*; and further manuscripts have since been found. Cf. Kuttner, *Projected Corpus*, pp. 345–51. See also the annual Bulletin of the Institute of Research and Study in Medieval Canon Law, *Traditio*, xi–xvii (1955–proceeding).

contained only a fragment of their total contents. Fortunately, many of these rejected or superseded decretals can now be recovered from the twelfth-century collections. Even merely statistically, the gain is striking: Maitland estimated on a basis of the evidence in the *Decretales* that Alexander III had dispatched one hundred and eighty decretal letters to England; and Brooke increased this estimate to two hundred and nineteen by consulting also the *Compilationes Antiquae*. By extracting those decretals discovered afresh in the twelfth-century canonical manuscripts, Holtzmann has shown that no less than three hundred and fifty-nine are now known to have been dispatched to England—and there is no reason to assume that even this provisional estimate is the final figure. In other words, to England alone, during a single pontificate, one hundred and forty forgotten decretals have been made once more available, and many are of considerable historical interest. The quantitative recovery alone, therefore, would justify a detailed analysis of these neglected manuscripts.[1]

But the gain is not quantitative simply. The older collections include fuller and more accurate versions of many decretals already well known. It has often been noticed that many decretal letters, whether in medieval manuscripts or even the best modern editions, are frequently unreliable in historical detail. This defect is due principally to two factors: the one relating to the technical and professional conventions of the canonists themselves; the other resulting from the carelessness or ignorance of medieval copyists. In the first place, a canon lawyer valued a given decretal for its juridical content only;

---

[1] Maitland, *Roman Canon Law*, p. 130; Brooke, *Effect of Becket's Murder*, pp. 219–224; Holtzmann, *Nachrichten*, p. 34; *idem*, *Dekretalen Gregors VIII*, pp. 113–23; *idem* and Kemp, *op. cit.*, pp. xvi–xvii. The total number of known decretals has to be revised constantly as further letters are discovered in manuscripts previously unnoticed. It must be admitted that Maitland did not claim his figure as an absolute or final total. But his argument does assume the figure to represent the true ratio of letters dispatched to England as compared with other countries. The decretal collections can never provide a complete picture of the total decretal issue, since they are based simply on the selection of letters made by particular canon lawyers. Evidence of numerous decretals never incorporated in professional collections can be discovered in cathedral and monastic cartularies. Moreover, the number of letters rediscovered in the canonical collections is even greater than the statistics given above suggest at first sight: many so-called decretals in the calculations by Maitland and Brooke were merely decretal chapters.

the historical circumstances giving rise to the judicial decision were of little moment to him, and were consequently a fit subject for abbreviation or even total excision. In this way many decretals have been seriously distorted in the process of inclusion in professional collections, the excision being most serious in the hands of the most juristically skilled authors. In diplomatic terms, both protocol and eschatocol were eliminated or drastically curtailed, and even the historical element of the contextus, the *species facti*, was liable to suppression. Further, as the canonist's skill grew, he tended to dissect the longer decretals into their component parts, and these he distributed through the various books and sub-sections into which he divided his collection.[1] In these circumstances, it became increasingly difficult to reconstruct the authentic textual shape of the original entity; and, at the same time, historians from Maitland to Morey have been greatly misled in their statistical calculations.[2] On two counts, therefore, a more accurate version may be discovered if we consult the earlier, more primitive, compositions, designed before the process of excision and dissection had made much headway. So much, then, for the defects due to professional conventions: there remains the problem of scribal inaccuracy.

Maitland noticed long ago how canonistic scribes were prone to distort or misinterpret references to names of persons and places, and his illustrations have been supplemented by later historians. In the many surviving transcripts of a single decretal involving the parishes of Potton and Sandy, he discovered eighteen variant readings of the former and ten of the latter.[3] And Holtzmann has more recently listed ten variants of Kenilworth, to which one more can be added from a Peterhouse manuscript, where it appears in an unusually accurate version.[4]

---

[1] Kuttner, *Projected Corpus*, pp. 345–6; Maitland, *Roman Canon Law*, pp. 124–5: showing how Innocent III dealt with a wide variety of topics in a single letter to the bishop of Ely (1204).

[2] Maitland, *Roman Canon Law*, p. 128; A Morey, *Bartholomew of Exeter*, Cambridge (1937), p. 44.

[3] Maitland, *Roman Canon Law*, pp. 122–3: Sandy appears as Sander, Santen, Sandeia, Sandria, Sandinia, Sandeta, Sandaia, Fand and Sandola.

[4] Holtzmann, *Nachrichten*, pp. 25–32: Kenilworth appears as Chinelwi, Chinel Wi, Chimel Wirch, Chimen Wl., Chinel W., Chunbt, Chwith, Exmtwth, Inthwobt and Knieleunede; cf. Peterhouse MS. 193, fol. ii. ra: Kinelworþe. See also W. Ullmann,

The problem hinges chiefly on the use of abbreviated forms of place-names and persons, which were liable to confusion. The slightest acquaintance with the work of decretal scribes will suggest many typical examples: thus London was subject to confusion with Laon, Lyons and Lund, in their Latin versions; York with Evreux; while Exeter was particularly difficult, being confused in specific instances with Lisieux, Brescia, Oxford, Huesca and Osma—and even with Bath, when Bartholomew of Exeter was intended.[1] If such familiar examples as these perplexed the decretal copyists, it is hardly surprising that the Hungarian province of Kolocsa presented even greater difficulties in abbreviated transcription, and was almost invariably re-copied as Cologne;[2] in the same way Dublin was occasionally confused with Durham, Ramsey with Reims, and Salisbury with Salzburg. In many instances the corruption of historical references was so extreme that it is no longer possible to reconstruct them with any conviction. Obviously, the more immediately dependent a transcript was on an original copy or on an archetypal collection, the more accurate was likely to be the abbreviation. The most extravagant misreadings are naturally found (except in a few uncharacteristic instances) in the remoter generations. Here then is another reason for dissatisfaction with the later collections when better texts are available in the ancestral manuscripts.

A precise example affords the most convincing argument. A decretal of Alexander III is included in the Gregorian *Decretales*, in Friedberg's vulgate edition, with the following details:[3]

Idem Herfordensi episcopo et abbati de Forde. Ex literis I. Salabriensis episcopi accepimus, quod defuncta persona ecclesiae de Laton., G.miles qui villam, in qua ecclesia sita est, a monasterio de Vinton. *etc.*

'A Scottish Charter and its Place in Medieval Canon Law', *Juridical Review*, LXI (1949), pp. 225–41; *idem*, 'A Forgotten Dispute at Bridlington Priory in its Canonistic Setting', *Yorkshire Archaeological Journal*, XXXVII (1951), pp. 456–73.

[1] The abbreviations Bathon., Brixen. or Brix., Lexou., Oxon., Oxom., and Oscen. (for Bath, Brescia, Lisieux, Oxford, Osma and Huesca respectively) were frequently confused with Barth. Exon., B.Exon., and Exon. (for Exeter).

[2] The abbreviation for Kolocsa was Coloc., which was very readily confused with Colon., the conventional form for Cologne.

[3] Friedberg, ed., *Corpus Iuris Canonici*, II: *Decretales Gregorii IX*, III. 38. 7.

Experience suggests at once that this letter was sent in reality to the bishop of Hereford and the abbot of Ford, though this could not be taken for granted on the text alone. It is conceivable that the German bishop of Herford was in fact the recipient of this letter, and is referred to quite accurately in the decretal inscription. But a knowledge of scribal failings suggests the correction from Herford in Germany to Hereford in England; and this deduction is amply confirmed by the following reference to the abbot of Ford in the diocese of Exeter. With the English provenance of the letter sufficiently established, the reference to 'I. Salabriensis' in the text is soon identified as Jocelin of Salisbury, and the place-name 'Vinton.' is readily recognized as a familiar abbreviation for Winchester. This simple example reveals how the typically distorted details in decretal transcriptions may be corrected by a process of supposition based on probability. But, if the original version is available in an earlier copy, then the deductive process is unnecessary. Deduction is, in any case, a defective instrument in such matters. The decretal discussed above is discovered with fuller and more accurate details in an English decretal collection, the Claudian Collection, made in or shortly after Urban III's pontificate (1185–7).[1] This early manuscript confirms the suggested emendations on all points but one: where Friedberg's version provides the reading 'Vinton.', the primitive collection records 'Wiltona', identifying therefore not Winchester but Wilton. This example merely typifies the numerous corrections which will result from an investigation of the twelfth-century manuscripts, and emphasizes once more the need for further research into the archetypal collections.

One further example illustrates the occasional excitement of an unexpected discovery. In his introduction to Ralph de Diceto's *Ymagines Historiarum*, Stubbs considered at some length the possible etymology of its author's name. The course and con-

---

[1] B.M. Cotton MS. Claudius A. IV, fol. 212rb, n.175. Elementary though such reconstructions seem to be, they depend in many instances on local knowledge: the inscription 'Riwallis et de Beglaus abbatibus et priori de Novoburgo' (*Tanner* VII. 15.15; Holtzmann, *Sammlung Tanner*, p. 143) is easily identified by English historians as addressed to the abbots of Rievaulx and Byland and the prior of Newburgh; but in an otherwise less obvious context the reference 'Beglaus' would clearly present some difficulty.

clusion of his enquiry need not detain us here in detail, but while examining a suggested derivation of the word Diceto from the Norfolk parish of Diss, he cited a lost letter of Alexander III to John of Oxford, bishop of Norwich.[1] The letter could no longer be discovered and was not included among the known collections of Alexander's decretals. Its existence was known only through brief summaries in the *Votaryes* and *Scriptores* of Bale, writing in the sixteenth century. In the decretal, according to Bale, Alexander:

> commaundeth that Wyllyam the new person of Dysse, for clayminge the benefice by inheritaunce, after the decease of his father person Wulkerell which begate him in his presthode, should be dispossessed, no appellacyon admitted.

This letter can now be examined in its authentic form in various decretal manuscripts conventionally associated with Worcester and described in consequence as members of the 'Worcester' family. The letter begins as follows:[2]

> Ad aures nostras sepius pervenisse cognoscas, quod defuncto Wlfkerel sacerdote, qui in ecclesia de Dische multis temporibus personatum habebat, Willelmus filius eius in sacerdotio genitus eiusdem ecclesie administrationem quasi hereditaria successione suscepit, et eam contra fundi dominum violenter detinere contendit. *Etc.*

And in this way accurate details and a little additional illumination are provided for arguments which Stubbs was able to base simply on second-hand and tenuous allusion.

These examples suggest all too briefly how historical enquiry may be furthered in many respects by an exploitation of the neglected manuscripts, both as to general historical problems and details of individual cases. But the manuscripts provide also the materials in which alone can be traced the development of the techniques and traditions in the schools of canon lawyers in the classical period of the emergence of canon law as a true

[1] W. Stubbs, ed., *Radulfi de Diceto Decani Lundoniensis Opera Historica*, Rolls Series (1876), I, pp. x–xviii.

[2] Trinity College Cambridge MS. R.14.9, fol. 86r; cf. H. Lohmann, 'Die Collectio Wigorniensis', *ZRG., Kan.Abt.*, XXII (1933), p. 104. The form 'Wlfkerel' is almost certainly corrupt; the variants 'Ulfkutel' and 'Bultekel' are found elsewhere, but the most likely form is 'Wulfketel'.

juristic science. It is for these reasons that the extant manuscripts, and particularly those with English associations, have
been chosen as a basis for this present study. Stephen of Tournai,
a distinguished canonist and contemporary of Alexander III,
referred to the 'inextricabilis silva' of Alexander's decretals.
From a canonistic point of view, the chief interest of the twelfth-
century collections is their evidence of the way in which the
canon lawyers gradually traced a path through this vast forest.

2. HISTORICAL DEVELOPMENTS

(a) *Ius Antiquum*

In the earliest Christian centuries, canon law consisted primarily of episcopal *acta* and the decisions of provincial and
oecumenical councils.[1] The decrees of the councils of Arles
(314), Nicaea (325), Constantinople (381) and Chalcedon
(451); the decisions and letters of Roman pontiffs, perhaps
even from the time of the epistle of Clement I to the Corin-
thians (c. 96), and that of Victor I on the Montanist heresy
(c. 189–98); papal decretal letters at least as early as the pontificate of Damasus I († 384) or his successor Siricius: all these
provided the substance of the primitive canon law.[2] Again,
among early canonical collections, there were the *Collectio
Romana* (not later than 352), which included the canons of
Nicaea and Sardica, and the vastly influential collection of
Dionysius Exiguus, completed at Rome c. 514. In Peitz's
judgement, the influence of the Dionysian collection on the
works of later canonists has been much underrated.[3]

These were the beginnings of the first epoch in the history of
canon law: the period of 'dispersion' and of *ius antiquum*, which

---

[1] For a general survey of the history of canon law to Gratian, see Fournier and
Le Bras, *Collections canoniques*; van Hove, *Prolegomena*; Plöchl, *op. cit.*, pp. 56 ff.; Le
Bras, 'Canon Law', *Legacy of the Middle Ages* (edd., C. G. Crump and E. F. Jacob,
Oxford, 1948 imp.), pp. 321–61; etc.

[2] For discussion of the *Ad Gallos Episcopos* of Damasus I as the first known decretal, see E. Ch. Babut, *La plus ancienne décrétale*, Paris (1904); and R. Naz, 'Lettres
décrétales', *DDC*, IV (1949), cols. 1064–5. But see also E. Caspar, *Geschichte des
Papsttums*, I (1930), pp. 261–3, for the view that the first decretal was issued by
Siricius after the death of Damasus.

[3] Mgr. P. W. Peitz, 'Dionysius Exiguus als Kanonist', *Schweizer Rundschau*, II
(1945–6); *idem* and G. Ebers, 'Gratian und Dionysius Exiguus', *Studia Gratiana*,
I (1953), pp. 51–82.

lasted from the earliest centuries until the publication of the *Decretum*.[1] In this period whatever codes of law existed were private in character and lacked the support of a universally recognized authority, although some were widely influential. A few of the most important collections may be mentioned briefly: the *Hispana*, at one time attributed to Isidore of Seville at the beginning of the seventh century; the Penitential of Theodore of Canterbury; the *Hadriana*, widely accepted in the empire of Charles the Great; the influential *Pseudo-Isidore*, of uncertain provenance, but most probably made at Reims or Le Mans c. 847–52;[2] a great flowering of collections from the end of the ninth century, including the *Collectio Anselmo dedicata*, the *Collectio Abbonis Floriacensis*, two works by Regino of Prüm, the famous *Decretum* of Burchard of Worms, together with its derivative the *Collectio XII partium*; and finally the collections of the Hildebrandine Reform: the significant *Collection in 74 Titles*, Cardinal Atto's *Capitulary*, Deusdedit's *Collectio canonum*, Bonizo of Sutri's *Liber de Vita Christiana*,[3] the collection of Anselm of Lucca, and Cardinal Gregory's *Polycarpus*, completed during the pontificate of Pascal II.

Up to this point, there had been little striking innovation in the technique of codification. Even the best collections had advanced little beyond a broad separation of subject-matter: there was little systematic ordering of contents, and canons were often transcribed simply in chronological sequence. There was no commentary or literary discussion of the juristic importance of the canons, except in a few cases where brief titles or summaries were introduced as chapter headings. Even Burchard of Worms, who was unusually original in handling the source material, introduced little schematic arrangement beyond a broad division of his canons into twenty books. But he clarified his plan by inserting also a list of titles as a prefatory table of contents.[4]

[1] Van Hove, *Prolegomena*, pp. 118–19.

[2] P. Hinschius, *Decretales Pseudo-isidorianae et Capitula Angilramni*, Leipzig (1863), pp. clxxxiii–ccxxxvi; H. E. Feine, *Kirchliche Rechtsgeschichte*, i, Weimar (1950), pp. 150–3; Plöchl, *op. cit.*, pp. 215 ff.; van Hove, *Prolegomena*, pp. 305–11; and for further discussions, see *passim* A. Stickler, *Historia Fontium Iuris Canonici*, i, Turin (1950); and B. Kurtscheid, *Historia Iuris Canonici*, Rome (1951).

[3] E. Perels, ed., Bonizo of Sutri: *Liber de Vita Christiana*, Berlin (1930).

[4] Fournier and Le Bras, *Collections canoniques*, i, pp. 368–71 and 414–21; van Hove, *Prolegomena*, pp. 239, 263, 298 and 320.

A most decisive contribution to the canonists' technique was made by Ivo of Chartres, Bernold of Constance and Alger of Liége. The novelty of their method lay in the attempt to reconcile the apparent conflicts in existing canon law, and a solution to this problem was discovered by distinguishing necessary and immutable laws from those which could be altered or abrogated by dispensation. By showing that law might vary to suit different times, persons and places, they achieved a harmony through a theory of the relativity and mutability of laws or *leges*. An early stage of this most fruitful development is seen in Ivo of Chartres' *Panormia* (briefer and simpler than his own *Decretum*). His work is distinguished for its intelligent arrangement of short commentaries, or rather explanations, of the main points of law in the individual chapters.[1] Alger and Abelard carried the development a stage further by attempting a reconciliation of conflicting opinions wherever they were discovered. Both were important in influencing the work of Gratian. Abelard's *Sic et Non* was significant in canonical as well as philosophical history, and his method of reconciling the *contrarietates* was reflected in Gratian's *Decretum*.[2] The work of Alger was no less decisive, and provided Gratian with much of the substance of the *Decretum*, published in its vulgate form ten years after Alger's death in 1131. Gratian borrowed from him both in method and manner, accepting one hundred texts and sixteen *dicta*.[3]

Yet, to understand these developments fully, they must be considered in a wider intellectual setting, since they were in no way confined to the writings of canon lawyers. The canonistic developments were merely one aspect of a general growth of the dialectical or scholastic method in thought and argument.

[1] Fournier and Le Bras, *Collections canoniques*, II, pp. 67–79 and 83–99; J. Migne, ed., 'Ivonis Carnotensis Opera Omnia', *Pat. Lat.*, CLXI, cols. 9–1344; van Hove, *Prolegomena*, pp. 331–2; Fournier, 'Yves de Chartres et le droit canonique', *Revue des questions historiques*, LXIII (1898), pp. 51–98 and 384–405; *idem*, 'Un tournant de l'histoire du droit', *NRHD*, XLI (1917), pp. 155–80; J. de Ghellinck, *Le mouvement théologique du XIIe Siècle*, Bruges-Paris (1948 ed.), pp. 445–59.

[2] Kuttner, 'Zur Frage der theologischen Vorlage Gratians', *ZRG.*, Kan.Abt., XXIII (1934), pp. 243–68; van Hove, *Prolegomena*, pp. 344–5.

[3] For Alger's works, see *Pat.Lat.*, CLXXX: 'De sacramentis corporis et sanguinis Dominici libri tres', and 'Liber de misericordia et iustitia'; van Hove, *Prolegomena*, pp. 334–5; Le Bras, 'Alger de Liége et Gratien', *Revue des sciences philosophiques et théologiques*, XX (1931), pp. 5–26.

Problems connected with universal concepts and the nature of reality were being discussed in a new dialectical framework. The writings of Anselm and Abelard had been extremely influential in guiding the development of philosophic method. In the realm of philosophical controversy, there were the rival schools of nominalists, realists and conceptualists—to mention only the more important. Conflicting attitudes to faith and in-intellectual enquiry were typified in the writings of Bernard and Abelard. All these factors conditioned the climate of philosophical, theological and canonical speculation in an age of extraordinary intellectual enthusiasm and originality. They help to explain, at least in part, the new temper and style in the canonical collections.[1]

Gratian came on the flood-tide of this movement and decisively influenced the development of canon law within its compass. The older canonical traditions and the new professional methods were drawn together in his hands, and a great collection of ecclesiastical canons was constructed in a dialectical pattern. Given a problem in law, the arguments are marshalled first on one side, then on the other. The authorities for both points of view are carefully arrayed, and from their differences and conflicts a harmony or synthesis is achieved, the whole presenting a clear picture of the classical dialectical argument: thesis, antithesis and synthesis.

The *Decretum* is divided into three parts. The first, concerned with the source of law and ordinations, is divided into one hundred and one *Distinctiones*. The second, composed of thirty-six *Causae*, deals primarily with judgements and transactions. The third treats of sacraments and sacramentals: this part also is divided into *Distinctiones*, but may have been intended by Gratian as a final *Causa* in Part II. The author's comments and attempted harmonies are placed between the individual chapters and canons, and are known as the *dicta Gratiani*.[2]

[1] Van Hove, 'De momento methodi scholasticae in elaboranda Concordia discordantium canonum', *Apollinaris*, Vatican City (1948), pp. 14–17 and 22; de Ghellinck, *Mouvement théologique*, pp. 494–9.

[2] Among recent discussions on the structure and composition of the *Decretum*, see Kuttner, 'New Studies on the Roman Law in Gratian's *Decretum*', *Seminar* (Annual Extraordinary Number of *The Jurist*), xi (1953), pp. 12–50; *idem*, 'De Gratiani opere noviter edendo', *Apollinaris*, xxi (1948), pp. 118–28; *idem*,

It would be impossible to exaggerate the influence of this book in the history of canon law. It was the major point of departure in the main stream of development: the 'Great Divide' in medieval canon law. Coming at a moment of crucial importance, summing up the best of well-established traditions, and expressing them in the new scholastic style, it swiftly captured the entire field of ecclesiastical law, ousted the earlier compilations, and became the standard text-book in the schools and the principal authority in the courts. It marks the beginning of the science of canon law.[1]

(b) *Ius Novum*

Once the *Decretum* had captured the minds and monopolized the interests of the canonists, it was never again necessary to attempt a canonical composition in the old style: wherever this was attempted, the work had little influence and was quickly forgotten. Such a work, of the most transitory historical interest, was the great collection of Cardinal Laborans. To such an extent had Gratian become the basis of canonistic scholarship, that the value of this collection has never been properly assessed, partly because it had no significant influence even in its own day.[2] And yet the *Decretum* was never recognized as authoritative in the same way as the *Decretales*. We could have no better evidence than this of the unofficial nature of canon law in the twelfth century, when the activities of numberless anonymous canonists can only be understood when it is realized that Gratian is the permanent backcloth to their thought.

'Graziano: L'Uomo e l'Opera', *Studia Gratiana*, I (1953), pp. 17–29; Ullmann, 'The Paleae in Cambridge Manuscripts of the *Decretum*', *Studia Gratiana*, I (1953), pp. 161–216. The earliest date of composition of the *Decretum* is likewise the subject of much discussion at present. The conventional estimate of c. 1140–1 or later is provisionally accepted in this volume, and is correct as far as the vulgate edition of Gratian's work is concerned. But the existence of much earlier recensions is argued now by Vetulani, who retraces its ancestry even to the pontificate of Pascal II: 'Le Décret de Gratien et les premiers Décrétistes à la lumière d'une source nouvelle', *Studia Gratiana*, VII (1959).

[1] Kuttner, *Scientific Investigation*, pp. 493 ff.; van Hove, *Prolegomena*, p. 345: *idem, De momento methodi scholasticae*, p. 17. The original name of Gratian's compilation was *Concordia discordantium canonum*; but twelfth-century canonists frequently called it *Decreta*, and the conventional name used by historians is *Decretum*; see Kuttner, *Projected Corpus*, p. 345; *idem, Scientific Investigation*, p. 495. Cf. Pius XII's address to the Gratian Congress at Bologna in 1952, *Acta Apostolicae Sedis* (1952), pp. 368–9.

[2] Van Hove, *Prolegomena*, p. 442.

From the mid-twelfth century to 1234 the canon lawyers devoted their energies to two principal tasks among many others: the first in time was the basic work of examining the *Decretum* in detail, explaining doubtful points, and writing commentaries on it.[1] At first almost exclusively, and even later predominantly, these commentaries or *Summae* were composed at Bologna. Although it is well established that distinguished schools of decretists developed swiftly in England and France and in the Rhineland, the more decisive and more permanently influential work was that of the school at Bologna.[2] That great Italian centre of legal studies is at times considered pre-eminently the home of anti-papal lawyers, learned in the Civil Law: it was in fact the home of both laws equally, and was at this time fashioning the most powerful weapons for the papacy in the coming ideological controversies.[3] What other school could boast of a succession of canonists to compare with those who wrote and lectured at Bologna in the fifty years which followed the publication of Gratian's work: Paucapalea, Rolandus Bandinelli (later Alexander III), Rufinus, Stephen of Tournai, John of Faenza, Cardinal Gratian, Simon of Bisignano, Gandulph, Sicard of Cremona, Peter of Spain, Bazianus, Melendus and (greatest of them all) the matchless Huguccio, to whom Innocent III owed so much of his canonistic skill and knowledge.[4] It is small wonder that Frederick Barbarossa viewed with apprehension the growth of canonistic jurisprudence at Bologna with such great advantage to papal ideology, and there is little doubt that his Authentic *Habita* was issued at Roncaglia in 1158 in

[1] The best survey of varied canonistic activities between the *Decretum* and the Gregorian *Decretales* is in Kuttner, 'Repertorium der Kanonistik, 1140–1234', *Studi e Testi*, LXXI (1937); see also *idem* and Rathbone, *art.cit.*, pp. 279–358.

[2] *Ibid.*, pp. 279–358: discussing primarily the literary activities of the Anglo-Norman school. For the school of canonists at Cologne, *ibid.*, pp. 296–303.

[3] H. Rashdall, *The Universities of Europe in the Middle Ages* (revised by F. M. Powicke and A. B. Emden, Oxford, 1936), pp. 131 and 136; de Ghellinck, *Mouvement théologique*, pp. 416–65; Ullmann, 'The Medieval Interpretation of Frederick I's Authentic "Habita"', *Estratto dagli Studi in memoria di Paolo Koschaker: L'Europa e il Diritto Romano*, Milan, I (1953), pp. 102 ff.

[4] J. F. von Schulte, *Die Geschichte der Quellen und Literatur des canonischen Rechts*, I (1875), pp. 109–72; van Hove, *Prolegomena*, pp. 433–6; Kuttner, 'Bernardus Compostellanus Antiquus', *Traditio*, I (1943), pp. 277–340. The outstanding importance of Huguccio's work is well known, and critical editions of his *De Consecratione* and *Summa* are at present in preparation.

C

part at least with the purpose of affording protection and privilege for lay students of the Civil Law, and so to strengthen their position at Bologna vis-à-vis the clerical canonists.[1]

Meanwhile, the ingenuity of the early decretists was spent either in glossing Gratian's text or in composing *summae*. The primitive gloss consisted of a brief interpretation of key words and phrases, written in the margins or between the lines of the manuscript in hand. Alternatively, it consisted of an apparatus of cross-references, written in the margin and identifying passages of cognate interest elsewhere, either in the same manuscript or in some other work of reference. The *summa*, in contrast, was a full-scale commentary, which could be written out as a separate treatise, though following in most cases the structure and text of the *Decretum*. As the glossators gradually expanded their marginal or interlinear explanations, the gloss itself took on the form of a literary composition with some of the character of the *summa*. The final stages of this development were reached in the great gloss-apparatuses, *apparatus glossarum*, which appeared in and after the first decade of the thirteenth century. These were full-scale treatises, written out separately or included in the manuscript of the *Decretum*. The most important was that of Johannes Teutonicus (c. 1215), which was accepted in the schools as the standard gloss, and so described as *Glossa Ordinaria*, until its supersession by the mid-century recension by Bartholomew of Brescia. And these were merely the principal types of literary commentaries: there were in addition *distinctiones, casus, notabilia, abbreviationes, quaestiones, transformationes* and various others.[2]

This long decretist tradition, at least as far as Bologna is concerned, was built up in two clearly defined stages: there was, firstly, a period of almost uninterrupted activity from 1140/50 until 1190, in which flourished that famous school of canonists already mentioned. This was followed by an interval beginning not later than 1190, during which the work was not resumed (except for a few isolated commentaries) until the appearance of the *apparatus glossarum* from 1210. Thereafter, the renewal of Bolognese interest in Gratian's text was revealed in an impres-

---

[1] Ullmann, *Authentic 'Habita'*, p. 102.
[2] Kuttner, *Repertorium*, pp. 228–71; van Hove, *Prolegomena*, pp. 438–42.

sive series of commentaries of which the more important were *Ecce vicit Leo*, *Ius Naturale*, the apparatus of Laurentius Hispanus, the *Glossa Palatina*, and the *Glossa Ordinaria* of Johannes Teutonicus.[1] The temporary halt in this literary activity may be explained by the coincidence of several interrelated factors; and of these the definitive character of Huguccio's *Summa*, recently published and winning swift and general acceptance, was perhaps the most significant.

But it was at that precise moment also that Bernard of Pavia published his *Breviarium* at Bologna—that epoch-making collection later known as *Compilatio Prima*, and composed predominantly of decretal letters issued in or after Alexander III's pontificate. The emphasis of Bolognese scholarship was shifted in consequence from a preoccupation with the *Decretum* to the decretal collections; and with this movement the ultimate triumph of the decretalists as distinct from the decretists was assured. It was a triumph prepared in the course of the preceding fifteen years by decretal canonists through Western Europe generally, in the English and French schools as well as in that at Bologna. But the person and the place were the means of the victory.

3. Decretals in the Twelfth Century

The rise of the decretals to importance in the twelfth century is one of the most striking developments in the whole history of canon law. Its true context is the centralizing policy of the post-Hildebrandine papacy, and the translation of papal theories of authority into precise legal form. Basically, there was nothing new in the concept of legislation by decretal letters, and popes had defined various points of law or doctrine in this fashion at least as early as the pontificate of Damasus or Siricius in the later-fourth century.[2] And recognition of the importance of decretal legislation, as distinct from the importance of the individual letters, was no less ancient. Reference has been made already to the influential collection of Dionysius Exiguus in the early-sixth century, and to *Pseudo-Isidore* in the mid-ninth;

---

[1] Kuttner, *Repertorium*, pp. 59 and 76 ff.; *idem*, *Compostellanus Antiquus*, pp. 284 ff.
[2] Cf. p. 12 and n.2, above.

whereas both had included many decretals as part of their contents, the latter collection is sometimes called the False or Forged Decretals, because of its inclusion of many putative or apocryphal papal letters allegedly from very early times.[1]

The circumstances which distinguish such legislation in the twelfth century are the astonishing acceleration in the rate of issue of papal rescripts, and the parallel growth of interest in them as a separate species of ecclesiastical law. These factors together produced a remarkably vigorous and creative school of decretal compilators in and after the closing decade of Alexander III's pontificate; and with the publication of *Compilatio Prima* they achieved a more or less unchallenged ascendancy over the whole field of canonical codification.[2] The salient features of their collections were a very remarkable concentration on decretal letters, as distinct from all other *canones*, and the contemporaneous emphasis in their selection. In fact they include the most recent decretals available at the moment of composition, a far smaller number of patristic and pre-Gratian texts, and the canons of the most important post-Gratian councils.

This was a very understandable development, fitting in with the papal policies already mentioned, since it was precisely by exploiting this weapon of decretal legislation that the popes were able to make their authority felt throughout the length and breadth of Western Christendom. But it was not a unilateral development. Persons involved in ecclesiastical disputes everywhere realized the advantages in referring their cases to a central judge of integrity, disinterested in the local issues involved. And bishops and ecclesiastical judges were glad to have definitive papal rulings, particularly as so many vital matters in law and theology were only now being decided.[3] At the same time, the pope could not hope to deal personally with the immense stream of questions flowing into the Curia, and the office of judge delegate was created to provide a remedy. The delegated judges were extremely active in all countries of Western Europe during Alexander III's pontificate. Usually the pope appointed

[1] Fournier and Le Bras, *Collections canoniques*, I, pp. 127–233. The collection also includes the *Capitula Angilramni* and the *Capitularia* of Benedictus Levita.

[2] For the date of *Compilatio Prima* (c. 1191), see van Hove, *Prolegomena*, p. 356; Friedberg, *Quinque Compilationes*, pp. vi and x.

[3] Friedberg, *Canonessammlungen*, pp. 1–2.

one or more judges to investigate the dispute in the district of its origin, and to bring it to a satisfactory conclusion. The delegate's jurisdiction was carefully defined, and limited in scope and time. He had no further authority once the issue giving rise to the papal commission had been decided. The rapid extension of this device resulted in an increase in the number of decretals issued, both through the matters in dispute, and to explain the office of the delegate and the procedure he was to follow.[1]

But the circumstances above all others which set the course for the decretal collectors to follow were the general acceptance and far-reaching influence of Gratian's *Decretum*. Gratian provided them now with a more certain foundation. Since the antique law was efficiently and adequately summarized in his work, they were able to start afresh, building their own collections of new law laid down in the most recent papal letters. This process was very like the emergence of ecclesiastical case law, though these private collections could not stand as authentic law books in their own right, as explained above.[2] They were books of convenient reference at first, intelligible only if it is remembered that the *Decretum* remained the basic text in the schools.

The growth of this new type of canonical collection can be traced clearly for the first time in the years immediately preceding the Third Lateran Council (1179). The earliest surviving collections were completed between c. 1174/5 and 1181, or shortly after; and many of these are of undoubted English provenance, both in contents and composition.[3]

Considering the ascendancy which the Bolognese canonists quickly achieved over the whole field of decretal codification, it could not be expected that they were unimportant in any phase of its development. But the role of the English canonists

[1] For the office of judge delegate, see Morey, *op. cit.*, pp. 44 ff.; Holtzmann and Kemp, *op. cit.*, pp. xvii–xxviii; R. Brentano, *York Metropolitan Jurisdiction and Papal Judges Delegate, 1279–96*, California (1959).

[2] But not exactly case law in the English sense. In canonical collections the details of actual cases, the *species facti*, were omitted as of no importance. Cf. F. Pollock and F. W. Maitland, *The History of English Law before the time of Edward I*, Cambridge (1923 imp.), p. 115.

[3] These matters are discussed at length in later chapters. The collection known as *Wigorniensis Altera* (B.M. Royal MS. 11 B. II, fols. 97–102) was apparently assembled at Worcester, and not much later than 1175. Cf. Kuttner, *Repertorium*, p. 283; Holtzmann, *Nachrichten*, p. 22. But see also Kuttner, *Repertorium*, pp. 273–6.

was second to none in the construction of many of the most primitive collections now surviving. Their contribution was vital in that formative stage, and exerted a permanent influence on the material contents of later, and more famous, collections composed on the continent. These English collectors displayed an almost incredible enthusiasm in assembling as many of the most recent decretals as they could acquire: starting with a very rudimentary technique, they soon evolved a convenient scheme of composition. But, within a few years, the value and significance of the decretal collections were more generally recognized, and by 1191 (if not earlier) leadership in this field also had been secured decisively by Bologna. From the publication of *Compilatio Prima*, the most significant work, by decretists and decretalists alike, was done in Italy. But it was not so in the beginning. The swift acceptance of Bernard's compilation so over-shadowed all earlier collections that they ceased to have any practical interest, and so passed out of use and knowledge; and in a similar way the Gregorian *Decretales* later obliterated the famous collections completed in the decades which preceded it.

Meanwhile, the structure of *Compilatio Prima* became the model for all later collections of any distinction. It was designed in five books under the headings: *Iudex, Iudicium, Clerus, Connubium* and *Crimen*. The five books were in turn subdivided into many special aspects; each of the subdivisions of the five 'books' is known as a 'title'. The whole composition was treated in a scientific manner, and purged of all irrelevant or non-juridical matter. Ten years later the Benedictine Rainer of Pomposa drew up a collection of decretals issued by Innocent III, but this was superseded by the great collections of two Englishmen —Gilbert (1202) and Alan (1206).[1] The elder Bernard of

---

[1] R. von Heckel, 'Die Dekretalensammlungen des Gilbertus und Alanus', *ZRG., Kan.Abt.*, XXIX (1940), pp. 116–357; Migne, ed., Rainer of Pomposa: 'Prima Collectio Decretalium Innocentii III', *Pat.Lat.*, CCXVI, cols. 1173–1272. Rainer's Collection was somewhat retrograde: he was not influenced schematically by *Compilatio Prima*, and his subject-matter arrangement is primitive, the longer decretals remaining unabbreviated. Very few MSS. of this collection survive, which suggests that its influence was not great. Hostiensis made no reference to Rainer's work in his review of the most important collections preceding the Gregorian *Decretales*: Hostiensis, *Henrici a Segusio Cardinalis Hostiensis Aurea Summa*, Venice (1605), col. 7.

Compostella completed his *Compilatio Romana* a little later, and in 1209–10 Peter of Benevento's *Compilatio Tertia* was published with a bull of authentication.[1] Next in order of completion, but containing earlier material, came *Compilatio Secunda*, drawn from the work of Gilbert and Alan by John the Welshman (1210–15). *Compilatio Quarta* was issued after the Fourth Lateran Council of 1215; and *Compilatio Quinta* was published with a bull of recommendation on 2 May 1226. Lastly, the Gregorian *Decretales*, deriving from the principal collections already mentioned, supplemented by more recent papal rulings, was declared authoritative in Gregory IX's *Rex pacificus* of 1234.[2]

[1] The date is discussed in Ullmann, *Scottish Charter*, p. 227. See also Friedberg, *Quinque Compilationes*, pp. 105–34; van Hove, *Prolegomena*, pp. 356–7. The bull of authorization enjoined its use 'tam in iudiciis quam in scholis'. Cf. the bull of authorization for the Gregorian *Decretales* of 1234: Friedberg, *Corpus Iuris Canonici*, II, cols. 1–4: 'Volentes igitur, ut hac tantum compilatione universi utantur in iudiciis et in scholis, districtius prohibemus ne quis praesumat aliam facere absque auctoritate sedis apostolice speciali.' See also the bull *Novae causarum* in which Honorius III promulgated the *Compilatio Quinta* of 1226; van Hove, *Prolegomena*, p. 357.

[2] For further details, see *ibid.*, pp. 355–61; Ullmann, *Scottish Charter*, pp. 226–31; *idem, Medieval Papalism*, pp. 13–16. A contemporary account of the main collections down to *Compilatio Secunda* is found in Tancred's prologue to his apparatus on *Compilatio Tertia*, printed by Ullmann, *Scottish Charter*, p. 229, n.11 (depending on the Durham Cathedral MS. C. III. 4, fol. 95ra), and by Schulte, *Quellen und Literatur*, I, p. 244. A further version is found in the Caius College Cambridge MS. 17.28, fol. 135ra., in a better recension. Hostiensis concludes his review of the most important collections preceding the Gregorian *Decretales* as follows: 'Et si ea quae premisi bene attenderis octo compilationes poteris invenire. Ideo bene congruebat ut Gregorius IX faceret opus novum, quare dictus Dominus Gregorius tantam confusionem et prolixitatem removere cupiens, ex dictis decretis, decretalibus epistolis, et dictis sanctorum patrum, ac legibus, antiquis compilationibus decretalium abrogatis, voluit necessaria et utilia redigere in hunc librum': *Aurea Summa*, col. 7.

CHAPTER II

The Decretal Letter in Canonical Commentaries

1. Introduction to the Theoretical Basis of Decretal Legislation

EVERY decretal letter is in essence a microcosm of the plenitude of power which medieval canonists and theologians believed axiomatically to be a necessary quality of the popes as heirs of St. Peter, Prince of the Apostles. Accepting this notion of a unique authority in St. Peter's see, it was a simple extension of doctrine to claim for the pope an unlimited primacy over the whole of Christian society.[1] In practical terms this concept of legislative and judicial supremacy was made effective through papal rescripts dealing with individual problems as they arose, and in more solemn matters through conciliar decrees concerned with more general questions and applicable to the whole Church. But canon lawyers before Gratian had not considered decretal letters the normal or almost exclusive expression of papal or canonical authority. They were merely one of several equally well-known, equally important, agencies. For this reason, the theoretical basis of decretal legislation had never been the subject of exact or urgent enquiry, though many canonical sources and papal letters had referred to it. This was scarcely surprising while the total number of decretals issued was not oppressive in any given period; but the publication of the *Decretum* coincided with an upsurge in the volume of letters

[1] In this theory, the Roman Church was considered the epitome of Christendom and the *sedes iustitiae*. Cf. F. Thaner, 'Ueber Entstehung und Bedeutung der Formel: Salva sedis apostolicae auctoritate in den päpstlichen Privilegien', *Sitz.KA.Wien*, LXXI (1872), pp. 807–51; J. B. Sägmuller, *Zur Geschichte des päpstlichen Gesetzgebungsrechts*, Rottenburg (1937), pp. 12 ff.

issuing from the Curia; and this development was in turn further stimulated by the decisive influence which Gratian's work itself exerted. Moreover, the decretals received in the older canonical collections were usually more important intrinsically or of wider application than the technical and judicial details discussed so frequently in the rescripts of Alexander III and his successors.[1] Still more decisive was the advance of canon law as a true juristic science, in which basic assumptions and long-familiar procedures were subjected for the first time to precise and analytical scrutiny.

The *Decretum* had provided the canonists with an acceptable summary of existing law and a stimulus to the scientific analysis of their material. A new emphasis in papal policy had already appeared before Gratian completed his collection, and was reflected in the steadily rising flow of decretals, mentioned above. But the general acceptance of the *Decretum* as a text-book, conveniently summarizing *ius antiquum*, produced a rapid acceleration in this process. An important change took place in the codification of law, and the collections made after Gratian found both their inspiration and the greater part of their substance in the most recent papal decisions. Not only was the sheer volume of letters increased beyond all recognition, but they dealt increasingly with procedural points and details of interpretation arising in the course of routine litigation, as well as with the great matters which had been their principal concern for so many centuries.

If we remember the time and the state of law when the *Decretum* was published, Gratian's discussion of the basis of decretal authority seems not disproportionate: he allowed it two Distinctions comprising thirteen chapters in all, together with three explanatory *dicta*, and referred to it as a secondary issue in several other contexts.[2] Considering the predominance which

---

[1] M. Cheney, *art.cit.*, pp. 181–3; Kuttner, *Projected Corpus*, p. 345. Letters of advice to ecclesiastical judges were usually issued in reply to questions submitted to the Curia for an authoritative ruling; letters of commission to judges delegate usually followed a process of impetration. Cf. Maitland, *Roman Canon Law*, pp. 100–31; Morey, *op. cit.*, p. 48; Holtzmann and Kemp, *op. cit.*, pp. xvii–xxviii.

[2] Friedberg, ed., *Corpus Iuris Canonici*, I (1879); J. H. Boehmer, ed., *Pat.Lat.*, CLXXXVII (1891 imp.). Gratian's discussion of the authority of decretal letters is found mainly in *Distinctiones* XIX and XX; relevant questions touching on papal authority are dealt with in *Causa* XXV, *Quaestiones* 1 and 2.

the decretals were soon to secure over the entire field of canon law, so brief a treatment may seem at first inadequate. But Gratian was not yet confronted with that 'inextricabilis silva' of decretals which sometimes perplexed the canonists in Alexander III's pontificate.[1] It is more surprising that the early decretists were so slow to carry his analysis much further, for they were plunged increasingly into the mainstream of development, as far as decretal legislation was concerned. They were assembling their own decretal collections at least as early as the mid-1170's,[2] and citing the new 'extravagant' laws in their commentaries by 1177–9 at the latest.[3] But, if they were slow to develop further the exposition which Gratian had already propounded, yet the basic assumption of the canonists from Gratian to Huguccio was invariable: that the pope could legislate by personal rescript was accepted as fundamental, and its essence never seriously questioned anywhere. It cannot be denied that the ever-increasing use of decretal letters was the subject of some disquiet and complaint, but their essential authority was not impugned by the critics. Stephen of Tournai, writing sometime after the death of Alexander III in 1181, deplored what he considered an excessive reliance on the latest papal rescripts to the rejection of the older canons.[4] His comments reflected the anxiety felt by some lawyers at the remarkable growth in importance of the numerous individual decisions. But his own earlier teaching, as a professional canonist when glossing the *Decretum*, had included a forthright statement

[1] M. Cheney, *art.cit.*, p. 183. It was Stephen of Tournai who spoke of the 'inextricabilis silva decretalium'.

[2] Kuttner, *Repertorium*, p. 147; M. G. Hall (Mrs. Cheney), *Roger Bishop of Worcester, 1164–79*, Oxford University B.Litt. thesis (1940), p. 64.

[3] Simon of Bisignano refers to 'extravagant' laws in his *Summa* on the *Decretum*, completed not later than 1179: Lambeth Palace MS. 411, fol. 25ra. (at *Decretum*, C.II, Qu.6): 'ut in extra, Sicut Romana ecclesia'; and 'ut in extra, Ex querimonia'. Simon was here referring to decretals of Alexander III: J-L 12293 and 13814. Cf. J. Juncker, 'Die Summa des Simon von Bisignano und seine Glossen', *ZRG., Kan. Abt.*, xv (1926), pp. 326–500; Holtzmann, 'Beiträge zu den Dekretalensammlungen', *ZRG., Kan.Abt.*, xvi (1927), pp. 47–50. An edition of Simon's *Summa* is now being prepared by T. McLaughlin: cf. *Traditio*, xiii (1957), p. 465.

[4] Cf. M. Cheney, *art.cit.*, p. 183: 'Rursus si ventum fuerit ad iudicia ... profertur a venditoribus inextricabilis silva decretalium epistolarum, quasi sub nomine sanctae recordationis Alexandri papae, et antiquiores sacri canones abiiciuntur, respuuntur, expuuntur.' The full text of Stephen's comment is in Migne, *Pat.Lat.*, ccxi, cols. 516–18, ep. 251.

of the binding force of papal rescripts. His later complaint concerned an abuse, but did not question the basic papal right.[1] This was axiomatic and never in dispute in the period.

2. GRATIAN AND THE DECRETALS

The legal force of decretal letters was discussed by Gratian most directly in his 19th Distinction, in which he considered the following three principal questions: are decretal letters authoritative when not included in the 'corpus canonum'; are all papal decisions, and therefore decretal letters also, legally binding; assuming an affirmative answer to these first two questions, in what circumstances may the validity of a papal ruling be rejected? The canons assembled by Gratian to deal with these problems can be briefly paraphrased as follows: all papal decisions relating to faith and doctrine, the needs of the Church and the morals of the faithful must be received as binding, for this was laid down in a canon by Pope Nicholas I.[2] And since all such rulings could not possibly be included within a single volume, their absence from the 'corpus canonum' must not be thought to deprive them of legal force: such a requirement would deprive of legal sanction the letters of Gregory I and even the Sacred Scriptures, when these are not included.[3] Moreover, a general sanction for all decretals had been provided by Popes Leo I[4] and Agatho, the latter declaring that all

[1] J. F. von Schulte, ed., *Die Summa des Stephanus Tornacensis über das Decretum Gratiani*, Giessen (1891), p. 29: 'Quia quidam dicebant, decretales epistolas non habere vim canonum vel decretorum, ostendit in hac distinctione, quia non minoris auctoritatis sunt, quam canones vel decreta.'

[2] *Decretum*, D. XIX: 'De epistolis vero decretalibus quaeritur, an vim auctoritatis obtineant, quum in corpore canonum non inveniantur.' *Ibid.*, c. 1: 'quanto potius, quae ipsa pro catholica fide, pro sanis dogmatibus, pro variis et multifariis ecclesiae necessitatibus et fidelium moribus diverso tempore scripsit, omni debent honore praeferri, et ab omnibus prorsus in quibuslibet opportunitatibus discretione vel dispensatione magistra reverenter assumi': from a council held in Rome by Nicholas I in 865, or a letter sent by him to the bishops of Gaul.

[3] *Ibid.*, 'Si ideo non esse decretales epistolas priscorum Pontificum Romanorum admittendas dicunt, quia in codice canonum non habentur adscriptae, ergo nec Sancti Gregorii, nec ullius alterius, qui ante vel post ipsum fuit, est aliquod institutum vel scriptum recipiendum, eo quod in codice canonum non habeatur adscriptum.'

[4] *Ibid.*, 'decretales epistolae Romanorum Pontificum sunt recipiendae, etiamsi non sint codici canonum compaginatae, quoniam inter ipsos canones unum Beati Leonis capitulum constat esse permixtum quo ita omnia decretalia constituta sedis apostolicae custodiri mandantur'.

decisions of the apostolic see must be observed 'tanquam ipsius divini Petri voce firmatae'.[1] It follows that the faithful must recognize the authority of the Holy See, even when it seems unbearable, as a Frankish capitulary and various papal letters had made clear.[2] Among other authorities, Gregory IV had ruled that disobedience to apostolic precepts should be punished with the loss of episcopal office;[3] St. Augustine had argued that decretal letters should be considered as part of the canonical writings;[4] and Leo I had strongly urged the necessity of unity with Peter, and therefore with the papal see.[5]

So much for the canonical texts which Gratian had gathered together. Here was a clear statement of the basic principle of a pervasive authority expressed in papal edicts of all kinds. But Gratian inserted at this point his first explanatory *dictum* and further canons, which qualified to some extent the argument developed in his texts so far. The validity of papal rescripts depends, according to Gratian's commentary, on their not conflicting with scriptural precepts or with papal statutes, previously existing. The story of Anastasius II provided a relevant example, since that pope had issued a ruling on the validity of ordinations conferred by heretics, conflicting with doctrines defined both before and after his own pontificate. In these circumstances, he had issued his rescript illegally and uncanonically, and was repudiated in consequence by the Roman Church.[6]

---

[1] *Ibid.*, c. 2: a decision of Agatho addressed to the bishops assembled at Rome in 680, or a letter which he issued between 678 and 681. Cf. Ivo of Chartres, *Decretum*, IV, 238, and *Panormia*, II, 101. The version in Ivo's *Decretum* agrees with Gratian's; but the *Panormia* has: 'tanquam ipsius divini praecepti voce firmatae': Migne, *Pat.Lat.*, CLXI, col. 515.

[2] *Decretum*, D. XIX, cc. 3 and 4.

[3] *Ibid.*, c. 5.

[4] *Ibid.*, c. 6.

[5] *Ibid.*, c. 7: including the Petrine text: 'Tu es Petrus, *etc.*', and concluding: 'Verum hanc petrae istius sacratissimam firmitatem, Domino, ut diximus, aedificante constructam, nimis impia vult praesumptione violare, quisquis eius potestatem tenat infringere, favendo cupiditatibus suis, et id, quod accepit a veteribus, non sequendo.'

[6] *Ibid.*, *dict.* post c. 7: 'Hoc autem intelligendum est de illis sanctionibus vel decretalibus epistolis, in quibus nec praecedentium Patrum decretis, nec evangelicis praeceptis aliquid contrarium invenitur. Anastasius enim *etc.*'; and *dict.* post c. 8: 'Quia ergo illicite et non canonice, sed contra decreta praedecessorum et successorum suorum haec rescripta dedit . . . ideo ab ecclesia Romana repudiatur, et a Deo percussus legitur fuisse hoc modo.'

And so, the Distinction, which had for the greater part expressed with perfect clarity the authority of all papal rulings and definitions, was now completed with this awkward reservation.

But Gratian took up the central theme once more, and developed it more explicitly, in his 20th Distinction. The principal issue considered by him in this section was as follows: decretal letters have equal force with conciliar canons, but what is their authority compared with scriptural works? To resolve this problem, Gratian now made clear a crucial distinction. Through the grace of the Holy Spirit some writings must be preferred to others, and for this reason the works of Augustine, Jerome and the Fathers are placed above some papal statutes. But the judgement of cases and scriptural exposition are two quite different matters, since both authority and knowledge are required in deciding affairs. Thus, Christ had said to Peter: 'Whatsoever you shall bind on earth, shall be bound also in Heaven'; and with these words He granted to Peter the keys of the Kingdom of Heaven: the one imparting knowledge and the other conferring power. Therefore, it is clear that, although the expositors of the Sacred Scriptures may surpass the popes in knowledge, they have not achieved the summit of papal power; and that is why, although they are to be preferred to the popes in scriptural interpretations, they must take second place to them in pronouncing judgements.[1]

A practical problem induced Gratian to return obliquely to this question in his 25th *Causa*, in which his primary concern was the canonical income of the 'ecclesia baptismalis'. But the question of wider implication arising was this: can the pope

---

[1] *Ibid.*, D. XX, introd. *dict.*: 'Decretales itaque epistolae canonibus conciliorum pari iure exaequantur. Nunc autem quaeritur de expositionibus sacrae scripturae, an exaequentur, an subiiciantur eis? Plurimi autem tractatorum, sicut pleniori gratia sancti Spiritus, ita ampliori scientia aliis praecellentes, rationi magis adhaesisse probantur. Unde nonnullorum Pontificum constitutis Augustini, Hieronymi atque aliorum tractatorum dicta videntur esse praeferenda. Sed aliud est causis terminum imponere, aliud sacras scripturas exponere. In negotiis definiendis non solum est necessaria scientia, sed etiam potestas. Unde Christus dicturus Petro: 'Quodcunque ligaveris *etc*'. . . . apparet, quod divinarum tractores scripturarum, etsi scientia Pontificibus praemineant, tamen quia dignitatis eorum apicem non sunt adepti, in sacrarum quidem scripturarum expositionibus eis praeponuntur, in causis vero definiendis secundum post eos locum merentur.'

exempt a monastery from the payment of tithe to the 'ecclesia baptismalis'? Such a right, if it were conceded, would seem in conflict with ancient rulings on the canonical division of diocesan incomes. The question is: can the pope override ancient canons by granting special privileges? This is a difficult problem, which Gratian resolved by explaining the extent and discretionary quality of papal authority.[1] To the objection that the 'prima sedes' should above all others preserve the conciliar statutes and decrees of earlier pontiffs, Gratian replied that the Roman Church confers their legal force and sanction on the canons, yet is not itself constrained by them.[2] It is the head and hinge of all the churches, and has the right to formulate laws from which no one may lawfully dissent; but, in conferring authority on the canons, it does not subject itself to them.[3] As the 'prima sedes', it should certainly respect what it has itself ordained, but it has no obligation to do so.[4] The Roman Church may grant concessions contrary to general decrees, and may concede by special privilege what the general laws forbid.[5] The canons themselves affirm that the right of interpreting laws is reserved to it, just as it has the power to lay them down; that is why such phrases as 'nisi auctoritas Romanae ecclesiae imperaverit' and 'salvo tamen in omnibus iure Sanctae Romanae ecclesiae', and other expressions of that kind, are used respecting its rights. Therefore, the Roman Church may strengthen some by granting special privileges, or may make concessions passing beyond the general rules, but with equity observed in all

---

[1] *Ibid.*, C. XXV, Qu. 1, introd. *dict.*: 'quia decimae iuxta decreta sanctorum Patrum quadripertito dividuntur, quarum una pars episcopis, secunda clericis, tertia fabricis restaurandis, quarta vero pauperibus est assignata. Decreta vero sanctorum canonum neminem magis quam Apostolicum servare oportet.'

[2] *Ibid.*, *dict.* post c. 16: 'Si ergo primam sedem statuta conciliorum prae omnibus servare oportet, et si pro statu omnium ecclesiarum necesse est illam impigro vigilare affectu; si ea, quae a Romanis Pontificibus decreta sunt, ab omnibus observari convenit . . . *etc.* His ita respondetur: Sacrosancta Romana ecclesia ius et auctoritatem sacris canonibus impertitur, sed non eis alligatur.'

[3] *Ibid.*, 'Habet enim ius condendi canones, utpote quae caput est et cardo omnium ecclesiarum, a cuius regula nemini dissentire licet. Ita ergo canonibus auctoritatem praestat, ut se ipsam non subiiciat eis.'

[4] *Ibid.*, 'Oportet ergo primam sedem, ut diximus, observare ea, quae decernendo mandavit, non necessitate obsequendi, sed auctoritate impertiendi.'

[5] *Ibid.*, 'Licet itaque sibi contra generalia decreta specialia privilegia indulgere, et speciali beneficio concedere quod generali prohibetur decreto.'

things: for the Roman Church is indeed the mother of justice, and so should not itself be found to deviate in anything from justice.[1]

Although the canons and Gratian's *dicta*, discussed above, refer in many instances to the Roman Church and not to the pope more specifically (an important distinction in certain later controversies[2]), there is little evidence that Gratian intended this emphasis in his choice of terms in most of the passages cited. It is equally true that he was concerned in the 25th *Causa* with papal *privilegia* more particularly than decretal letters; but his exposition of papal authority was no less relevant to these, and later canonists drew together his separate arguments into a single theme. The final impression conveyed by Gratian's treatment is one of firm support for papal discretionary power in conferring favours and defining law, in pronouncing judgements and in legal exposition. The difficulty raised by the proviso at the end of the 19th Distinction is partly illusory, when properly understood, and should not be stressed disproportionately. As far as the Sacred Scriptures at least are concerned, it could be taken for granted that popes would not normally seek to alter their fundamental precepts.[3] Nevertheless, the case of Anastasius presented some difficulty, and decretists in the later-twelfth century (as well as the *Correctores Romani* in the sixteenth) were sometimes disturbed by the limit which Gratian had seemed to place on papal initiative in this context, and

---

[1] *Ibid.*, 'Sacri siquidem canones ita aliquid constituunt, ut interpretationis auctoritatem sanctae Romanae ecclesiae reservatur. Ipsi namque soli canones valent interpretari, qui ius condendi eos habent . . . Valet ergo, ut ex praemissis colligitur, sancta Romana ecclesia suis privilegiis quoslibet munire, et extra generalia decreta quaedam speciali beneficio indulgere, considerata tamen rationis aequitate, ut quae mater iustitiae est in nullo ab ea dissentire inveniatur.'

[2] Cf. J. Watt, 'The Early Medieval Canonists and the Formation of Conciliar Theory', *Irish Theological Quarterly*, XXIV (1957), pp. 13–31. The crucial importance of this distinction is fully recognized, but is not of principal concern in the present context: for a full discussion of this subject, including Gratian's treatment of the case of Anastasius, see B. Tierney, *Foundations of the Conciliar Theory*, Cambridge (1955), pp. 23–46 and 248–50.

[3] Maitland, *Roman Canon Law*, p. 12: in Maitland's well-known phrase, it could be assumed that popes would not 'attempt to repeal the Ten Commandments'. Cf. the broader concepts of the 'princeps legibus solutus' and 'quod principi placuit legis habet vigorem', familiar to canonists and Roman Civil lawyers alike; see F. Schulz, 'Bracton on Kingship', *EHR*, LX (1945), pp. 136–76.

sought to qualify the reservation he had expressed.[1] It must be admitted that Gratian had left unresolved certain difficult questions. Thus, if a decretal might conceivably contain a ruling in conflict with fundamental or scriptural precept, who could adjudicate in that eventuality? And what was the exact significance of the 'corpus canonum' which figured so prominently in the 19th Distinction?

3. CLARIFICATION OF DEFINITIONS BY THE DECRETISTS

Two questions, therefore, were left open for elucidation by later canonists: how, against the background of legislative and technical developments in the period, was a decretal letter to be defined more precisely; and, with this settled, how was its authority to be fitted into the general pattern of papal legislative and judicial supremacy? The former question was decided quite quickly; the latter not satisfactorily before Huguccio's *Summa*.[2] As to the question of definitions: the earliest commentators were content for the most part to repeat Gratian's imprecise generalizations.[3] But the drift of events would not permit this attitude to last for long, and in face of the swelling stream of decretals issuing from the Curia, canonists were compelled to examine more closely the forms and purposes of papal rescripts. Their early definitions are typified in Stephen of Tournai's *Summa* (1160–70), where a decretal letter is described as a papal rescript sent to any bishop or ecclesiastical judge on some doubtful point of law when the Roman Church had been consulted.[4] A more detailed analysis is found in some of the

---

[1] Huguccio's views are fully discussed below. For the *Correctores Romani*, see Boehmer, *ed. cit.*, cols. 109–10: 'Notatio Correctorum C. VII (f), *Anastasius*. Minime est sensisse Anastasium ordinatos ab Acacio post latam in ipsum sententiam, rite fungi acceptis officiis potuisse . . . Habetur autem haec eadem Anastasii Papae II epistola in corpore canonum, quod Romana ecclesia semper approbavit, ut infra D. XX, *De libellis*, est adnotatum. Ita sine causa reprehenditur hoc loco Anastasius a Gratiano.'

[2] For Huguccio's commentary, see Pembroke College Cambridge MS. 72, fols. 128ra–129rb. Cf. Caius College Cambridge MS. 676, fols. 9va–10vb: an English gloss slightly later in composition.

[3] F. Thaner, *Die Summa Magistri Rolandi nachmals Papstes Alexander III*, Innsbruck (1874), p. 6; Schulte, *Die Summa des Paucapalea über das Decretum Gratiani*, Giessen (1890), p. 20. Cf. *De multiplici iuris*, Pemb. MS. 72, fol. 68ra.

[4] Schulte, *Summa Stephani*, p. 2: 'Decretalis epistola est, quam dominus apostolicus, aliquo episcopo vel alio iudice ecclesiastico super aliqua causa dubitante et ecclesiam Romanam consulente, rescribit et ei transmittit.' Cf. Caius MS. 676,

extant manuscripts (but not all) of the commentaries by Rufinus (1157–9) and Simon of Bisignano (1177–9).[1] Its authorship is uncertain at present, in the absence of more consistent manuscript evidence; but, whatever its origin, the following classification of the various kinds of decretals had become generally accepted by the end of Alexander III's pontificate:

Decretal letters are either universal and general or they are special. The former are sent to all or many provinces, while the latter are addressed to individuals. Special decretals are in turn subdivided into several categories: some define or limit a point of law, and are important even outside their immediate circumstances, unless specifically limited to time or person;[2] others mandate a course of action but do not require immediate compliance unless questions of faith are involved;[4] others prohibit action but, again, do not require immediate compliance unless the matter forbidden is altogether illegal;[5] and others, finally, grant indulgence or dispensation by virtue of the pope's discretionary powers, but these have no importance outside their own special circumstances.[6] This was a satisfactory basic

---

fol. 173 vb: 'Decretalis epistola: que ad consultationem alicuius rescribitur.' See also Hostiensis, *Aurea Summa*, col. 9.

[1] The classification of decretals given in this chapter is based on MSS. of Rufinus and Simon of Bisignano, but no presumption is made concerning its authorship. H. Singer, ed., *Die Summa Decretorum des Magister Rufinus*, Paderborn (1902), pp. 42–4, provides a very elementary analysis in his main text and a fuller version in the footnotes. Two MSS. of Simon of Bisignano preserve variant arrangements: Lambeth Palace MS. 411 has no analysis of decretal species; but B.M. Addit. MS. 24659, fol. 4v, includes a useful classification in the marginalia.

[2] Singer, *Summa Rufini*, p. 42: 'Sunt enim decretales epistolae quas ad provincias vel personas pro diversis negotiis sedes apostolica direxit'; and n.2: 'Decretalium epistolarum quaedam sunt universales, quae universis provinciis mittuntur, omni robore fultae; quaedam speciales, alicui episcopo super aliquo (negotio) remissae. Specialis aliquandoque diffinit; et tunc trahi potest ad consequentiam, nisi diffinitio detur pro tempore vel pro persona vel alicuius tali *etc.*' Cf. Addit. MS. 24659, fol. 4v: 'quandoque diffinit, docens quid iuris sit, et hoc optinet'; Caius MS. 676, fol. 9v: 'aut diffinit et tunc pro lege observatur'.

[4] Singer, *Summa Rufini*, p. 42, n.2: 'Quandoque imperat: nec est transgressor, si statim non obtemperat, nisi imperet papa de fidei articulis.'

[5] *Ibid.*, 'Quando prohibet: nec est transgressor, si statim non obediat, nisi prohibeatur omnino illicitum, quando precatur (=deprecatur), et tenetur acquiescere.' Cf. Caius MS. 676, fol. 9v: 'Aut prohibet vel precipit et tunc omnino observatur.'

[6] Singer, *Summa Rufini*, p. 42, n.2: 'Quandoque indulget: et tunc non est trahenda ad consequentiam. Duo sunt quibus roboratur apostolica sententia, scilicet discretio et dispensatio sibi tradita.'

D

classification, and later canonists found little need to add to it. Huguccio and similar later commentators expanded or refined the various points of detail, but added little in essence to what had already been established.[1]

4. THE NATURE OF DECRETAL AUTHORITY IN THE HANDS OF THE DECRETISTS

In considering the nature of decretal authority, Gratian had stated the basic right in general terms, equating the force of decretals with that of conciliar canons and papal decrees. The earliest decretists were again content merely to paraphrase these brief conclusions. Thus, Paucapalea (1140–8) stated simply that decretal letters have equal force with conciliar canons;[2] and Rolandus Bandinelli (ante 1148) repeated this general principle, appending Gratian's argument that, whereas Augustine and other writers are to be preferred in scriptural exposition, the canons have greater weight in deciding cases.[3] According to Rufinus (1157–9), decretal letters have the same authority as canons and decrees because of the primacy of the Roman Church; and this emphasis, by no means an innovation, provided a key to the deeper examination of the nature of decretal authority by later canon lawyers.[4] Rufinus himself repeated without elucidation Gratian's limitation of the validity of papal decisions to matters not in conflict with already existing doctrine;[5] and so at this stage there was still no serious attempt to probe more deeply into the nature of the problems involved. But the scope of enquiry was gradually widened in the hands of the most advanced decretists, until a first fully-satisfactory analysis was produced in Huguccio's *Summa*. This great treatise is still accessible in manuscript only, except for occasional brief and select quotations, though a critical edition is now in pre-

---

[1] The work of the English glossators is discussed by Kuttner and Rathbone, *art.cit.*, pp. 317–21 and 347–53.

[2] Schulte, *ed. cit.*, p. 20.

[3] Thaner, *ed. cit.*, p. 6.

[4] Schulte, *Summa Stephani*, p. 30. Cf. *De multiplici iuris*, Pemb. MS. 72, fol. 68ra: 'Quod decretales epistole eiusdem auctoritatis et canones et decreta propter primatum Romane ecclesie *etc.*'

[5] Singer, *Summa Rufini*, p. 42: 'que omni devotione sunt custodiende, nisi preceptis evangelicis vel decretis sanctorum patrum inveniantur adverse'.

paration.[1] Therefore, a final assessment of Huguccio's doctrine on any important point of law cannot be made at present; but his commentary on Gratian's 19th Distinction throws much revealing light on his attitude to papal authority expressed in decretal letters. His argument proceeds by way of question and answer as follows:[2]

Consider the statement that decretal letters are of equal weight with canons and decrees. Is it not true that, whereas a decretal rests on papal authority alone, a canon has that advantage but is further strengthened by the support of the whole council? Quite the contrary: so far is this from being true that a decretal letter has in fact the greater authority. If a decretal appears in conflict with existing canons, it need not be assumed that the pope is ignorant of the law, but rather that he wishes to derogate from it, as he has the right to do.[3] He has the power of uttering and interpreting the canons: these are faculties reserved to him both tacitly and expressly, and he has the right to grant dispensations. Does this power then include the right to decide even matters of law and faith in general? Alexander III's decretals show that this is indeed the case. Thus, the decretal *Licet praeter* (which Alexander sent to the archbishop of Salerno, c. 1174–6) decided among other matters that a betrothed woman should be restored to her first spouse even if she had been later given to another; and the decretal *Cum Christus* (which he sent to the archbishop of Reims in 1177, to combat heresies spreading dangerously in France) defined the orthodox teaching on the nature of Christ.[4] These examples show how the pope might

[1] Details of progress on this great work of collaboration are given by Kuttner, *Traditio*, XIII (1957), p. 465.

[2] Pemb. MS. 72, fols. 128ra–129rb.

[3] *Ibid.*, fol. 128ra: 'dicunt quod canon prevalere quia nititur auctoritate (*MS.* : auctoritatem) pape et totius concilii, sed decretalis sola auctoritate pape. Econtra tamen dico quod potius decretalis preiudicare debet, quia cum apostolicus . . . decretalem constituit contrariam canoni ex certa scientia videtur velle derogare canoni quia ei licet.'

[4] *Ibid.*, 'In canonibus enim condendis supertacite vel expresse reservantur (*MS.*: reservatur) interpretatio et dispensatio. *Etc.*' *Licet praeter* is J-L 14091; *Cum Christus* is J-L 12785. The latter was sent to the archbishop of Reims in 1177, and included the definition: 'sicut verus Deus, ita verus est homo, ex anima rationali et humana carne subsistens'; it should be compared with a similar letter which Alexander had sent to the archbishops of Bourges, Reims, Tours and Rouen in 1170: J-L 11809. Huguccio's comment on the *Cum Christus* is highly significant: 'Item peccant illi qui

deal with important general principles relating to morality and faith in the course of his decretals. In similar ways, he might also regulate matters of administration and appointments: he could restore a deposed bishop to office, even when a successor had already been elected.[1]

But what of the objection with which Gratian had opened his discussion: what of decretals which are not included in the 'corpus canonum'? It would be inconvenient in practice to insist on such a condition. Moreover, a general sanction for all decretals was provided by the rulings of Popes Leo and Gelasius, as Gratian had noted.[2] But is this an acceptable solution, to justify a papal claim by appealing to a papal decision; were not the popes themselves interested parties in the matter; can their 'domestic testimony' be accepted in such a situation? Indeed it can, for there is no doubt about the truth of what these popes had stated.[3] The solution resides in the special quality of the apostolic see and its Petrine foundation. The popes derive their authority from the see, not in their own persons: 'non sit ratione persone sed propter auctoritatem sedis'.[4] The see gained its dignity from Peter, and through it his power has been transmitted to his successors. There are some indeed who question the authority of the Roman see, and deny that it is the head of all the churches; but these are contumacious, their opinions savouring of heresy and schism. They deny that the apostolic see

dicunt Christum non esse aliquid secundum quod est homo, cum apostolicus et sic Romana ecclesia hoc approbaverit, et sub interminatione anathematis hoc esse tenendum, ut in Extra, Cum Christus.'

[1] *Ibid.*, 'Hic dicitur ad illum quod si quis episcopus fuerit depositus, et alius substitutus, si dominus papa eum restituit, substituto preferri debeat.'

[2] *Ibid.*, fol. 128rb: 'Hic ostendit quod decretales non ideo minus sunt recipiende quod non continentur in corpore canonum quia non omnes possunt (*MS.*: posset) ibi contineri. *Etc.*'

[3] *Ibid.*, 'Sed nonne Leo et Gelasius erant apostolici; quia ideo ergo in propria causa valet testimonium domesticum? Dico non dubitabatur de veritate eorum.'

[4] *Ibid.*, 'Hoc non sit ratione persone sed propter auctoritatem sedis, unde caute dixit apostolice sedis et non dixit apostolici. Item sit propter dignitatem persone quam (*MS.*: que) locus in dignitate Petri obtinet, et quantam (*MS.*: quando) dignitatem et potestatem habuit Petrus . . . tantam habuit quilibet eius successor.' These views were not original to Huguccio; cf. those set forth by Cardinal Humbert in the previous century in discussing the relationship between the pope and the Roman Church: Ullmann, 'Cardinal Humbert and the Ecclesia Romana', *Studi Gregoriani*, IV (1952), pp. 111–27. See also Innocent III's interpretation: Migne, *Pat.Lat.*, CCXVII, col. 670, Sermo IV.

can make canons, or that it has the authority to make them; and they assert that its statutes need not be observed. Those guilty of offences of this kind should be excommunicated as heretics.[1] But a distinction must be drawn between those who deny the papal right in principle and those who refuse to submit to it in practice. The latter are not heretical, though they sin mortally.[2] Basically the whole position rests on Petrine supremacy: there is no salvation without the faith of Peter, and opposition to the apostolic statutes and to the primacy of the Roman see opens up the road to damnation. The Roman Church has the undoubted right to issue decrees for other churches. If Gratian's final reservation meant that a pope could not alter the decisions of his predecessors, then this was not in fact a true opinion. Having considered a statute already existing, the pope may revoke it if he wishes, even when it embodies a perfectly sound decision. He may not contradict the scriptural precepts or hinder matters which are necessary to salvation; nor may he act contrary to the well-being of the Church as a consequence. If this is what Gratian meant by his reservation, Huguccio concluded, then his teaching holds good: otherwise he was in error.[3]

A great advance to juristic maturity is obvious in Huguccio's treatise. Despite the incidental flaws in its treatment, his analysis had easily outstripped that of all earlier decretists. The

---

[1] Pemb. MS. 72, fol. 128va: 'Sunt enim quidam qui contumaciter apostolicam sedem esse caput omnium ecclesiarum negantes, dicunt ipsam non posse condere canones vel decreta, nec habere auctoritatem condendi ea, et statuta ab ea non esse observanda; isti tales scisma et heresim sapiunt, et ipso genere delicti tanquam heretici excommunicati sunt.'

[2] *Ibid.*, fol. 128 va.

[3] *Ibid.*, fol. 128vb: 'Christus prefecit Petrus omnibus, et in soliditate fidei eius ecclesiam collocavit . . . tamen dicitur ecclesia fundata super fidem Petri quia ad instar fidei Petri salvantur omnes fideles, et quia ipse primus posuit fundamentum fidei in gentibus, et quia tanquam saxum immobile ecclesiam contineat.' Huguccio explains that by 'ecclesia' he means 'unitas fidelium', not 'ecclesia triumphans': 'id est ecclesie scilicet unitatis fidelium . . . quod ideo dico ne tu intelligis ecclesiam triumphatam super fidem Petri fundatam.' As to the accusation that the pope cannot decree anything contrary to the good statutes of his predecessors, Huguccio concludes: 'Quod non credo esse verum, nam etiam bona statuta potest revocare inspecta causa, dummodo non tangat precepta veteris vel novi testamentorum, vel articulos, vel ea que sunt necessaria ad salutem, vel que pertinent ad generalem statutum (? statum) ecclesie, et ideo non approbo quod hic dicit magister nisi de talibus intelligat.'

widest implications of decretal legislation are explored by him against a backcloth of the possible objections which might be raised against them. Passing far beyond the limits of the questions originally discussed by Gratian, a clear statement is made of papal supremacy and the plenitude of papal power, of which each decretal letter is an isolated expression.[1] This is a very different interpretation of Huguccio's teaching from that advanced by Carlyle on admittedly tenuous foundations.[2] On a basis of certain brief extracts previously published by Schulte, Carlyle concluded that Huguccio was somewhat hesitant in support of decretal authority where a papal letter appeared in conflict with a decree or a conciliar canon. It is certainly not easy to agree with this verdict in the light of the evidence cited above; and even the extracts which Schulte had published hardly support so general a deduction.[3] The evidence in Huguccio's commentary on Gratian's 19th Distinction suggests in fact the very opposite conclusion.

The following brief points from an English gloss, composed at the close of the century, will serve as a postscript to Huguccio's analysis, for its authors were well acquainted with his work. If the genuineness of a decretal is called into question, and its authenticity remains unestablished by the evidence of oaths and witnesses, the letter may be rejected once with impunity. But, in the event of disobedience to a papal mandate, the penalty of excommunication should be imposed on the offender, its severity increasing in proportion to his persistence in the offence.[4] Both power and knowledge are necessary in judging cases, for the greatest knowledge is not sufficient without authority. In

---

[1] But cf. pp. 29–31, above: Huguccio's commentary on *Distinctio* XIX included certain arguments already found in Gratian's *dictum* in *Causa* XXV.

[2] R. W., and A. J. Carlyle, *A History of Medieval Political Theory in the West*, II, pp. 192–3. This great study is not always reliable when dealing with canon law: see *ibid.*, pp. 160 ff., where it is argued that there was no clear-cut and precise notion of the nature of canon law 'in the Middle Ages'.

[3] Schulte, *Quellen und Literatur*, I, pp. 164–5; *Decretum*, C. II, Qu. 6. In discussing a point of appellate procedure, Huguccio had used the expression: 'sed plus credo antiquo decreto et novo concilio quam decretalibus'; it would be rash to assume that he intended this comment to define a general principle on the respective importance of canons, decrees and decretals.

[4] Caius MS. 676, fol. 10ra: 'venitur tamen contra mandatum domini pape semel impune'; 'Nota quod inobediens pape, primo minori excommunicatione, deinde si perstiterit maiori feriendus est.'

matters of faith the decision belongs to Peter alone, and there is no salvation for failure to obey the apostolic precepts.[1]

5. DECRETAL DIPLOMATIC

And so by the end of the twelfth century, through the technical perfection of Bernard of Pavia's *Compilatio Prima* and the maturity of juristic analysis reflected in Huguccio's *Summa* the ascendancy of the decretals was assured. Not only had the new 'libri extravagantium' become the standard form of canonical codification, but the nature and purpose of the decretals themselves had been satisfactorily expounded in literary commentary. There was one further problem of an essentially practical nature: the development of diplomatic science in the hands of the canonists.[2]

As the stream of decretals issuing from the Curia widened, the problem of forgeries was raised in an increasingly acute form: it was a problem bearing both on the grant of rights and immunities in papal *privilegia*, and the enunciation of judicial decisions in decretal letters. The progress in dealing with the former is sufficiently known from the records of some of the more famous disputes of the period: the Canterbury and York dispute over the primacy in England;[3] the various isolated references to the critical autopsy of chancery documents in twelfth-century papal letters (the Spanish monastic and cathedral archives are particularly rich in evidence of this kind);[4] the well-known disputes involving English and Welsh ecclesiastics

---

[1] *Ibid.*, fol. 10vb: 'In causis decidendis necessaria sunt scientia et potestas. Unde peritissimi, nisi habeant potestatem, causas decidere non possunt. Questio etiam fidei soli Petro reservatur.'

[2] For papal diplomatic, see H. Bresslau, *Handbuch der Urkundenlehre für Deutschland und Italien*, Leipzig, II (1931), pp. 361–70; A. Giry, *Manuel de Diplomatique*, Paris (1925), pp. 454–62; R. L. Poole, *Lectures on the History of the Papal Chancery down to the Time of Innocent III*, Cambridge (1915), pp. 76–97, 142 ff., and 162–5; A. Bouard, *Manuel de Diplomatique*: II. *Diplomatique papale* (1949); L. Santifaller, 'Beschreibstoffe im Mittelalter', *Mitteilungen*, LXI (1953).

[3] Poole, *op. cit.*, pp. 142 ff.; J. Raine, ed., *Historians of the Church of York*, Rolls Series, II, pp. 112 ff.; H. Boehmer, *Die Fälschungen Erzbischof Lanfranks von Canterbury*; Foreville, *op. cit.*, pp. 48–60, 64–76 and 276–326.

[4] The many Papsturkunden volumes in the *Abhandlungen* provide ample evidence from the various provinces of the Western Church. Thus, for England, cf. Holtzmann, ed., *Papsturkunden in England*, I (1930), pp. 372–3, ep. 109a; *ibid.*, II (1935), pp. 388–9; for the Spanish Peninsula, cf. P. Kehr, *Papsturkunden in Spanien: Katalanien*, II (1926), pp. 413–17, epp. 118–19; *ibid.*: *Navarre und Aragon*, II (1928), pp. 345–8, ep. 46; pp. 393–4, ep. 78; pp. 472–6, epp. 134–5. All these letters (and many

during Innocent III's pontificate (such as those involving Thomas of Marlborough, Robert of Clipstone and Giraldus Cambrensis).[1] Not only have we details of the critical examination of documents in Pope Innocent's presence, but there is even the record of instructions which he sent to the archbishop of Reims and the clergy of Milan on the detection of forged epistles.[2] His pontificate has been justly recognized as marking a decisive stage in the systematization of papal diplomatic, but the contribution of earlier popes has been unduly overshadowed in the process. In Alexander III's pontificate, canon lawyers were already including in their decretal collections separate sections concerned with documentary forgeries.[3] The decretals of Lucius III, Urban III and Celestine III are also well known to have dealt at times with this problem, which had a significant place in the history of clerical privilege.[4] But the commentaries of the decretists have been largely unknown or neglected, and that by Huguccio is once more most revealing, and especially important since he included the future Pope Innocent III among his pupils.

If the authenticity of a decretal is called into question, the first remedy (in Huguccio's opinion) is to refer to the papal registers for confirmation. If there is no trace of the letter contained there, then recourse must be had to internal evidence and presumption: is the decretal acceptable by reason of its style, because it smacks of the curial conventions; and is it

others) record the critical examination of papal documents and legal instruments, and abound in such phrases as: 'in forma atque bullatura, annis Domini et indictione et aliis multis peccare'; 'filo serico vel saltem lineo'; 'nec ex stilo dictaminis nec ex bulla aut scriptura comprehendere potuerimus, quod aliquid falsitatis in se contineat'; etc.

[1] Cf. W. D. Macray, ed., *Chronicon Abbatiae de Evesham ad Annum 1418*, Rolls Series (1863), p. 141: 'De itinere abbatis et Thome monachi, et causa itinerum eorundem ad curiam Romanam' (1204); *ibid.*, p. 161, Innocent III's comment: 'Huiusmodi privilegia quae vobis ignota sunt, nobis sunt notissima, nec possunt falsari.' But Poole argued that Innocent was himself mistaken in accepting an ancient document as genuine: it was parchment when it should have been papyrus; *op. cit.*, pp. 148 ff.

[2] For typical letters of Innocent III on these matters, see Friedberg, ed., *Decretales*, V, 20, 4; Migne, *Pat.Lat.*, CCXIV, cols. 322–4: Register I. 349; *ibid.*, CCXV, cols. 1459–60: Register XI. 144; etc.

[3] Cf. Friedberg, *Canonessammlungen*, p. 22: *Parisiensis II*, XIV, De falsariis; but see also *ibid.*, n.3.

[4] R. Génestal, *Le Privilegium Fori en France*, Paris, II (1924), pp. 30–7.

acceptable in its substance, because of its agreement with canonical equity? Examine the whole document with a view to its possible forgery: nor is it enough to establish simply that the letter was made in the chancery, for it must be made there with the knowledge of the pope or by some recognized authority.[1] It is a forgery too if something has been subtracted or altered, or if there is any defect in bullation or parchment, in thread or script.[2] A forger may be convicted on the evidence of a spurious seal or a style differing from that of the Curia; and on conviction such a forger should suffer the appropriate penalty, though a bishop may not punish him without a papal mandate, unless it was an episcopal and not a papal letter in question. A clerical forger should be deprived both of benefice and office, and condemned to perpetual imprisonment in a monastery. For a layman, the Roman Law decreed that a freeman should lose his possessions and be sent into exile, and that a slave should be sentenced to death.[3]

---

[1] Pemb. MS. 72, fol. 128ra: 'Sed quid si dubitetur an sit decretalis, recurrendum est ad registrum; quod si ibi non continetur, recurrendum est ad presumptionem, scilicet quia ab hominibus habetur et dicitur (*MS.*: dicetur) esse decretalis quia stilum redolet curie, et quod a canonica non discrepat equitate.' *Ibid.*, fol. 128va: 'Quia non fuit facta de conscientia pape vel in cancellaria, vel ibi facta non fuit de conscientia pape, vel principis, vel alterius prelati *etc.*' Huguccio's reference here to the 'cancellaria' is most interesting, since that technical expression seems not to have been in general use at the time, though it was used occasionally: cf. Lucius III's reference, *Decretales*, I, 3, 10. The Roman Chancery was not officially known as 'cancellaria' until Innocent III's pontificate; see H. W. Klewitz, 'Kanzleischule und Hofkapelle', *Deutsches Archiv*, Weimar (1940–1); and Nicolo del Re, *La Curia Romana*, Rome (1952), pp. 245 ff.

[2] Pemb. MS. 72, fol. 128va: '. . . aliquid est additum a falsatore vel subtractum vel vitiatum, sive in bulla sive in carta sive in filo sive in litteris, et de omnimoda tali falsitate hic agitur.' Cf. Innocent III's much-quoted phrase: 'tam in charta quam bulla, tam stilo quam filo'. (Register VII. 34.)

[3] Pemb. MS. 72, fol. 128va: 'sed qualiter potest convinci falsarius per testes, per sigillum dissimile, per litteras dissimiles, per modum scribendi, et per multas alias presumptiones . . . episcopus non possit punire falsarios ante susceptum mandatum domini pape, sed distinguitur utrum falsaverint litteras domini pape vel ipsius episcopi. In primo casu potest episcopus eos custodie mancipere sed non punire donec mandatum pape suscipiat . . . in secundo casu potest eos punire . . . de talibus si clerici sunt . . . officio et beneficio privati perpetuo retrudantur in monasterium . . . si laici sunt . . . nobis licentiam diffiniendi dare quod Romana lex statuit de talibus . . . ut portentur et in omnibus bonis proscribantur si liberi sunt, si vero servi, ultimo supplicio afficiantur. Pena enim falsi non est capitis amissio nisi in servis . . . in liberis pena falsi non est capitis amissio, sed deportatio et omnium bonorum confiscatio.'

According to the English glossators, in the English gloss mentioned above, a decretal letter may be false through surreptition,
or by the discovery of some lie in the statement of law or in the
facts of the case, or by defect of concealment; and, if the decretal
is defective in any of these respects, the matter involved should
still be decided by the rescript's authority, but according to
equity rather than by its literal tenor. But a decretal may also
be false through defect of form: in its seal, thread or mem-
brane, though abrasion, in its script, or in many other ways;
and, if the decretal is defective in any of these respects, it must
be rejected and its forger punished.[1] In one respect the English
glossators diverge in emphasis from Huguccio's commentary:
the latter had stated that, in the case of a doubt concerning a
decretal's authenticity, recourse should be had in the first place
to the papal registers, but the former asserted that he must prove
it to be a true decretal who alleges it to be so. He must prove it
by oath and with witnesses; and the letter may once be rejected with impunity, should he fail in this.[2]

Although there is no disharmony between Huguccio and the
English glossators in basic principles, there is nevertheless a
significant difference in their emphases. For the former, the
greater interest lies in juristic exposition, in concepts of papal
authority and the theoretical basis of decretal legislation, in the
practical work of the papal chancery and in questions of administration. For the latter, the more immediate interest is in the
receipt and interpretation of the individual rescripts in local
courts and by particular recipients. To some extent this difference may be explained simply by geographical factors, since,
for the English canonists, concerned with practical problems
far away from Italy, proofs by oath and witnesses were more

[1] Caius MS. 676, fol. 10ra: 'Rescriptum comperitur falsum per surreptitionem;
vel quando mendacium invenitur in narratione iuris, vel facti, vel in fraude tacendi.
In omnibus his modis auctoritate rescripti procedendum est, non quidem secundum
tenorem eiusdem sed secundum equitatem. (Vel comperitur falsum) per formam
adulterinam, si in bulla fuerit falsitas, vel in filo forte consuto, vel in membrana,
vel in abrasione, vel in litera, et denique multis aliis modis. Omnibus his modis
reprobatur rescriptum, *et punitur falsarium.*' This final comment with triple under-
lining was in fact added to the gloss in a second layer of commentary, by a different
though contemporary hand.

[2] *Ibid.*, fol. 10ra: 'Si autem dubitetur utrum sit decretalis, probet eam decretalem
esse is qui eam allegat iure iurando vel testibus; si autem defecerit, non audiatur.'

feasible than the inspection of the papal registers. But, when allowance has been made for this consideration, Huguccio's analysis remains in its central emphasis deeper in thought and ranging more comprehensively over all the relevant problems, while the English glossators reveal a more practical turn of mind in discussing problems within a more restricted setting. Perhaps there are some grounds here for receiving with caution the recent reassessment of the work of the English canonists, and especially the suggestion that the conventional picture of 'an English school primarily bent upon satisfying the practitioner's needs is quite mistaken and based on one-sided evidence'.[1] The literary achievements of English canon lawyers, and the variety of their interests, have certainly been neglected; but the older view of an English school of canonists preoccupied to an unusual degree with practical and procedural problems is not without some foundation. The contrasting emphases in Huguccio's *Summa* and the English glosses provide merely an isolated example, on which alone it would be rash to build too much. In the broader sweep of canonical history, the crucial influence of English canonists in the primitive phases of decretal codification is a far more powerful argument. Only the Italians showed comparable initiative in assembling the earliest decretal collections, in which we discover a hitherto unexplored, or at best only partly understood, argument for the 'practical outlook' theory as applied to English or Anglo-Norman canonists.

6. General Conclusions

Whereas the earliest decretists had been content to assert dogmatically the binding force of decretal letters, and to affirm their

---

[1] The matter is one of emphasis, not of essence. Kuttner and Rathbone, *art.cit.*, pp. 290–2, justly argue against an extreme emphasis being placed on the practical interests of the English Canonists to the neglect of their other achievements. Nevertheless, there is a difference of approach to many problems in Huguccio's *Summa* and the Caius gloss: cf. pp. 41 and 42, above. But see also the remarkable comment in Caius MS., fol. 173v: 'Quidam tamen meticulosi iudices seu simplices omnino exequuntur mandatum pape etiam licet est iuri contrarium . . . Si iuri naturali fuerit contrarium non est sequendum, quia ius naturale papa non potest immutare.' The extraordinary implication here is that a papal decretal might define something contrary to Natural Law, and that (in such a case) it was open to the recipients to ignore it. It is also true that the Caius gloss incorporates much of Huguccio's teaching.

equality of authority with other legislative devices, later canonists were compelled to examine more exactly their theoretical
justification, and to relate it to the question of papal jurisdictional authority. They were compelled to analyse the purpose and form of the decretal itself, and to consider many
practical aspects connected with its use. The striking contrast
between the discussions of Paucapalea and Rolandus on the one
hand, and Huguccio and the English glossators on the other,
reflects at once the actual and immense extension of the use of
decretals as a normal instrument of legislation in the years following the publication of the *Decretum* and the growth to maturity
of the new canonistic science to which the *Decretum* had itself in
part given birth. The legal force and theoretical basis of decretal letters had been examined and asserted confidently. It remains to see what use the canon lawyers were making of it in
practice.

CHAPTER III

The Technical Evolution of Decretal Collections

1. Introduction to the Technical Problems

THE importance of twelfth-century decretal collections as historical source material is partly fortuitous. Were it not for the loss of contemporary papal records and the merely fragmentary survival of the records of receipt in the various countries of Western Europe, the canon lawyers' collections would be of small interest to the general historian, since it was due to these circumstances that many decretal letters are now known in canonistic sources only. That is why the collections are so valuable in the wider context. But their *raison d'être* was essentially practical; and this too has its intrinsic interest. In their true context, their greatest interest lies in the evidence which they provide on the growth of canonical science: in them we discover how the decretal lawyers transformed their somewhat crude early collections into highly systematic compilations, which set the standard for canonical collections for the rest of the Middle Ages. The decisive period for this development was from the closing years of Alexander III's pontificate to the publication of *Compilatio Prima*.

The most obvious features of the earliest surviving collections are their simplicity of structure and juristic immaturity: some include no more than ten or twelve decretals, transcribed simply in order of availability to the collector. Their immediate successors, though naturally more substantial in contents, show little advance towards a schematic arrangement: they have no structural plan of composition or juristic framework of discussion, no division of material into books and titles, and no literary treatment of the points of law in the individual letters. In other words, there is little to distinguish them in appearance from the typical cartularies of the same period, except that the latter are usually more accurate transcripts and less ruthlessly contracted, whereas the canon lawyers paid scant attention to the details of authentication—for reasons already stated. Therefore, it is illusory to speak of technical accomplishment at all in this period, since it was virtually non-existent. But very few of the prototypal collections have come down to us, and their structure and contents must frequently be deduced from later, derivative, collections. Even the latter are strikingly primitive in construction, though seldom as devoid of plan and purpose as may appear at first sight. There is almost invariably some groping towards a subject-matter arrangement, or perhaps a unity and emphasis suggesting the provenance of the source material or the interests of the author. And there is this further consideration that, while the contents of a collection were still very slight in substance, there was obviously no need for a systematic plan of composition.

The British Museum manuscript, conventionally known as *Wigorniensis Altera* (Royal MS. 11 B. ii, fols. 97–102), affords a perfect illustration of an English primitive collection devised on a basis of personal and local interests.[1] It is a very small collection, perhaps the earliest now surviving, and includes no more than ten decretals sent by Alexander III to papal judges delegate. With only one exception, these letters were addressed to English judges: including four to Roger of Worcester and one to Bartholomew of Exeter. The manuscript itself belonged to Worcester Cathedral Priory in the Middle Ages, and the letters cannot be positively dated later than the mid-1170s. It is well known that Roger of Worcester and Bartholomew of Exeter were among the most distinguished judges delegate in England at that time; and it is clear enough, therefore, that *Wigorniensis Altera* was derived in some way from the judicial records of Bishop Roger and his ecclesiastical colleagues.

No less revealing is the *Collectio Belverensis* (Bodl. MS. e Mus.

---

[1] Holtzmann, *Nachrichten*, p. 22; Kuttner, *Repertorium*, pp. 283–5. Two of the twelve decretals are missing from Kuttner's analysis. For a complete analysis, see Appendix I, below; the collection is also discussed more fully in Chapter IV, Part 2.

249, fols. 121–35), again of very early date in composition.[1] This work was assembled in several quite separate stages. Following a transcription of the canons of the Council of Tours (1163), the opening ten decretals were derived from a source identical with that of *Wigorniensis Altera*. These are followed by nine letters, transcribed in two separate sequences of seven and two respectively; and five of the first seven letters in this part were received by Gilbert Foliot, as bishop of London. The canons of the 1175 Council of Westminster are entered next; and the whole work is completed with a further group of nine decretals, assembled in two separate stages, received either at Canterbury or by Cistercian abbeys. The collection as an entity, though it was certainly not designed as a single composition, is now found in a volume of materials connected with the career of Gilbert Foliot, which belonged in the Middle Ages to Belvoir Priory, from which the collection takes its name. Both *Wigorniensis Altera* and *Belverensis*, therefore, illustrate very clearly the personal associations or local influences which can sometimes be traced in the most primitive collections. But evidence of this kind is unhappily less frequent in later collections, which are derivative rather than original. As an author's technical skill grew, together with the number of decretals available to him, the contents of his collection were rearranged to suit a more convenient pattern of reference; and in this way the original motives and stimuli of the earliest collectors were obscured from the historian's vision. For these reasons the primitive collections are most valuable for the historian, though less so for the canonist.

Other primitive collections, in contrast, reflect not so much the careers and activities of identifiable persons, but a selection of topics by professional canonists as a first stage in the development of an ordered plan of composition. Typical of such work is the *Collectio Cantabrigiensis* (Trinity College MS. R. 9.17, fols. 72–107).[2] This collection is named simply after its present location in Cambridge; and, though it was once believed to be

---

[1] Holtzmann, *Nachrichten*, p. 22; C. N. L. Brooke, 'Canons of English Church Councils in the Early Decretal Collections', *Traditio*, XIII (1957), pp. 471–9. For a complete analysis, see Appendix II, below; see also Chapter IV, Part 2.

[2] Holtzmann, *Nachrichten*, p. 21; *idem, Register Papst Alexanders*, pp. 69–80; Kuttner, *Repertorium*, p. 278; Ch. Lefebvre, 'Collection de Cambridge', *DDC*, II (1937), cols. 1270–3; Friedberg, *Canonessammlungen*, pp. 5–21. The collection divides

of English origin, it is now thought to have been composed by French canonists in or after 1178. It can be analysed in two parts: the first concerned with procedural and judicial problems, and the second with the canon law of marriage. In all probability, the manuscript as it now survives is merely a fragment of a much larger collection; even so, it records in a characteristic way the beginnings of a professional interest in the selection and classification of subject-matter which were ultimately to produce a satisfactory pattern of composition. But most early collections have no clear style of composition, and little discernible arrangement of their contents. The *Collectio Cantuariensis* (Royal MS. 10 B. IV, fols. 42–58) will serve as a typical example of these. Completed at Canterbury towards the closing years of Alexander III's pontificate, it has no overall plan of composition, though there is undoubtedly some grouping of cognate topics within it.[1] Nor is this Canterbury collection a single or integrated composition in reality: it is merely the independent work of at least three collectors and several scribes, brought together on separate folios and bound up within a single volume.

These few examples, chosen at random from the many surviving decretal manuscripts, illustrate the variety of styles of composition in the earliest collections, and reveal at the same time their juristic immaturity. It is obvious enough retrospectively that a satisfactory pattern of composition would be achieved only when each collection was devised in several parts, and all decretals of related interest placed together in appropriate sections. This was the first and most elementary development, and an important step in the longer process by which a fully satisfactory scheme of composition was gradually evolved.

at n.74: items 2–74 might appear suitably in a book entitled 'Ad informandum iudices in diversis casibus quandoque emergentibus' (Cf. *Wig.* VII); items 75–100 are concerned exclusively with marriage questions. Cf. J. Juncker, 'Die Collectio Berolinensis', *ZRG., Kan.Abt.*, XIII (1924), pp. 301–5; and Lefebvre, *art.cit.*, cols. 1271–2. The dating limits of the collection are 1177–9: it includes the decretal *Cum Christus* (*Cantab.* 37, fol. 87r., J-L12785: Feb. 18th, 1177), but has no knowledge of the Third Lateran Council of 1179.

[1] Holtzmann, *Nachrichten*, p. 22; Kuttner, *Repertorium*, p. 282; see also Chapter IV, Part 2, below. As a typical example of the grouping together of decretals of cognate interest, see *Cantuar.* I, 5–8, fols. 43v–44r; these four items all appear in *Wig.* II, 31, 19, 14 and 35 (cf. H. Lohmann, 'Die Collectio Wigorniensis', *ZRG., Kan.Abt.*, XXII (1933), pp. 94 ff.).

In this process many separate strands of development can be traced, some of merely local or transient interest, others of wide influence and permanent importance. In the discussions which follow, two significant lines of development have been selected for illustration. The first reveals the growth of a pattern of composition in a single English primitive family, the second involves the most famous members of the principal lines of systematic transmission. The complex interconnexions between the many families and traditions are increasingly resolved in Holtzmann's studies; here, for brevity, the overall structure of the collections is examined first, leaving for later consideration the treatment of the separate letters.

2. THE 'WORCESTER' TRADITION

The 'Worcester' tradition was an English development whose details are only partly known at present. Its name is derived from the so-called 'Worcester' family, a group of interrelated English collections composed between c. 1181 and 1194 or later. The name is in fact open to some objection, being received from the *Collectio Wigorniensis* (Royal MS. 10 A. II, fols. 5–62), an authentic Worcester collection and an early member of the family, but not the earliest survivor as was formerly believed.[1] Nevertheless, the description is now so widely accepted that it would be merely confusing to suggest a more appropriate title. Six members of this once numerous family now survive, and several other extant collections reveal the influence of its tradition, receiving much of its substance and something of its technical conventions. Chief among these are three great collections known as *Tanner*, *Sangermanensis* and *Abrincensis;* but, unlike some members of the 'Worcester' family proper, these are already available in printed analyses.[2] Only three

[1] The oldest member in fact is *Trinitatis*. Holtzmann's list in *Nachrichten* (1945), p. 22, and *Sammlung Tanner* (1951), pp. 92–4, agrees with this view; but his more recent discussion in Holtzmann and Kemp, *op. cit.* (1954), p. xii, describes *Wig.* as the oldest member of the group. This description has been repeated in later studies; cf. Brooke, *Canons of English Church Councils*, p. 475. See Chapter IV, Part 4, below.

[2] *Tanner*: Oxford Bodl. MS. Tanner 8, pp. 591–720; Kuttner, *Repertorium*, p. 294; Holtzmann, *Sammlung Tanner*, pp. 83–145; Kuttner and Rathbone, *art.cit.*, p. 284. For *Sang.* and *Abrinc.*, see H. Singer, 'Neue Beiträge über die Dekretalensammlungen vor und nach Bernhard von Pavia', *Sitz.KA.Wien*, CLXXI (1913), pp. 68–400; Holtzmann, *Nachrichten* p. 23; Kuttner, *Repertorium*, pp. 98–9.

E

members of the family itself have so far been published.[1]

The family archetype has not survived, but its details can be deduced from its earliest descendants. They are reflected most directly in three closely interrelated collections: *Trinitatis* (Trinity College MS. R. 14.9, fols. 82–8), *Wigorniensis* (mentioned above) and *Claustroneoburgensis* (Klosterneuburg MS. 19, fols. 36–87), composed in that order in or after 1181. All three were devised in seven parts on a subject-matter basis, though this is not at first apparent in the Klosterneuburg manuscript, as a result of scribal deficiencies, and is somewhat hypothetical in the Trinity manuscript, which is now merely a fragment.[2]

The major divisions of such a collection are known as 'books' or *libri*, and the broad scope of their subject-matter is indicated by such a typical example as the introductory heading of Book I in *Wigorniensis*: 'De statu et iure coniugii sive contracti sive contrahendi.' There was no further analysis of narrower topics within the books at this stage of development, though there was undoubtedly some interior grouping of letters of cognate interest.[3] The obvious defect in this technical phase was that the classification of topics was still far too general to serve much practical purpose, and the component books were too lengthy to remain undivided, including in one instance as many as eighty-one decretals.[4] But the technical advance that had been

---

[1] F. Schönsteiner, 'Die Collectio Claustroneoburgensis', *Jahrbuch des Stiftes Klosterneuburg*, II (1909), pp. 1–154; Lohmann *loc. cit.*, pp. 36–187; C. Duggan, 'The Trinity Collection of Decretals and the Early Worcester Family', *Traditio*, XVII (1961), pp. 506–26.

[2] Lohmann, *loc. cit.*, pp. 39–40; the *Trin.* fragment begins towards the end of Book II, and breaks off shortly after the beginning of Book IV; the *Claustr.* MS. has no formal division of its material in book-form, but its underlying pattern of composition is the same as that in the other two collections. On the dates of composition of *Wig.* and *Claustr.*, see Lohmann, *loc. cit.*, pp. 51–3: the family archetype evidently included one decretal dated 23 January 1181 (*Wig.* VII, 59=*Claustr.* 291: J-L14365); but nothing later than the death of Alexander III in the same year is found in either collection. On internal evidence alone, the dating limits for *Trin.* are 1178–1181: the earlier limit being fixed by the decretal *Cum essemus Venecie*, J-L14334, and the latter by the absence of any material later than Alexander's death. But the close relationship between *Trin.* and the other two collections establishes 1181 as the earliest date of completion for all three.

[3] *Wig.* II. 26, 27 and 28 appear within the single title 'De decimis' in later systematic collections: cf. *Decretales* III. 30, 9, 11 and 10; Lohmann, *loc. cit.*, pp. 170–1, etc. But exact groupings of this kind are not typical in *Wig.*

[4] Lohmann, *loc. cit.*, pp. 125–49: *Wig.* VII, 1–81.

already made was considerable; and the canonists' skill in designing and using such a work should not be underestimated. Nevertheless, a marked improvement was made in the later 'Worcester' collections. Each book was now subjected to the same treatment as that applied to the whole collection in the earlier period, and was subdivided into numerous component sections concerned with precise aspects of the general theme of the book. These subsections are known as 'titles' or *tituli*; and, within the 'Worcester' tradition, this phase of development is best illustrated in the two late collections: *Cottoniana* (Cotton MS. Vit. E. xiii, fols. 204–88) and *Peterhusensis* (Peterhouse MSS. 114, 180, 193 and 203).[1]

Thus, to summarize the main stages of technical development within the 'Worcester' family: the early collections were first divided into seven books, and in the later collections each of these books was subdivided into numerous titles. The first stage produced a broad classification of subject-matter, while the second isolated more specialized aspects within the books. Whereas, to quote a typical example, in the first book of *Wigorniensis* all decretals relating in any way to the canon law of marriage were placed together without discrimination under the heading 'De statu et iure coniugii sive contracti sive contrahendi', in the first book of *Cottoniana* and *Peterhusensis* all such decretals were redistributed according to carefully defined aspects of the wider subject. Through the rubricator's negligence, these titles do not appear by name in the appropriate parts of the Cotton and Peterhouse manuscripts, but they may be exemplified by analogy with the relevant titles in *Compilatio Prima*: 'De clandestina desponsatione', 'De divortiis', 'De secundis nuptiis', 'Qui filii sint legitimi', 'De consanguinitate et affinitate', and many others of equally exact implication.[2]

3. THE *APPENDIX* TRADITION

In striking contrast with the tradition described above, the canonists of the *Appendix* tradition began their classification with

---

[1] The structure and dates of composition of these collections are fully discussed in Chapter IV, Part 4, below.

[2] Friedberg *Quinque Compilationes*, pp. 44 ff. Cf. *Abrinc.* VIII, 1. De nuptiis voventium et conversorum; 2. De sponsa de futuro cognita; 3. De fide coniugii; etc. (Singer, *loc. cit.*, pp. 386 ff.).

a framework of precisely defined topics. This is not altogether surprising when we remember that the earliest collection recording their technique is the famous *Parisiensis II*, whose author was perhaps the same Bernard of Pavia whose *Breviarium* was destined as *Compilatio Prima* to be the classical model for all later works.[1] In other words, the earliest collections in this style were already divided into titles, though not into books; and their authors revealed thereby a high standard of juristic training. This early realization of the practical value of the system of titles was of the utmost advantage, enabling canonists to refer very readily in their decretal records to the most exact legal questions. This was an advantage achieved only in the closing phases in the 'Worcester' tradition.

But the prototypal collection, *Parisiensis II*, which was completed about the year 1179, was not in fact a simple decretal collection at all. It represented, rather, an extension of pre-Gratian traditions into the decretal era, intermingling ancient canons with more recent papal letters.[2] Its principal interest in this discussion lies in its plan of composition, which was to influence so greatly the most advanced decretal canonists of the time. The collection is divided into ninety-five titles, comprising two hundred and thirty-six chapters in all. From a subject-matter viewpoint the arrangement in the sequence of titles is capricious; there is no ordered development to explain their relative positions: 'De novis statutis' is found (simply to cite a characteristic example) immediately preceding 'De his qui ex concubinis filios habent', and this is followed in turn by 'De officio archidiaconi'.[3] Therefore, the overall plan of composition was unsatisfactory. But the isolation of special aspects of law into ninety-five titles was a marked step forward; and it is a fact that many later famous collections, including *Compilatio Prima* and the *Decretales*, received with extensions and modifications many of the title-headings in this seminal collection.[4]

[1] Van Hove, *Prolegomena*, p. 352; Friedberg, *Canonessammlungen*, p. 21.

[2] *Ibid.*, pp. 26 ff.

[3] *Ibid.*, pp. 22–4: *Paris. II*, 3, 4 and 5.

[4] For the influence of *Paris. II* on the titles of later collections, see Friedberg, *ibid.*, pp. 24 ff. Many of these titles were ultimately taken into *Compilatio Prima*, though in extended forms: (1) *Paris. II*, 22: 'De filiis presbiterorum'; cf. *Comp. I*,

Still more influential, but advancing the same stylistic tradition, is the *Appendix Concilii Lateranensis,* from which the tradition derives its name. The provenance of this collection has been the subject of some dispute, and conflicting theories of English or Italian authorship have been developed. But, if the evidence for English authorship appears the more convincing, yet the *Appendix* was a fountain-head in the mainstream of the most highly developed collections on the continent.[1] It would be unrealistic to suggest a date of composition for the work as a whole, since it was built up in several separate stages, and the various extant recensions are not identical either in contents or in dates of completion. The collection in its *editio princeps,* based on a manuscript now lost, begins with the canons of the 1179 Lateran Council, followed by forty-nine titles, which, with the exception of the last two, are systematic in technical style. The basic work in this vulgate version was completed within the limits c. 1181–5, and the final form included material as late as 1188–90.[2] The concluding title in the *editio princeps* is not discovered in any of the surviving *Appendix* manuscripts, and has been shown by Holtzmann to depend on an excerpt from the lost register of Alexander III[3]. But some titles were closely copied in contents and arrangement by later authors in the mainstream of systematic codification; and the majority of the chapters were ultimately received into *Compilatio Prima* or *Compilatio Secunda,* and from these into the Gregorian *Decretales.*[4] Yet, the collection exceeds *Parisiensis II* in

1.9: 'De filiis presbiterorum ordinandis vel non, nec in paternis ecclesiis tollerandis'; (2) *Paris. II,* 42: 'De scismaticis et ordinatis ab eis'; cf. *Comp. I,* 5.7: 'De scismaticis et ordinatis ab eis et alienationibus factis'; (3) *Paris. II,* 81: 'De cognatione spirituali'; cf. *Comp. I,* 4.11: 'De cognatione spirituali et filiis ante vel post compaternitatem genitis'; etc.

[1] P. Crabbe, ed., *Concilia omnia tam generalia quam particularia,* Cologne, ii (1551), pp. 836–944; Lincoln Cathedral MS. 121, fols. 1–61; St. John's College Cambridge MS. 148/F. 11, fols. 82–4 (a previously unknown fragment); Holtzmann, *Nachrichten,* p. 23; Kuttner, *Repertorium,* pp. 291–2; *idem* and Rathbone, *art.cit.,* pp. 283–4; Friedberg, *Canonessammlungen,* pp. 63–84; A. Amanieu, 'Appendix Concilii Lateranensis', *DDC,* i (1935), cols. 833–41; and Chapter V, Part 3, below.

[2] Amanieu, *art. cit.,* cols. 833–41.

[3] The *editio princeps* was by P. Laurens: see Holtzmann and Kemp, *op. cit.,* p. xiii. Cf. Holtzmann, *Register Papst Alexanders,* pp. 13 ff. See Chapter V, Part 3, below, for a full discussion of this question.

[4] Notice especially the correspondence between *Appendix* X: 'De appellationibus'; *Compilatio Prima* I, 20: 'De appellationibus et recusationibus'; and *Decretales* II, 28:

importance more through the greatly larger number of its chapters than through any further significant technical development. The disposition of titles remained unsatisfactory, since there was still no consistently logical arrangement of topics throughout the collection as a whole, although it is quite clear that both *Parisiensis II* and the *Appendix* include some groups of titles arranged in unbroken sequence because of their related interests.[1]

It was by an extension of this group concept to the sequence of titles that a notable improvement was achieved in various later collections typified by the *Compilatio Bambergensis*, composed in France during or shortly after the pontificate of Lucius III (1181–5).[2] The French author of this famous work was largely indebted for his material to an early recension of the *Appendix*, or at least to some closely related common source; but he refashioned the overall plan of composition, so that inexact titles were subdivided more precisely, and the sequence of titles readjusted to suit a logical pattern of juristic exposition throughout. An ordered arrangement of major subjects can now be traced through the titles, proceeding from criminal causes to those dealing with clerical status, thence to questions of ecclesiastical property and judicial procedure, and finally to the canon law of marriage.[3] This schematic arrangement had effectively regrouped the titles into several major divisions or books, though this was not obvious at once in the manuscript format. Moreover, the canons of the Third Lateran Council, which had appeared as a preface in the edited version of the *Appendix*, were retained as an entity in *Bambergensis*, appearing

---

'De appellationibus et recusationibus et relationibus.' There is an extremely close identity between all three collections in contents and arrangement. Almost all chapters in *Appendix* are found in *Compilatio Prima* or *Compilatio Secunda*; and a majority of its chapters and titles were received into the *Decretales*; see Amanieu, *art. cit.*, cols. 839–41.

[1] E.g., Friedberg, *Canonessammlungen*, p. 22: *Paris. II*: 5. 'De officio archidiaconi'; 6. 'De officio archipresbyteri'; 7. 'De officio primicerii'; 8. 'De officio sacristae'; 9. 'De officio custodis'; etc. Select lists of titles from the principal systematic collections are cited below; cf. pp. 55–7, below.

[2] Friedberg, *Canonessammlungen*, pp. 64–5.

[3] Holtzmann, *Nachrichten*, p. 23; Kuttner, *Repertorium*, p. 292; Friedberg, *Canonessammlungen*, pp. 84–115; P. Daudet, 'Bambergensis', *DDC*, II (1937), cols. 84–9. *Lipsiensis* and *Casselana* were derived from *Bamb.*; see Kuttner, *Repertorium*, pp. 292–3; Daudet, *art.cit.*, col. 88; Naz, 'Collection de Leipzig', *DDC*, VI (1957), col. 400. See now W. Deeters, *Die Bambergensisgruppe*, Bonn (1956).

in this instance as an appendix.[1] The most satisfactory plan would have been to distribute these canons also through the various titles according to their subject-matter; and this further advance was in fact achieved in the *Compilatio Brugensis*, assembled in central or northern France about the same time that *Compilatio Prima* was completed in Italy (c. 1191), though neither collection was directly dependent on the other.[2] The author of *Brugensis* derived the bulk of his material from the *Appendix* and *Bambergensis*, or from their related and derivative compilations. But he drew also on the local archives in the province of Reims, and in so doing provided evidence of the greatest interest on the origins of the decretal collections.[3] Meanwhile, the final stage was reached in Bernard of Pavia's *Compilatio Prima*, in which the concept of a general pattern for the whole work was formally recognized by its division into five books under the headings *Iudex, Iudicium, Clerus, Connubium* and *Crimen*. After this, it was unusual for any canonist acquainted with his work to depart from Bernard's method.

Many other collections would have to be cited for a comprehensive treatment of these technical developments: *Tanner*, *Sangermanensis* and *Abrincensis* among the English and Anglo-Norman collections: *Lipsiensis* and *Casselana*, derivatives of *Bambergensis*, among continental works—to name only a few of the more familiar.[4] For simplicity, only the general outlines have been sketched above. But, in conclusion, the main phases of development in the *Appendix* tradition may be illustrated more precisely with select blocks of titles from the principal collections already discussed.

> *Parisiensis II* (Italian, c. 1179).[5]
>   1. De consuetudine.

---

[1] Friedberg, *Canonessammlungen*, pp. 114–15.

[2] Holtzmann, *Nachrichten*, p. 23; Kuttner, *Repertorium*, pp. 297–9; Friedberg, *Canonessammlungen*, pp. 136–70; P. Le Mercier, 'Collection de Bruges', *DDC*, ii (1937), cols. 1118–20. But *Brug.* is not in the *App.-Bamb.-Comp. I* tradition.

[3] All but thirty-four chapters in *Brug.* are found also in *Appendix, Bamb.* and their derivatives. The historical significance of the unique element in *Brug.* is discussed in Chapter V, Part 4, below.

[4] Van Hove, *Prolegomena*, pp. 350–5; Holtzmann and Kemp, *op. cit.*, pp. xi–xvi; Kuttner and Rathbone, *art. cit.*, pp. 283–4; cf. also pp. 49, n.2 and 54, n.3, above. For *Compilatio Prima*, see Friedberg, *Quinque Compilationes*, pp. 1–65.

[5] Friedberg, *Canonessammlungen*, p. 22.

2. De prioribus et posterioribus synodis.
3. De novis statutis.
4. De his qui ex concubinis filios habent.
5. De officio archidiaconi.
6. De officio archipresbyteri.
7. De officio primicerii.
8. De officio sacristae.
9. De officio custodis.
10. De electione.
11. De venatoribus.
12. De sagittariis.
13. De clerico percussore.
14. De falsariis.
    etc.

Appendix Concilii Lateranensis (? English, 1181–5, to c. 1190).[1]
1. Canones Concilii.
2. De simonia et ne merces pro ecclesiae consecratione recipiatur, vel pro moniacatione vel pro sacramentis ecclesiae, vel pro licentia docendi; neve prelati vices suas ad causas terminandas, vel regimen ecclesiarum sub annuo pretio committant; neve subditos taliis vexent, vel poena pecuniaria mulctent.
3. De dolo et contumacia et calumnia alterius partium punienda.
4. De decimis praestandis.
5. De coniugatis et sponsis monasterium ingressis vel ingredi volentibus.
6. De sponsalibus et matrimonio contractis sive contrahendo.
7. De potestate iudicum delegatorum et de variis literis diversis temporibus impetratis.
    etc.

Bambergensis (French, 1181–5).[2]
1. De symonia et ne merces pro ecclesiae consecratione recipiatur vel pro monachatione vel sacramentis ecclesiae.
2. Ne prelati vices suas sub annuo pretio aliis committant ad causas terminandas, vel sub annuo pretio presbiteri ad ecclesiarum regimen statuantur, licet ecclesia ad annuum censum dari possit.
3. Ne aliquid exigatur pro licentia docendi.

---

[1] *Ibid.*, p. 64.
[2] *Ibid.*, pp. 93–5.

4. Ne clerici illicitis exactionibus vel taleis vexentur, neve laici pena pecuniaria mulctentur.
5. De pactionibus licitis et illicitis in rebus ecclesiae.
6. Clericum sine auctoritate episcopi non posse constituere ecclesiam suam censuariam, vel ecclesiam occupare, vel in alium transferre ad evitandam controversiam.
7. De illis qui inciderint in canonem datae sententiae, vel incidere viderentur, cum non incidant, et qui sint ad sedem apostolicam transmittendi propter absolutionem.
   etc.

Brugensis (French, c. 1191).[1]
1. De fide Catholica.
2. De Iudeis.
3. De haereticis coterellis et piratis.
4. De schismaticis et symoniacis et de his qui prohibitas tam in excessibus corrigendis quam in spiritualibus administrandis venalitates exercent.
5. De usuris.
6. De raptoribus et furibus puniendis.
7. De sacrilegis ex iniectione manus in clericos, templarios, religiosos et violatione ecclesiarum.
8. De Romani pontificis auctoritate et dignitate.
9. De promotione summi pontificis at aliorum prelatorum qualiter fieri debeat.
   etc.

4. THE DISMEMBERMENT OF DECRETAL LETTERS

By various paths the canonists had now achieved a satisfactory method of handling the general structure of their collections. Meanwhile, a further and less obvious problem lay within the individual letters, and the second main technical development was concerned with the dissection of the separate decretals whenever this seemed desirable. The division and subsequent subdivision of a collection would have produced an entirely satisfactory result if each decretal had dealt with a single point of law and with that alone. But it was seldom so in reality. In many instances, several quite unrelated topics were discussed in the course of a single rescript, especially when the pope was dealing with a questionnaire submitted to him by an

[1] *Ibid.*, pp. 140–3.

ecclesiastical judge on various matters arising in the execution of his judicial office. The question arose: how should the decretal canonist deal with such a letter, when he came to incorporate it in his collection?

In the earliest stages this problem could be avoided without serious inconvenience. While the entire collection was still comparatively brief and devoid of schematic arrangement, there was little disadvantage in diversity of subject-matter within its separate items. But once an orderly arrangement of topics had been introduced into the collection as a whole, it was clearly inconsistent if a conflict of unrelated interests was retained within its component parts. Once more the solution to this problem is obvious enough retrospectively: each letter was dissected into its component chapters, and each chapter placed according to its subject-matter in the most appropriate book or title, exactly as if it were an entirely separate decretal. The canonists of the 'Worcester' family failed completely to grasp the importance of this technical device, and revealed their juristic inexperience compared with those of the *Appendix* tradition. The canonists of the former showed little general application of this fruitful idea even in their finest collections, within the primitive 'Worcester' family; whereas their contemporaries in the latter had already applied the technique extensively in the earliest known recension of the *Appendix* itself.[1] The 'Cheltenham' Collection appears at first sight an exception to this general distinction, but is not so in fact. It is a work of complex origin, being a 'Worcester' collection in substance and technical tradition for much of its contents; but it also reveals the technique of decretal dissection in other parts, where it is derived from a systematic collection in the Bamberg-Leipzig tradition.[2] The absence of decretal dissection elsewhere in the 'Cheltenham' Collection, as well as in collections of the 'Worcester' family as a whole, was a serious disadvantage, as can best be shown by examining the treatment of a single letter.

The decretal *Licet praeter*, addressed by Alexander III to the

---

[1] For details of the various recensions of *Appendix*, see *ibid.*, pp. 67–71; for examples of the dissection of individual decretals, notice especially J-L 13162, 13790, 13946, 14027, 14091, etc.

[2] This matter is fully discussed in Chapter IV, Part 4, below.

archbishop of Salerno c. 1174–6, includes no less than sixteen component chapters, dealing with several quite unrelated topics: the first three and the last are concerned with the canon law of marriage; the fourth and the fifth with the immunity of clerks; and the others with various equally unrelated questions. Now, in the earliest 'Worcester' collections, the whole of this decretal is found intact in a single book concerned ostensibly with the canon law of marriage, under the general heading: 'De statu et iure coniugii sive contracti sive contrahendi.' Obviously, the decretal was included in this section simply because its opening chapters were connected in interest with the general theme of the book; but, as a result, no less than ten chapters were placed at the same time under a heading bearing no relation to their contents.[1] This was a most unsatisfactory way of designing a professional collection. And yet the fault was aggravated rather than diminished in the later collections of the same tradition. The book of marriage decretals was broken down into many titles in the Cotton and Peterhouse manuscripts, each title being concerned with one narrowly defined aspect of the wider subject. But the decretal *Licet praeter* remained still undissected, and was placed as an entity in one of these closely circumscribed subsections.[2] In this way, much of what had been achieved in structural evolution was lost through failure to apply to the individual letters the same principle which had already been accepted for the whole compilation.

All collections of the *Appendix* tradition, in contrast and with the exception of *Parisiensis II*, divided *Licet praeter* into its component chapters, placing each in the most appropriate title.[3] Therefore, this tradition, almost from its inception, provided

---

[1] Lohmann, *loc. cit.*, pp. 84–5: *Wig.* I, 28a–q, *Licet praeter*, J-L 14091 and 13946. The unsuitability of this arrangement is obvious from the rubrics which appear in *Wig.* for the individual chapters of this single letter: e.g., I. 28b: 'De filiis compaternis non copulandis'; I. 28d: 'De accusatione et testimonio laicorum contra clericos'; I, 28e: 'De confessione clerici coram iudice seculari facta'; I, 28i: 'De clerico faciente sponte duellum'; and I, 28m: 'De decimis et oblationibus.'

[2] Peterhouse MS. 193, final quire, fol. 6rb: *Pet.* I, 3a–o; B.M. Cotton MS. Vit. E. XIII, fol. 210v: *Cott.* I, 3. The Cotton MS. is seriously damaged at this point.

[3] *Wig.* I, 28a–q is distributed in nine different positions in *Appendix:* VI, 8; V, 1; XXXII, 1, 2; VIII, 8; XXVI, 4, 5; VIII, 9; XXXVIII, 1; XXVI, 6, 7; V, 4. Alternatively, the same decretal is scattered in *Compilatio Prima* as follows: IV, 4, 3; IV, 11, 1–2; II, 13, 14; II, 1, 6; V, 12, 1; II, 13, 15; II, 18, 6; I, 12, 1; V, 10, 8; and III, 28, 1.

a far superior technique to that discovered in the 'Worcester' family, even at the peak of its development. And this was the technical style transmitted to *Compilatio Prima* and finally to the Gregorian *Decretales*, its overriding advantage being that each component division or title was now concerned exclusively with a single and precise issue, all irrelevant discussion being excised or placed in a more suitable section elsewhere. Thus, if we consult any title in a collection designed in this style, we find that every chapter deals exclusively with the subject named in the title-heading under which it is placed.

Hitherto, all decretal collections have been classified as 'primitive' or 'systematic'.[1] The essential point of this distinction is that a collection is considered systematic when divided into titles, if it also applies a thorough dismemberment of the individual decretals. In the absence of these characteristics, no collection is considered truly systematic. It must be admitted that this convention is not entirely satisfactory, since it entails describing even the most advanced collections in the 'Worcester' family as primitive, though they lack only the device of decretal dissection to make them systematic in the most complete sense.[2] Nevertheless, if this basic distinction is accepted, the difference between the two categories is clear enough for the purpose of classification.

5. ABBREVIATION TECHNIQUES IN DECRETAL COLLECTIONS

Quite apart from the problems connected with the general design of decretal collections and with the composite character of the decretals, there is the further question of conventional abbreviation. For practical purposes, it can be assumed that the structure of papal documents had become stabilized by the

---

[1] Holtzmann, *Nachrichten*, pp. 21–4; *idem* and Kemp, *op. cit.*, pp. xi-xvi; van Hove, *Prolegomena*, pp. 350–5; Kuttner, *Repertorium*, pp. 272 ff.

[2] The existing classifications leave something to be desired. Both *Chelt.* and *Cott.* were first described as systematic by Kuttner, and later as primitive by Holtzmann. If the distinction rests essentially on the adoption of the principle of decretal dissection, then *Cott.* is undoubtedly primitive; but *Chelt.* is hybrid, being partly derived from a systematic source in the Bamberg-Leipzig group. Again, both *Cott.* and *Pet.* are described by Holtzmann as 'primitive pre-Compilatio Prima' collections, but neither was completed before 1193, that is to say two years after the publication of *Compilatio Prima* itself.

later-twelfth century. The diplomatic formulae and cursive traditions were now well established. Problems connected with the interior structure of the sentences and the methods of accentual stressing have no interest for us in this chapter, but the standardized draftsmanship of the whole document has. Every decretal letter, as well as every Privilege, was drawn up in three main parts: protocol, contextus (or text) and eschatocol (or final protocol). It is quite obvious that from a juridical point of view many parts of such a document have little or no significance except in their immediate setting. The protocol and eschatocol make no contribution to canonical theory, however vital they may be in establishing the diplomatic authenticity of the document. Even in the text there is no juridical importance in the *arenga* and *narratio*.

In these circumstances, the canon lawyers decided on a policy of ruthless elimination and abbreviation of those parts in which they had no interest. In so doing they produced a characteristic style of transcription quite distinct from that of the contemporary monastic and cathedral scribes, who copied out accurately all the diplomatically important details.[1] In the hands of the canonists the protocol was abbreviated even to the extent of distortion;[2] the eschatocol was usually eliminated entirely (unfortunately with the loss of the date of issue); and the text itself was drastically reduced. The protocol was replaced by a shortened form of the pope's name and that of the recipient: the pope's number was inserted, though it had not appeared on the original. The text was divided into two parts: the *pars historica* (or *species facti*) and the *pars dispositiva* containing the vitally interesting canonistic discussions. In brief, the treatment meted out to the decretal letter was a drastic reduction of protocol and eschatocol, and a preservation only of the juridically important part of the text.[3]

[1] Cf. Kuttner, *Projected Corpus*, p. 345.

[2] The difficulties resulting from such practices have been explained in the opening chapter, above. Abbreviation and distortion of the *inscriptio* make it difficult in many instances to identify the recipient.

[3] But occasionally full and accurate transcriptions are found in the early collections. Cf. *Belver*. MS., fols. 125r–126v: 'Alexander III episcopus servus servorum Dei venerabili fratri B(artholomeo) Exoniensi episcopo, salutem et apostolicam benedictionem. Sicut dignum est et omni consentaneum rationi, graves et difficiles questiones ad examen apostolice sedis deferri, ita etiam nobis ex mini-

The skill and thoroughness with which this principle was applied grew with the advance of decretalist technique in other respects. Almost the whole document can be discovered in some of the earliest transcripts;[1] but this is very rarely true in their successors. From a professional point of view these archival devices were entirely advantageous. From the historical point of view they were disastrous. The canonists had destroyed or distorted precisely those points in which the historian is most naturally interested: details of persons and places, dates and the historical setting of canonistic discussions. This is why there is so much to be gained by retracing the individual letters beyond the version which appears in the well-known but later compilations, back as closely as may be to the original transcription. Frequently, it is only by these means that the authentic historical details can now be rediscovered.

It follows that the details of any single chapter, as they appear in a decretal collection, will seldom represent the whole contents of the original decretal. If there has been dismemberment, in the interests of a fully systematic technique, the chapter will be merely a part of the original letter. Alternatively, it is possible that part of the document has been omitted in a general elimination of non-juridical elements. In either instance, there is something missing from the copy as it stands. The earliest collectors adopted a somewhat cavalier attitude to this defect, but their more technically accomplished successors realized that it would be better to indicate where something had been omitted. Accordingly, they adopted the convention of writing 'etc' or 'etc et infra' or 'et infra' or 'paulo post', to signify where an excision had been made; the English author of the *Collectio Claudiana* wrote 'post alia' wherever his version had omitted part of the full decretal.[2] More important than these was the device

---

sterio suscepte sollicitudinis imminent easdem questiones prout nobis Deus dederit *etc.*' The *arenga* is thus retained in its entirety; but this was very unusual in later collections, in which the *inscriptio* (at the very least) was heavily abbreviated: cf. the above example as it appears in *Brug.* VII, I: 'Item Bartholome Exon. ep. Sicut dignum est *etc*'; and *Bamb.* X, I: 'Alex. III Exon. ep. Sicut dignum est *etc.*' In this case, in spite of drastic abbreviation, the references remain quite accurate; in many instances it was otherwise.

[1] Cf. p. 61, n.3, above: *Belver.* provides a particularly accurate transcription. See Appendix II, below.

[2] B.M. Cotton MS. Claudius A. IV: *Claud.* 153, fol. 210rb: 'Alexander III

of the systematic collectors who wished to show where a decretal had been dismembered: by each component chapter they wrote 'pars capituli' or 'pars capitis', followed by the principal *incipit* of the full decretal.[1] This proved a very useful method, enabling the parent letter of each fragment to be quickly identified.

Finally, the normal paleographical abbreviations are found in decretal manuscripts no less than in their contemporaries of all kinds, and decretal scribes added to them by the use of their own common-form abbreviations. The conventional phrases and formulae of the papal chancery, which occur repeatedly in decretal letters are seldom transcribed in full in the manuscripts. To select from numerous instances of this kind: 'appellatione remota' was usually written as 'ap.re.'; 'nulla contradictione facta' as 'n.co.fa.'; 'obstaculo appellationis remoto' as 'ob.ap.re.'; and, a very common example, 'fraternitati tue per apostolica scripta precipiendo mandamus quatinus' as 'f.t.p.ap.s.p.m.q.'. Similarly, familiar introductory or concluding phrases were usually curtailed, as in letters of commission to judges delegate, such as 'Sane si uterque vestrorum etc' and 'Sane si his exequendis etc'. All of which helped to give a concise and professional appearance to the collection.

6. General Conclusions

An attempt has been made in this chapter to explain the technical achievement of decretal canonists between the years 1174/5 and 1191, and to describe how their collections were gradually developed from primitive and disorderly transcriptions into the perfect scheme of Bernard's *Compilatio Prima*. As stated in the beginning, only the general outlines of selected lines of development have been traced, the selection being made for the sake

Carnotensi episcopo, post alia. Questioni autem *etc.*'; J-L 13835. This is a single chapter from the decretal *Cum sacrosancta Romana* (cf. *Cantab.* 15, and *Compilatio Prima* I, 21, 16; Friedberg, *Quinque Compilationes*, p. 8). Such an example illustrates very clearly the confusion which might result from the practice of scribal abbreviation: the *incipit* is 'Questioni autem' in *Claud.*, 'Cum sacrosancta' in *Cantab.*, and 'Sane quia nos' in *Comp. I.*

[1] Friedberg, *Canonessammlungen*, pp. 45–6. The phrases 'pars capituli' and 'pars capituli quod sic incipit', and many other similar variations, are found widely used in systematic collections, and occasionally in primitive works. To cite a typical example from *Compilatio Prima*: I, 2, 3: 'Alex. III Winton. ep. P.c.Quamvis simus. Ceterum si *etc.*' implies that the chapter *Ceterum si* is part of the decretal *Quamvis simus.*

of clarity and illustration. The hybrid collections, which represent no single school or tradition in particular, the transitional collections, which do not fit exactly into any of the phases or categories described above: all these have been neglected for the greater part. In the following chapter, all primitive collections of English provenance will be examined, partly for their technical interest, but chiefly for their wider historical significance. Meanwhile, in conclusion, the technical advance of the decretal collectors can be summarized in a single example. The whole of Book III in the primitive *Trinitatis* appears under the heading: 'De personis ecclesiarum et earum institutione et earum ornatu'. If the individual items in this book are traced to their locations in the systematic *Compilatio Prima*, it is seen that the elements of a single book in the former appear in five different books or fifteen titles in the latter. The principle of decretal dissection is shown by the way in which letters composed of several different parts, left undismembered in *Trinitatis*, are broken down and distributed through the titles in *Compilatio Prima*. Thus, the single decretal *Trin.* III, 12–13 is scattered through five separate titles in *Compilatio Prima*, and parts of *Trin.* III, 17 are found in two. In the following table, the items in *Trin.* III are listed first in numerical order, all appearing under a single heading; the second column identifies their corresponding positions in *Compilatio Prima*, together with the various title-headings under which the chapters are placed in the systematic collection.

Trin.	*Comp. I*	
1	III. 2.9:	De cohabitatione clericorum et mulierum *etc.*
2	I. 10.5:	De servis non ordinandis et eorum manumissione.
3	I. 22.1:	De officio legati.
4	II. 20.24:	De appellationibus et recusationibus.
7	V. 21.3:	De clerico percussore.
8	V. 10.9:	De homicidio voluntario vel casuali.
10	III. 7.1:	De institutionibus.
12a	III. 7.2:	De institutionibus.
12a	III. 2.7:	De cohabitatione clericorum *etc.*
12b	III. 5.4:	De prebendis.
13a	III. 33.15:	De iure patronatus *ete*

13b	I. 21.4:	De officio et potestate iudicis delegati.
15	II. 20.32:	De appellationibus *etc.*
16	IV. 6.3:	Qui clerici vel voventes matrimonium contrahere possunt.
17ab	II. 20.4:	De appellationibus *etc.*
17c	V. 16.3:	De crimine falsi.
18	I. 9.2:	De filiis presbiterorum ordinandis vel non, nec in paternis ecclesiis tollerandis.
19	V. 34.4:	De sententia excommunicationis et absolutione.
21	V. 15.4:	De usuris.
25	I. 9.7:	De filiis presbiterorum *etc.*

CHAPTER IV

The English Decretal Collections

1. The Present State of the Question

Having considered the state and nature of canon law in the later-twelfth century, the expansion of decretal legislation as part of papal centralizing policies in the period, the development of decretal collections by professional canon lawyers, and the principal traditions in codification by English and continental canonists, it now remains to examine the specifically English aspects of these questions, and to determine the historical value of the English collections. Their richness and value contrast sharply with their neglect by English historians. For the whole of Europe at least twenty-seven primitive collections have come down to us, of which no less than fifteen are undoubtedly English in origin and authorship. Of the rest, three are members of a Roman or Spanish family, with curial influences; four are French, and five Italian. Even merely statistically the proportion of English survivals is astonishing; but still more remarkable is the extent of English influence on collections made elsewhere in Europe. It is a proof of the neglect of this vital source material that, whereas six of the twelve continental collections and two of the fifteen English collections have been textually examined and analysed by continental scholars, none had been considered in any detail by English historians until very recently; and not one of the twenty-seven had been investigated for its wider significance in English history.[1]

---

[1] Holtzmann, *Nachrichten*, pp. 21–3. Among English collections, *Wig.* and *Claustr.* have been analysed by Lohmann and Schönsteiner respectively; and there is a brief analysis of *Wig.Altera* in Kuttner, *Repertorium*, p. 283. Among continental collections, *Eberbac.*, *Dertus.*, *Paris. I*, *Cantab.*, *Aureaev.*, and *Berol.* have been analysed by Holtzmann, Friedberg or Juncker; full details of these collections are given in Chapter V, Part 2, below. For illustration of the value of the primitive collections

In a brief but illuminating incursion into the field of canon law in the Middle Ages, Maitland set at rest many previously debated problems concerning the English Church, and laid down the course for future similar enquiries. Zachary Brooke later continued and expanded what Maitland had begun. Even when it is no longer possible to agree entirely with their conclusions in this context, it would be impossible to ignore our debt to these historians. But, in attempting to elucidate the course of papal decretal legislation in England in the later-twelfth century, neither referred to decretal collections preceding Bernard of Pavia's *Compilatio Prima* (c. 1191), which for reasons which are now very obvious must be considered as the *terminus ad quem* of decretal codification for Alexander III's pontificate. Therefore, they failed to appreciate the specialist and limited value of the collections which they cited, and their conclusions can be shown to have little relevance to the evidence on which they were based.[1]

Although certain aspects of the thesis advanced by Maitland and Brooke have been called into question by more recent historians (by Barraclough, Mrs. Cheney, and Kuttner and Miss Rathbone), the basic problems remain unexplored in detail, due to the neglect of the immense manuscript resources now available in canonical collections and canonistic commentaries.[2] The primary tasks undertaken in this chapter are, therefore, to examine the substance, structure and interconnexions of all extant English primitive collections; to determine from them the interests, motives and objectives of the English canon lawyers; and, finally, to relate this evidence to the general politico-ecclesiastical problems of the day. All English primitive collections have been classified by Holtzmann in three main groups or families: the 'English', 'Bridlington' and 'Worcester' families respectively.[3] It is admittedly difficult to devise a

in examining particular problems, see Brooke, *Canons of English Church Councils*, pp. 471-9; etc. See also now my article 'The Trinity Collection of Decretals and the Early Worcester Family', *Traditio*, XVII (1961), pp. 506-26. Cf. p. 124, n.2, below.

[1] The nature of this problem has been fully explained in Chapter I, Part 1, above.

[2] See especially Barraclough, *EHR* (1938), pp. 492-5; M. Cheney, *art.cit.*, pp. 177-97; Kuttner and Rathbone, *art.cit.*, pp. 279-80.

[3] Holtzmann, *Nachrichten*, pp. 22-3. A more complete discussion of these families may be read in my unpublished Cambridge Ph. D thesis: *Twelfth Century Decretal Collections and their Importance in English History*, 2 Vols. (1954); the second volume

satisfactory nomenclature in view of the complicated relationships both within and between the families, and the varied provenance of otherwise closely related collections; and so these conventional descriptions have been accepted here to avoid confusion, but it should be realized at the outset that they are by no means satisfactory in all cases.[1] In the same way, the conventions observed in naming the individual collections require some brief clarification. It must be understood that most collections preceding *Compilatio Prima* are of uncertain provenance. In some cases a place of origin can be suggested provisionally; and in a few rare instances the author's identity can be deduced from internal evidence. But on the whole the problems of identification remain impenetrable. In these circumstances, the general practice adopted hitherto is this: wherever the place of origin can be reasonably established for a given collection, it is named accordingly; but in all other cases it takes its name from the location, past or present, of the surviving manuscript, whichever seems more appropriate. Thus, *Parisiensis II* is now found in the Bibliothèque Nationale in Paris, and so acquires its name as the Paris II Collection, whereas *Wigorniensis* was almost certainly composed at Worcester, though it is now in the British Museum, and is known as the Worcester Collection. Briefly, then, associations of past or present location or of probable origin explain the conventional names both of the separate collections and of the family groups which they compose, though such descriptions are seldom apt when applied to a family as a whole.[2]

2. The 'English' Family

From the historian's viewpoint, the 'English' family is the most interesting of all groups of primitive collections. The canon lawyer is naturally more interested in systematic collections,

---

includes a provisional analysis of all members of the 'English' family, and select analyses from the 'Bridlington' and 'Worcester' groups, together with comparative tables.

[1] The name 'Worcester' family is a misnomer, based on the false assumption that *Wig.* is the oldest surviving member of the group.

[2] The 'Bridlington' family is so-called because the earlier of its two surviving members belonged originally to Bridlington Priory, but there is little doubt that the family archetype was composed in the Canterbury province.

which reveal a scientific and mature appreciation of the juridical subject-matter, altogether to a lawyer's taste, but quite lacking in the earliest works. Yet the very opposite is true of the historian, since in his judgement the older the version the greater is likely to be its historical reliability.[1] That is why the 'English' family is so valuable to historians of the English Church, since it is the most primitive of all the surviving groups, and shows more clearly than any other how English canonists accumulated their raw materials in the earliest collecting phases, and moved gradually towards a conscious pattern of composition in the construction of their decretal collections. The family name is perhaps the least satisfactory of existing conventional descriptions, being both imprecise and subject to confusion, though it is too well-established to be readjusted now.[2] Seven members of the family (listed below) are known at present, and it is best to summarize briefly the salient features of each in turn.

(1) The Worcester II Collection: *Wigorniensis Altera*: Royal MS. 11 B. II, fols. 97–102.
(2) The Belvoir Collection: *Belverensis*: Bodl. MS. e Mus. 249, fols. 121–35.
(3) The Canterbury Collection: *Cantuariensis*: Royal MS. 10 B. IV, fols. 42–58 and 59–65.
(4) The Rochester Collection: *Roffensis*: Royal MS. 10 C. IV, fols. 137–55.
(5) The Fountains Collection: *Fontanensis*: Bodl. MS. Laud Misc. 527, fols. 24–45.
(6) The Durham Collection: *Dunelmensis*: Durham Cathedral MS. C. III, 1, fols. 5–18.
(7) The Royal Collection: *Regalis*: Royal MS. 15 B. IV, fols. 107–18.

The earliest extant 'English' collection is the Worcester manuscript *Wigorniensis Altera*: this brief work is among the

---

[1] By older we mean depending more immediately on the archetypal text; date of completion or transcription need not be a material consideration in this context: among 'Worcester' collections, *Chelt.* was completed (and probably transcribed) later than *Claustr.*, but it is textually more faithful to their common source.

[2] The name 'English' family, as applied to only one of three known English groups, is clearly unsatisfactory. To avoid such ambiguity, the name 'Canterbury' family might have been a better choice.

oldest post-Gratian collections surviving in the whole of Europe, and is certainly one of the earliest decretal collections composed in England. In date of composition it is conceivably as early as 1173–4, though three of its items can be dated only within the limits of Alexander III's pontificate (1159–81) or Roger of Worcester's episcopate (1164–79).[1] The manuscript itself belonged originally to Worcester Cathedral Priory, though it is now in the British Museum;[2] and of its ten decretals all but one were received by English ecclesiastics, advising them on legal and judicial problems arising in the course of their delegated jurisdiction.[3] The chief personal interest within the collection centres on Bishop Roger of Worcester, who received no less than four of its ten items; and this fact, coupled with his great reputation as a papal judge delegate and the medieval presence of the manuscript in Worcester, makes it very likely that he was connected in some way, if only indirectly, with its composition. Beyond doubt the collection is the work of an English canon lawyer, based on decretals received by Roger and his English judicial colleagues. And yet the transcription is not itself the ancestral version, since it has textual faults which were not repeated in derivative collections.[4] This is a most surprising fact considering the Worcester provenance of the extant manuscript.

[1] Appendix I: *Wig.Altera*, 6. J-L 13163 and 14132, 1164–79; 9. J-L 13164, 1164–79; 10. J-L 13873, 1159–81. Apart from these three letters which cannot be dated precisely, the final dating limit is suggested by: 7. J-L 12253 and 14146, 1159–17 January 1174; 8. J-L 13982, c. 1173; and 12. J-L 12293, 2 June 1173–4.

[2] The MS. was certainly at Worcester in the thirteenth century: the inscription 'Liber monasterii Wygornie' appears on the title folio, and two thirteenth-century letters involving the monks of Worcester are found on fols. 55v and 128v respectively.

[3] Appendix I: *Wig.Altera*, 11. J-L 12020, 2 March 1171–2: to Archbishop Henry of Reims. This decretal and the final item (12. J-L 12293, 2 June 1173–4: to Archbishop Roger of York) were added to the collection after the first recension, and are omitted from Kuttner's analysis, *Repertorium*, p. 283. Therefore Roger of Worcester received no less than four of the eight decretals composing the first draft. For Roger, see Morey, *op. cit.*, pp. 45 ff.; Hall, *Roger of Worcester*; etc. Alexander III described Roger and Bartholomew as the two great luminaries of the English Church: in the picturesque phrasing of Giraldus Cambrensis this metaphor was extended to twin candelabra, illuminating all England with their brilliance; J. S. Brewer, ed., *Giraldi Cambrensis Opera*, Rolls Series, VII (1877), p. 57.

[4] Only two decretals retain their inscriptions in this version: Appendix I: *Wig.Altera*, 1 and 7. On the other hand, four decretals retain their dates: *ibid.*, 1, 3, 11 and 12. See Plate I, below.

The Belvoir Collection is so-named from its medieval location in the Benedictine cell at Belvoir, a dependency of St. Albans Abbey; and the volume in which it is now incorporated is composed of varied materials relating to the career of Gilbert Foliot, bishop of London.[1] Like most of the members of the so-called 'English' family, the Belvoir Collection is not strictly an integrated collection at all, conceived as an entity. It is built up from several quite independently devised components, drawn together for the first time in a single volume. Thus it shows very clearly how decretal materials were frequently assembled in the most primitive phases. At least four clearly distinguished elements can be identified in its composition, revealing precise and personal interests, transcribed in several stages by many different copyists.[2] The first component is related to *Wigorniensis Altera*, but is closer to their common source in textual details: the decretal inscriptions appear here with unusual fulness and accuracy, and each decretal is preserved intact.[3] But the second component marks a distinct break in the continuity of the manuscript; and in subject-matter and provenance alike the decretals which follow contrast

[1] There is some reference to this collection in Brooke, *Canons of English Church Councils*, pp. 471–9. A full analysis is provided in Appendix II, below.

[2] The decretals are preceded by various papal letters chiefly to Foliot, Henry II and Archbishop Rotrou of Rouen. The decretal collection is transcribed in several different hands, and built up as follows: (*a*) Canons of the Council of Tours, in double columns, fols. 121ra–122rb; decretals, in single column, fols. 122v–129r. (The canons and decretals are written in different but contemporary hands.) (*b*) A second group of decretals, following on the previous folios without intermission and possibly in the same hand, fols. 129r–131rb, reverting to double columns at fol. 129v; an appendix of two letters on the Becket canonization, with a further change of hand, fols. 131rb–132ra. (*c*) The canons of the 1175 Council of Westminster, with a further change of hand (or hands), fols. 132ra–133va. (The final item 'Ex concilio Spanensi' is an independent transcription.) (*d*) A final group of decretals, written in two stages: 1. Fols. 133va–134va; 2. Fols. 134va–135rb. These four major divisions correspond with the analysis suggested in the present chapter, though it is clear that each part is itself of composite character.

[3] Appendix II: *Belver*. I, 9: 'Alexander tertius episcopus servus servorum Dei venerabili fratri R(ogerio) Wigorniensi episcopo, salutem et apostolicam benedictionem. Inter cetera *etc.*'; I, 11: 'Alexander III episcopus servus servorum Dei venerabili fratri R(ogerio) Eboracensi archiepiscopo, salutem et apostolicam benedictionem. Fraternitatem tuam *etc.*' Both these inscriptions were entirely omitted from *Wig.Altera*, and in this respect the *Belver*. text is superior; but *Wig.Altera* includes four dates which do not appear in the *Belver*. MS. It is evident that both transcriptions derive from an archetypal source now lost: they cannot be mutually interdependent.

sharply with those in the preceding section. The subject emphasis is now switched from the work of the papal judges delegate to matters involving churches and the status of clerks; while at the same time the personal interest is shifted from Roger of Worcester to Gilbert of London. Four of the nine letters in this part of the collection were received by Foliot personally in London, and the two concluding items(transcribed in a different hand) relate to the canonization of the martyred Becket.[1] The third component is again distinct in nature, being a transcription of the decrees of the 1175 council held at Westminster, and agreeing in provenance very well with the preceding decretals.[2] The final component is a further group of decretals, transcribed in two sections, whose main though not exclusive emphasis is on the religious orders and tithe payment, and whose stress in provenance is jointly shared by Canterbury and various monastic houses.[3] It follows that no single date of composition can be suggested for the Belvoir Collection as a whole: there is nothing in the first two parts which can be dated with certainty later than 1174; the conciliar decrees were published in 1175; and the final section includes one letter that can be dated in 1175. But various items in all three decretal components can be dated only by Alexander III's pontificate (1159–81); and with that essential proviso it may fairly be inferred that the collection as a whole was completed soon after 1175.[4]

The historical interest of the Belvoir Collection can, therefore, be summarized as follows: although the collection was not conceived as an entity, it is a revealing example of the way in which English decretal collectors assembled their raw materials in the earliest stages. Three personal or regional influences have been traced in the gradual build-up of the manuscript, linked with Roger of Worcester and Gilbert of London, and with an

---

[1] Appendix II: *Belver*. II, 8: J-L 12201, 12 March 1173; and II, 9: J-L 12203-4, 13 March 1173.

[2] The latest discussion of these canons is in Brooke, *Canons of English Church Councils*, pp. 471–6.

[3] Appendix II: *Belver*. IV, 1–8.

[4] Apart from decretals which cannot be dated more precisely than Alexander III's pontificate, the latest positive date in any part of the collection is 23 March 1175: *Belver*. IV, 2: J-L 12448 and 14314: 'Dat. Ferent. X Kal. Aprilis.'

intermingled monastic and Canterbury interest. Coinciding with these, and reflecting in the first two instances the activities of the bishops concerned, three distinct emphases in subject-matter have been detected: on the jurisdiction of judges delegate, on churches and clerical status, and on the religious orders and their payment of tithes. Such evident features of personal or particular influence and subject-matter selection are of deep significance in a wider context. It was from such beginnings as these that later and more famous collections were (in part at least) developed, and that later canonists derived an important part of their source material. And it is a point of further interest that the canons of the Council of Westminster, forming the third component in the Belvoir manuscript, include three extracts from contemporary decretal letters, intermingled with the canons of well-known and ancient councils, thus proving that by 1175 at the latest, within three years of the Avranches settlement, English bishops were citing the new extravagant laws in their synods, setting them side by side with the canons of great councils.[1]

Later members of the 'English' family are less interesting from the viewpoint of personal associations than the Belvoir Collection, but they are richer in substance, and show how professional skill developed gradually within the primitive framework. In some we detect the first beginnings of the systematic conventions, which were finally to render obsolete the entire range of primitive works. The Canterbury Collection is typical of these. In subject-matter selection and in transcription it is an authentic Canterbury composition, completed two or three years after the 1179 Lateran Council, and was almost certainly at Canterbury towards the close of the century. In manner of assembly it resembles the Belvoir Collection, lacking an integrated conception, and illustrating once again the gathering together of several quite independent works, bound up for the first time within a single volume. It is composed of three groups of decretal letters and an appendix of conciliar canons.[2]

---

[1] Appendix II: *Belver.* III, 1: 'Ex decretali epistola Alexandri pape III. Si quis sacerdos *etc.*'; 2. 'Decernimus etiam eiusdem epistole auctoritate *etc.*'; 13. 'Alexander papa ad W(illelmum) Norwicensem episcopum *etc.*'

[2] The Canterbury Collection is built up as follows: (*a*) Decretals, fols. 42vb–57vb. (*b*) Decretals, fols. 58ra–58vb. These two sections are quite independent of one

In no part of the manuscript is there a formal division of subject-matter into books or titles, though there are occasional groups of decretals of related interest transcribed in a single sequence in the first part; but even this arrangement is not consistently developed. The extent of subject-matter arrangement will best be seen from a selection of the marginal comments or 'rubrics', appearing in a number of hands, different from that of the text and mostly written in elaborate style. In the list below, the selected comments are numbered according to a provisional numeration of the decretals themselves:[1]

1. Corpora excommunicatorum proiicienda extra cimiteria.
4. Sententiam in intrusores prolatam quater in anno renovandam.
5. Qui focarias non dimiserint.
6. De pastore eligendo.
7. Ut monachi et canonici clericos representent. Ne monachi adquirant iura patronatuum ecclesiarum.
10. Infra xiiii annum constitutum non institui personam.
11. Occupatores ecclesiarum cogendos eas dimittere.
12. In ecclesiis vacantibus potiendos iconomos.
13. Nolentes dare decimas per excommunicationem esse cogendos.
14. Contempnentes habitum et tonsuram inter apostatas esse numerandos.
15. Uxorati compellantur ecclesias dimittere. Simplex beneficium possunt retinere.
16. Res ecclesie pignoratas ab herede sacerdotis esse luendas.
20. Iudex delegatus potest causam delegare.
37. Si ante citacionem reus peregre profectus est.
38. Cum aliqua sub disiunctione mandantur.
39. Appellationem non tenere in excessu publico.
40. Usque ad quod tempus delegati jurisdictio duret.
41. Recusationem non admittendam ubi appellatio inhibetur.
    etc.

another in composition and transcription, and have some material in common.
(c) Decretals, fols. 59vb–61vb; again quite independent of the previous sections.
(d) Canons of the Third Lateran Council, fols. 62ra–65ra; this part was transcribed by at least three different hands. An analysis of the Canterbury Collection is provided in Appendix III, below.

[1] *Cantuar.* MS., fols. 42vb–52vb. The marginalia are effectively 'rubrics', though not literally so. The decretals are not numbered in the MS.; a provisional numeration is suggested here for convenience. Cf. Appendix III and Plate III, below.

The first component of the Canterbury Collection was completed within the limits 1179 and 1181 or slightly later;[1] the
second and third parts within the limits 1176 and 1181;[2] the
additional presence of the canons of the 1179 Lateran Council
makes it reasonable to suggest an overall date of assembly of
1179 to 1181 or soon after. A statistical breakdown of the collection on a basis of the provenance of its individual items reveals a situation of the greatest possible significance. The most
striking feature from this viewpoint is the high proportion of its
letters received originally in the Canterbury province. The first
component includes sixty-two items, of which at least fifty-four
were received in England, but only one in the province
of York; nineteen of these letters were received at Canterbury itself (including no less than eleven of the first thirteen
items), twelve at Exeter, and nine at Worcester.[3] The second
component is too brief for significant analysis. But the third
component is composed of twenty-two items, of which sixteen
were received in England; but in this instance only one letter
was received at Canterbury, and four in the province of York.[4]
Therefore, the Canterbury Collection reveals at once what is in
fact the most remarkable feature in the whole range of English
primitive collections: namely the high proportion of their total
contents of Canterbury, Exeter and Worcester provenance; or,
to stress the personal aspect, the large proportion of decretals
received by Richard, Bartholomew and Roger, their respective
bishops. The first and very obvious conclusion is that the

[1] These dating limits are established by the inclusion of the decretal *Inter ceteras*,
J-L 13878 and 14346, 1179–81, to the archbishop of York: *Cantuar.* MS., fol. 51v.
[2] The dating limits for the second part are fixed by the decretal *Cum sacrosancta*,
J-L 13768–70 and 13835, 1176–80, to the bishop of Chartres: *Cantuar.* MS., fol.
58r; and for the third part by the decretal *Nosti sicut*, J-L 12753, 1176, to the bishop
of Worcester: *Cantuar.* MS., fol. 60v. Both parts also include letters which can be
dated only by Alexander III's pontifical years: 1159–81. It is unlikely that they
were composed as early as 1176.
[3] *Cantuar.* MS., fols. 42v–57v. Appendix III, below: to Canterbury, *Cantuar.* I,
1, 3–7, 9–13, 32–5, 39, 50, 57 and 59; to Exeter, *ibid.*, 16, 17, 24, 27–9, 31, 40, 43–5
and 48; to Worcester, *ibid.*, 2, 17, 18, 22, 47, 54, 55, 57 and 61; to York, *ibid.*, 38;
to continental recipients, *ibid.*, 26, 30, 42, 46, 56, 58 and 60: to Florence, Rouen
and Jumièges, Reims, Rouen and Amiens, Salerno, Séez and Piacenza respectively.
The concentration of English decretals suggests a dependence on local records.
[4] *Cantuar.* MS., fols. 59v–61v. Appendix III, below: to Canterbury, *Cantuar.* III,
12; to recipients in the province of York, *ibid.*, 2, 4, 5 and 19.

English primitive collections are undoubtedly English in the provenance of their contents, depending on decretals received originally in the island. They were not derived at this stage from the papal registers. The second conclusion is that the decisive influence in this English development was the judicial activities of the three bishops already mentioned. This remarkable phenomenon is not simply coincidental; nor does it merely reflect the actual ratios of letters sent out from the chancery. Quite the reverse: its explanation lies at the heart of a just understanding of the course of papal decretal legislation in England after the death of Becket, emphasizing the importance of a few great English bishops in the spread of canon law in the island at that time. Their influence was made effective chiefly in their work as judges delegate and in the stimulus which they provided to the accumulation of the latest papal rulings which passed through their hands. Thus, in illustration of this theory: the Canterbury Collection begins with a sequence of thirteen decretals, of which no less than nine were addressed to the archbishop personally, while three more have a general interest for the Canterbury province and so in all probability came also into his hands.[1] It is possible to see in this arrangement a derivation directly from the Canterbury records, and more particularly from the decretals received there by Richard. This Canterbury derivation is the basic and initial element on which the rest of the work is constructed, being supplemented later with decretals of more varied provenance, but with a notable proportion received at Exeter and Worcester.

Closely related to the Canterbury Collection is a manuscript from the neighbouring and dependent see at Rochester. The Rochester Collection is similar in composition and style to the Canterbury Collection, being likewise derived from several separate sources, while the basic Canterbury derivative is common to both. But the Rochester manuscript is a beautiful and finished composition, transcribed somewhat later than its original construction, and completed in its surviving form not much earlier than the close of the century. The original composite character of the collection is here concealed in a single

---

[1] *Cantuar.* MS., fols. 42v–44v. Appendix III, below: *Cantuar.* I, 1–13.

continuous transcription. The collection opens with a preface of the decrees of the Third Lateran Council, followed by one hundred and twenty-five items, of which roughly the first seventy-five were drawn from a source in common with the first component of the Canterbury Collection. Within this section not more than fifteen items were of continental provenance.[1] Thereafter the collections diverge both in substance and interest, and with the change in filiation there is a parallel change in the provenance of the letters. Of the forty-eight concluding items of the Rochester Collection, no less than twenty-three were received by continental bishops, so that the non-English elements increase in proportion from one-eighth to one-half where the collector shifted from one source to another.[2] There is little doubt that the Rochester collector was indebted (whether directly or indirectly) to a continental source for the completion of his work, just as he had drawn on a Canterbury archetype for his opening materials. But in completing his collection he drew also on English sources later than anything discovered in the Canterbury Collection: five decretals of Lucius III (1181–5) are intermingled with the predominantly continental letters at the close.[3] Thus the final elements of the Rochester Collection are themselves of composite character, as the Canterbury archetype had already been, blending letters of Alexander III to continental bishops with those of his successor to English prelates, though it cannot be taken for granted that this

[1] *Roff*. MS., fols. 139v–149r. This provisional estimate allows for some uncertain inscriptions. To continental recipients, fols, 140r, 142v, 143v(3), 146v, 147r(2), 148r and 148v: to Séez, Reims, Syracuse, Piacenza, Rouen and Jumièges, French prelates, Biseglie, Salerno, Florence and Poitiers respectively. An analysis of the Rochester Collection is provided in Appendix IV, below: *Roff.*, 30, 46, 49, 51, 52, 80, 84, 88–9, 94 and 99; 82, 85, 86 and 91 are uncertain; 38 is addressed to Lisieux in this MS., but to Exeter elsewhere.

[2] *Roff*. MS., fols. 149r–154r. English and continental decretals and conciliar canons are intermingled here; but notice especially the sequence of non-English decretals on fol. 149r–v: one uncertain (MS.: Tiburnic.), Séez, Gran and Kolocsa, Triers, Lucca, Pisa and one uncertain (MS.: Auctaven.). Appendix IV, below: *Roff.*, 104–110.

[3] *Roff*. MS., fols. 151v–154r: (1) 151v: J-L 14964, to Baldwin of Worcester, 7 July, 1182–3; (2) 151v: J-L 14963, to John of Norwich, 1181; (3) 153v: J-L 15185, to John of Norwich, 1181–5; (4) 153v: J-L 14029, to John of Norwich, 1181–5, previously dated 1159–81; (5) 154r: J-L 14965, to Walter of Coutances, bishop of Lincoln, 1183–4. Appendix IV, below: *Roff.*, 119, 121, 145, 146 and 150.

blending was achieved for the first time in the manuscript which now survives.[1]

In this way the Rochester Collection adds a further point of interest, illustrating clearly for the first time in this survey of 'English' collections the interchange of material between English and continental canonists. But where the collection is not indebted to continental sources, it repeats the preponderance of letters received at Canterbury, Exeter and Worcester, as already noticed in the Canterbury Collection. In this instance, forty of the first seventy-five decretals were received at one or other of these three places.[2] Finally, the varied sources of the Rochester Collection are reflected in the dates of composition of its parts. There is no matter later than 1181 in the part dependent on the Canterbury archetype;[3] the limits of the second and composite section are 1183–5;[4] and the collection ends with a single letter issued by Celestine III in 1193.[5] Since the manuscript is a single transcription, with the probable exception of its final item, the date of completion of the work as an entity must be fixed at 1183–5 or later, with a single addition in or after 1193.

Two further 'English' collections have links with the province of York. The Durham Collection is so described from its present location in the Durham Cathedral Library; and the Fountains Collection, though now in the Bodleian at Oxford, belonged originally to the Cistercian abbey in Yorkshire. The Durham manuscript is composed of several parts of varied style and purpose, an *arbor consanguinitatis* and several canonical treatises. It is the product of several sources and many different hands. The opening section is composed of thirty-five items, either decretals or conciliar canons; then follow in turn the

[1] It is quite probable that further research on the continental primitive collections will reveal a source of the type on which the Rochester Collection partly depended. Cf. *Collectio Florianensis*: St. Florian Library MS. III, 5, fols. 173–83.

[2] *Roff.* MS., fols. 139v–149r: to Canterbury: 139v–140r(6), 144r(2), 144v(2), 145r, 145v, 146r–146v(4) and 148r; etc. Appendix IV, below: *Roff.*, 27–9, 32–4, 54, 55, 63, 65, 68, 71, 74, 76, 77, 83, 93; etc.

[3] The dating limits are fixed by the inclusion of the decretal *Inter ceteras*, J-L 13878 and 14346, 1179–81 (*Roff.* MS. fol. 141r; Appendix IV, below: *Roff.* 40) and the absence of decretals later than the death of Alexander III in 1181.

[4] These limits are fixed by the inclusion of five decretals of Lucius III; cf. p. 78, n.3, above.

[5] *Roff.* MS., fol 154r: *Prudentiam tuam*, J-L 17019, 17 June 1193, Celestine III to John, dean of Rouen.

decrees of the Third Lateran Council, an abbreviation of
Gratian's *Decretum*, the canons of the 1163 Council of Tours,
two further groups of decretal letters, and an appendix of
decretals of Lucius III transcribed in at least three separate
stages.[1] In spite of the presence of the manuscript in the province of York, there is nothing in its decretal sections to dissociate it from the 'English' family with its emphasis on letters
received in the province of Canterbury. Three separate groups
of decretals (intermingled with conciliar canons), comprising
thirty-five, forty-five and seventeen items respectively (or almost
one hundred items in all), include no more than nine decretals
received in the north. In contrast with this, nineteen of the first
thirty-five items were received at either Canterbury, Worcester
or Exeter.[2] And in the closing group of seventeen items, no
less than twelve were received in England, but only two of these
in the northern province.[3] Apart from the decretals of Lucius
III, which must be dated post 1181, no material elsewhere in the
collection can be dated later than that year. The first group of
decretals can be fixed between the limits 1179 and 1181; and
these are also the most likely limits for the assembly of the work
as a whole.[4]

[1] The Durham Collection is intermingled with varied canonical material as
follows: (*a*) Decretals, fols. 8va–10vb. (*b*) Canons of the Third Lateran Council, and
an *arbor cansanguinitatis*, fols. 11ra–12vb. These first two parts are written in double
columns. (*c*) An abbreviation of Gratian's *Decretum*, fols. 13ra–14ra, written in
triple columns. (*d*) Canons of the Council of Tours, followed by decretals, fols.
14rb–16vb; beginning in triple columns but reverting to double columns at fol.
15r. (*e*) Decretals, fols. 17ra–18ra: at least one folio is missing between fols. 17 and
18. (*f*) Appendix of decretals of Lucius III, fol. 18ra, written in at least three
different hands.

[2] *Dunelm.* MS., fols. 8v–10v: to Exeter: 8v, 9r(2), 9v and 10v(4); to Worcester:
8v(3), 10r(2) and 10v; to Canterbury: 9v(2), 10r and 10v(2); to York province:
8v(2), 9r(2) and 10v. In some cases a single decretal was received by more than one
recipient, and occasionally in both the southern and the northern provinces: in
this first group of decretals in the *Dunelm.* MS. five decretals were received in the
north, but two of these were received also in the south.

[3] *Dunelm.* MS., fols. 17r–17v: to Canterbury: 17r(4); to York province: 17v(2);
etc. At least one folio is missing after the seventeenth item, but there is an unidentified fragment and one further English decretal on fol. 18r.

[4] The first group of decretals can be dated by its inclusion of the decretal *Inter
ceteras*: *Dunelm.* MS., fol. 10v; cf. p. 75, n.1, above. This is followed by the decrees
of the 1179 Lateran Council; the remaining groups of decretals cannot be precisely dated, but include nothing later than the death of Alexander in 1181;
and the appendix of decretals of Lucius III must be dated 1181–5.

The Fountains Collection presents a very similar picture.
It is a composite work of several independent collections bound
up together in the single volume. There can be no doubt that the
manuscript was transcribed in part at least at Fountains, since
an extract from the Fountains cartulary is incorporated integrally within it.[1] The collection opens with a group of fifty items
of varied date and provenance: the letters in this part are predominantly English, but with French and Italian decretals
intermingled with them (as in the final part of the Rochester
Collection).[2] The now familiar Exeter and Worcester emphasis
is once again in evidence, with eleven decretals received by
Bartholomew and eight by Roger.[3] The cohesion of the Exeter
material is particularly striking in this case: eight letters to
Exeter appearing at one stage in an almost unbroken sequence.[4]
There is no reason to doubt that the Fountains Collection was
indebted in this part to a southern English collection, perhaps
with some direct dependence on Exeter. But immediately following this first group of decretals, there is a marked break in
manuscript continuity, both in its physical composition and in
the substance of the letters. Beginning on a fresh folio and
written in a different hand is found a transcription from the
Fountains cartulary of papal *privilegia* which strictly speaking
have no place in a decretal collection at all. These are followed
in turn (but in this case without a break in transcription) by a
further group of decretals revealing the typical Canterbury and
continental influences already noticed in several connexions.[5]
The whole is completed with a further and separate batch of

[1] The Fountains Collection was assembled in these stages: (*a*) Decretals, including both primitive and systematic techniques, fols. 24r–31v. (*b*) Cartulary of
Fountains Abbey, fols. 32r–37r. (*c*) Decretals, fols. 37r–39v. (*d*) Decretals, including
the canons of the Council of Tours among the concluding items, fols. 40r–45v.
These components were designed and transcribed independently of one another,
except that (*c*) follows immediately upon (*b*) without a break and in mid-folio.

[2] *Font*. MS., fols. 24r–31v: to continental recipients: 26v(2), 27v(3), etc. Cf.
Roff. MS., fols. 149r–154r.

[3] *Font*. MS., fols. 24r–31v: to Exeter: 26v, 27v, 29r–30r(8) and 30v; to Worcester:
24r, 24v, 27v–28r(4) and 31r(2).

[4] *Ibid*., fols. 29r–30r: there is a single unidentified letter in this otherwise unbroken sequence of decretals to Bartholomew of Exeter.

[5] *Ibid*., fols. 37r–39v: this section includes both English and continental decretals
intermingled with conciliar canons; but at least sixteen of its twenty-nine items are
of English provenance.

decretals, comprising forty-one items of which four were sent to Exeter and six to York.[1]

There are no decretals in the Fountains Collection later than the death of Alexander III; the Lateran decrees are not included in this manuscript, but at least one decretal can be dated between 1179 and 1181.[2] On the other hand, one letter of Lucius III appears among the abbey charters, which fixes the date of transcription of the cartulary after 1181.[3] The second group of decretals must also, therefore, be later than 1181 in transcription, though this could never have been deduced from internal evidence within the decretal collection. The dates of composition of the various parts may be provisionally suggested as follows: 1179 or later for the opening component; and 1179–81 or later for the second. The separate components of this so-called collection are, once again, independent of one another in provenance and origin. In several instances a single letter occurs in each of two components, and one decretal is found in all three sections.[4] In places the composition is technically more advanced than in the 'English' collections discussed so far, revealing traces of systematic techniques and conventional abbreviations.[5]

The final member of the 'English' family is in some ways the most interesting of them all. Revealing no certain association of place or person, it is identified by its present location among the Royal Manuscripts in the British Museum, and is therefore known simply as the Royal Collection or *Regalis*. The appearance of the manuscript is very disappointing at first sight: ill-arranged in layout, hastily and carelessly transcribed in places, and contrasting markedly with the beautiful *Roffensis* described above. Whereas the latter had been a show piece or presentation

---

[1] *Ibid.*, fols. 40r–45v: to York province: 40r(2), 41r(2?), 42r and 45r(2); to Exeter: 40r(2), 42v and 43v(2); Conciliar canons: 43v–44r(6), 45v(2), etc.

[2] *Ibid.*, fol. 40r: *Inter ceteras*; cf. p. 75, n.1, above.

[3] *Ibid.*, fol. 36v.

[4] *Ibid.*, fols. 29r, 38r and 40r: these three chapters are all parts of a single letter to Bartholomew of Exeter: J-L 13917, 1162–81.

[5] Some decretals remain undissected in *Font.*, especially in the opening folios; cf. *Font.* MS., fol. 24r: *Super eo quod* (J-L 13162, 1167–9, to the bishop of Worcester) retains its ten chapters in this single position. But the abbreviation conventions 'et infra' and 'etc et infra' are found on some later folios; cf. *Font.* MS., fols. 27v–31r.

G

copy, the Royal Collection seems more like a rough hand-book of reference for the practising or teaching canon lawyer.[1]

Yet beneath this somewhat forbidding appearance, the collection is far in advance technically speaking of its English contemporaries. Although it has no clearly indicated division into books and titles, there is an underlying arrangement to suit a subject-matter pattern. Still more striking is the author's use of the systematic conventions of decretal dissection and textual abbreviation.[2] The collection is composed of one hundred and twenty-six items, about one-quarter of which have brief chapter headings or summaries, which are effectively 'rubrics', and indicate the extent of subject-matter analysis to suit an overall pattern of composition. The following select examples are numbered according to a provisional numeration of the decretal chapters themselves:

7. Posteriores littere non preiudicant prioribus, nisi in eis facta fuerit mentio priorum et earundem possessionum.

12. Clericos uxoratos simplex habere posse in ecclesiis beneficium.

39. Non prorogatur causa ultra prefixum diem.

43. Quod ecclesie sub conditione datur, non revocatur.

44. Qui in monasterio (*MS.*: monesterio) converti volunt laici, medietatem rerum suarum suis ecclesiis relinquant.

47. Ut decimas reddant monachi.

58. Ubi tenetur solvere debitum uxori quamvis cognoverit consanguineam eius.

59. Si quis contraxerit cum consanguinea eo nesciente, et postea mota fuerit questio, tamen tenebitur matrimonium.

60. Johannes filiam suam cuidam iuveni Stephano nomine simplicibus verbis desponsavit, que, antequam ad nuptias pervenit, morte preventa est. Utrum vero soror defuncte cum eodem iuvene posset contrahere matrimonium, dominus papa consultius ita respondit.

---

[1] The volume also includes a formulary book in a contemporary hand for the guidance of judges delegate: Royal MS. 15 B. IV, fols. 75 ff. Cf. Cheney, *English Bishops' Chanceries, 1100–1250* (1950), p. 128. See Plate II, below.

[2] The decretals are not always dissected in this work, but they are in many instances: the decretal *Super eo quod* (J-L 13162, 1167–9, to the bishop of Worcester), appears in *Cantuar.* MS., fol. 46v, as a single item composed of twelve chapters; the same decretal is distributed in five different positions in *Regal.* MS., fols. 109r, 110v, 111r, 111v and 112v.

63. Si aliquis duas in prima vel secunda consanguinitatis linea contingentes duxerit, utraque careat. Si in ulteriori linea, secunda tantum.

64. Adulter adulteram in uxorem ducere posse, nisi alter machinatus fuerit mortem prioris viri, vel eo vivente fidem dederit.

81. Donationes ecclesiarum absque auctoritate (*MS.*: auctoritae) episcopi non valere.

83. Electus disponere de rebus ecclesie non potest, nisi electione eius confirmata.

92. Indignum est ut in subdiaconum ordinatus ecclesiastico careat beneficio.

93. Simoniace ad sacerdotium promotus aut ad religionem inducatur, aut ecclesiasticum habeat beneficium et sacerdotali careat officio.

94. Qui matrimonium contraxerit aut separetur aut ecclesiam amittat.

95. Laico non concedantur decime.

96. Possidens patrimonium sacerdotis tenetur res ecclesie pro necessitate sacerdotis pignoratas ecclesie restituere.

97. Non licet alicui distrahere sive in perpetuum locare.

102. Vi et metu facta in irritum revocanda.

103. Monachos de Cist (erciensis ordinis) ecclesias vel iura patronatuum adquirere non decet.

111. Tenet appellatio ubi est inhibita. Pensionem nomine ecclesie per illusionem non esse solvendam vel recipiendam.

117. Nisi transactio apostolica auctoritate confirmetur non inter ecclesias sed inter personas facta videtur.

Thus, as a significant illustration, chapters 58–61 in the select list given above could be appropriately placed under the title 'De statu et iure coniugii'; and so forth.[1] It is clear that a good sense of subject selection and arrangement pervades the work without being taken to its full application. The collection cannot be dated with certainty later than 1181, since it includes no letters later than the death of Alexander; but various canons of the Third Lateran Council and at least one decretal from the period 1179–81 are included within it;

---

[1] *Regal.* MS., fols. 112va–113ra; etc. The typical items listed above are found respectively on fols. 108r(2), 110v, 111r, 111v(2), 112v(4), 113r, 114v, 115r, 116r(5), 116v(3), 117r and 117v. The items are not numbered in the MS. itself; the numeration cited above is adopted for convenient reference.

so that c. 1181 or later is the fairest suggestion for its date of completion.[1]

The provenance of the separate letters is once again strikingly English, though exact numerical ratios are less easy to establish in this collection owing to the application of the systematic devices. But if the contents are provisionally classified in one hundred and twenty-six items, only twenty decretal chapters can be shown to bear non-English inscriptions.[2] Due to the dissection of the individual letters, regional, local or personal influences are less obvious than in most primitive collections. But the Canterbury, Worcester and Exeter emphasis is again repeated, with a greater proportion of letters in this instance addressed to Exeter.[3] Thus the Royal Collection is a remarkable work, well advanced technically, but a member nonetheless of the primitive 'English' family in substance. In the final analysis, its date of composition, though probably c. 1181 on the basis of internal evidence, must remain conjectural.

3. The 'Bridlington' Family

The 'English' family, discussed above and including the most primitive of all English decretal collections, is chiefly valuable for the evidence it provides on the basic stimuli and resources from which the collections were gradually evolved in England. The 'Worcester' family, still to be discussed, reveals most clearly the typical lines of technical development within the schools of the more advanced English canonists. Two manuscripts remain outside these major groupings, and are known as the 'Bridlington' family, their reference details being as follows:

[1] Two canons of the 1179 Lateran Council appear on *Regal*. MS., fol. 108r; the decretal *Inter ceteras*, J-L 13878 and 14346, 1179–81, is distributed in three places: *ibid.*, fols. 107va, 114vb and 115rb.

[2] The inscriptions are not reliable in all cases, but decretals of certain or probable continental provenance are found on the following folios: 107v(2), 108r(2), 108v, 109r, 109v, 111r(?), 111v, 112v(2), 114v, 115r, 117r(3), 118r(?) and 118r(2).

[3] *Ibid.*, fols. 112r-v: a sequence of three letters to Exeter; fols. 115v–116r: a sequence of nine letters to Exeter. The provenance is uncertain; Kuttner and Rathbone, *art. cit.*, pp. 282–3, n.10, suggest a Worcester origin; the formulary book for judges delegate (cf. p. 82, n.1, above) includes a local interest involving Bury St. Edmunds; but the most striking concentration of decretals within the Royal Collection itself is of Exeter provenance.

(1) The Bridlington Collection: *Bridlingtonensis*: Bodl. MS. 357, fols. 80–133.

(2) The Claudian Collection: *Claudiana*: Cotton MS. Claudius A. iv, fols. 189–216.

The two 'Bridlington' collections are closely interrelated for roughly half their contents. The Bridlington Collection, which gives its name to the group, belonged in the Middle Ages to Bridlington Priory, and was almost certainly transcribed in a north-country scriptorium (perhaps in the priory itself) about 1182 or shortly after.[1] The Claudian Collection was completed five or six years later; its place of origin is uncertain, and it is identified simply by its present location in the Cottonian Collection in the British Museum.[2] There is nothing in this manuscript to dissociate it in any way from the province of Canterbury.

Both works are closer in style to the 'English' than to the 'Worcester' collections, but are far more satisfactory than the former in arrangement and transcription. Each collection is transcribed as an entity, advancing beyond the obvious and very rudimentary composition of the 'English' works, but with nothing technically comparable with the book and title framework of the 'Worcester' collections. Their interest and value lie partly in their contents and partly in their style of presentation. A sense of completion and unity is achieved by a continuous and integrated transcription of the whole work and an unbroken numeration of the individual decretals through the entire composition: the decretals are in fact numbered in the manuscripts, reaching a total of one hundred and ninety-three items in the Bridlington and two hundred and sixteen in the Claudian version. An elaborate apparatus of rubrics,

---

[1] The volume includes William of Malmesbury's *De Gestis Pontificum*; the flyleaf bears the inscription: 'Liber sancte Marie de Bridelington. Qui hunc alienaverit, anathema sit'; and fol. 1r is inscribed: 'Liber sancte Marie de Brillinctuna.' See N. R. Ker, *Medieval Libraries of Great Britain* (1941), p. 8; H. Omont, *Zentral.blatt für Bibliothekswesen*, ix (1892), p. 203: it is suggested that the list of books transcribed in the B.M. Harley MS. 50, fol. 48v, may record the medieval library of Bridlington Priory, but the Bridlington Collection cannot be identified in the list. The date of the decretal collection is discussed later in this chapter.

[2] The collection was certainly compiled in the Canterbury province not earlier than 1185; the dating limits are fixed by the inclusion of three decretals of Urban III (1185–7): *Claud. MS.*, fols. 209rb, 210ra and 216ra.

summarizing the juridical contents of each chapter, gives a distinctive appearance to this family in contrast with all other English primitive works. There was of course nothing original in the concept of rubricated or marginal comments, and several of the collections already described included them in one form or another.[1] Their distinctive feature in the 'Bridlington' collections is the important and obvious role which they play in the scheme of composition, which may be seen to best effect in a few select examples. Generally speaking, a single rubric suffices for a whole decretal, and is incorporated within the main body of the transcription as an integral part of its basic structure: it is not merely a marginal addition. In such instances, the rubric emphasizes the main point of law in the decretal to which it appears as an introduction. But many decretals within the collections have several component sections (for the collections are primitive and their decretals usually undissected),[2] and for these there are supplementary rubrics supplied for each of their various components. The following examples are simply characteristic of the 'Bridlington' conventions:[3]

Bridlingtonensis:

    i. *Rubric*: Sive deficiat clericus super homicidio infamatus in purgatione canonica, sive testibus ordine iudiciario convincatur, eadem pena percellitur et officio et beneficio privatur.

   ii. *Rubric:* Archiepiscopus accepto iuramento iudicio sisti, quem eius suffraganeus excommunicavit, absolvere potest, qui post excommunicationem ad (*MS.*: ab) ipsum appellavit; et post absolutionem eius causam audire poterit. Nam si appellavit ante excommunicationem, non indiget absolutione. Nec ad eum mittendus est quis a quo appellaverit.

---

[1] Cf. the Canterbury and Royal Collections discussed above.

[2] Since the items are numbered in the 'Bridlington' MSS., it is simplest to identify them here in that way. For examples of undissected decretals, see *Claud.* 7, 12, 26, 28, 29, 32, etc; for undistributed blocks of conciliar canons: *Claud.* 23, 24 and 84. But there is increasing evidence of decretal dissection in the later parts: see *Claud.* 146, 148, 149, 156, etc., in all of which the phrase 'post alia' appears after the decretal inscription.

[3] *Bridl.* i and ii are found in exactly comparable positions with similar rubrics in *Claud.*; *Claud.* 84, not included in *Bridl.*, is composed of the canons of the 1179 Lateran Council in a rather unusual sequence: elsewhere the conciliar canons usually begin with *Licet de vitanda*, laying down the requirements for a valid papal election. In *Claud.* this is 84.17, appearing with the rubric: 'Ex concilio eiusdem Alexandri: Non nisi a duabus partibus electus Romanus pontifex habeatur.'

Claudiana:

84. *Rubric:* Ex concilio Alexandri pape tertii in Lateranensi ecclesia beati Johannis.

(i) *Rubric:* Persone et cause peregrinantium sint sub episcoporum custodia.

etc.

Such an extensive apparatus was quite unusual in English collections of this style and period, and its lengthy comments were not at all characteristic of primitive families in general. The 'Bridlington' style is worked out most completely in the Claudian Collection, which has also a very full marginal gloss of a most elementary kind, composed chiefly of numerical cross-references to other chapters elsewhere in the same collection. Usually the gloss is much slighter in substance in the Bridlington Collection, and some of its rubrics appear within the marginal comments in the Claudian version.[1] Once more a few select examples should make these matters clear:[2]

Claudiana marginalia:

1. Infra lxiiii contra; dicitur enim ibi quod criminalem causam dominus papa nulli committit, nisi persone prius coram eo appareant. Infra cxxiii et ccix; secus si crimen est notorium, ut infra cxxii.

19. Qui tales litteras impetrat expensas adverse parti solvet, ut infra lxi, *etc.* Secus est si littere prime dolo suppresse fuerint, ut infra clv, pa. ii.

---

[1] The rubrics in *Bridl.* and *Claud.* are frequently much fuller than those for the corresponding passages in collections of the 'Worcester' family. Cf. *Bridl.* 26 and *Wig.* II, 8 (Lohmann, *loc. cit.*, pp. 91–2): *Bridl.* 26b: 'Monachi assignent vicariis suis sufficientem sustentationem de beneficiis ecclesie. Quibus si non fuerint assignata, non detur sed auferetur cura animarum'; *Wig.* II, 8b: 'De vicariis monachorum.' Notice especially the long rubric for *Bridl.* 11, quoted above. But the 'Worcester' collection *Trin.* has a full apparatus of rubrics: Trinity College MS. R. 14.9, fols. 82r–87v.

[2] All *Bridl.* decretals have rubrics, but the primitive gloss references are confined to the following: 1, 2, 3, 12c, 13, 23g, 50, 59, 62b, 71a, 74, 83, 89, 91, 94, 95, 97, 103, 106, 126, 131 and 158. These are mostly very brief references, and the comments at 12c and 97 are written in a later hand. Owing to later trimming of the *Claud.* MS. many marginal references have been lost, and it is impossible to attempt their total reconstruction. As an example of a *Bridl.* rubric appearing in the *Claud.* marginalia, cf. *Bridl.* 32b and *Claud.* 38b: *Bridl.* rubric: 'Ubi tollitur remedium appellationis, tollitur et recusationis'; *Claud.* margin: 'Ubi tollitur remedium appellationis, tollitur et recusationis; infra clxii, ca. iii, contra.' See also Plate IV, below.

77. Nota, quod, licet causa commissa sit appellatione remota, iudex tamen suspectus recusari potest, ut hic dicitur ob manifestas inimicitias vel alias suspiciones. Hec enim causa, ut dicitur infra lxxix, commissa fuit abbati de Leicestria et abbati de Lilleshall appellatione remota, et tamen, ut in ista epistola dicitur, recusantur quod consonat illi quod dicitur infra (*MS.*: contra) clxii, pa. iii. Sed est contra hoc quod dicitur supra xxxviii, pa. ii; secus est si expressa fuerint nomina locorum non personarum, ut infra lxxix, et cv.

But not only are these two collections comparable in appearance and style of transcription, they correspond closely in contents and composition. They derive in part from a single source, which may be described as the 'Bridlington' archetype, and the details of this common origin can be deduced from their collation. So exact is the parallel for roughly half of their items that it might be supposed at a first consideration that the Claudian version, being later in completion, was directly derived from the Bridlington version. But it is quickly apparent for several different reasons that such a conclusion is quite without foundation.[1] The family archetype is reflected in each derivative, but, whereas in the Claudian manuscript it appears in a single unbroken sequence at the beginning of the completed collection, it is itself divided in the Bridlington manuscript, where it appears in two quite separate sections with additional letters interpolated between them. The Bridlington version could not, therefore, stand between their common origin and the Claudian manuscript, for it would be inconceivable that the common basis, having once been broken, would be restored to its former unity in a later derivative. To express the matter more explicitly: the 'Bridlington' archetype is represented by chapters 1–107 in *Claudiana*, and by chapters 1–40 and 68–119 in *Bridlingtonensis*. Elsewhere the collections are independent

---

[1] The inscriptions are sometimes fuller in *Claud.*, and some passages in *Bridl.* are omitted from the corresponding decretals in the later work: thus *Bridl.* 19b appears as *Claud.* 19, but *Bridl.* 19a does not exist in *Claud.* Again, there are variations in phrasing which could not be explained if an immediate textual relationship existed between the two MSS.: thus *Bridl.* 3 has the rubric: 'Clericus licet non possit ecclesiasticus tamen patronatus vendicare ex donatione militis' (which certainly seems a careless transcription), where *Claud.* 3 has the clearer version: 'Clericus licet non possit ecclesiam, ius tamen patronatus vendicare *etc.*' Still more cogent arguments result from a collation of the MSS.

of one another in their completed forms; and, therefore, though so closely related, they cannot be textually interdependent.[1]

The 'Bridlington' collections are transitional in style, since they are not entirely devoid of subject-matter arrangement and have a better manuscript format than the 'English' collections. But they have no consistent separation of topics into books or titles, and such subject-matter arrangement as does exist can best be seen by analysing their authors' treatment of a few major interests throughout the collections. The two hundred and sixteen items in *Claudiana* could be provisionally classified under the five following headings: marriage questions, procedural and judicial problems, churches, clerical status and the religious orders; and the following statistical analysis provides a sufficient insight into the distribution of these topics throughout the work:

Marriage questions:[2] at least fifty-six decretals touch on marriage and related questions. They are widely scattered in the archetypal section of the collection, but occasionally grouped in small local concentrations. Where the collection is not dependent on the archetype there is a striking difference: the long sequence of decretals 123–52 deals exclusively with the canon law of marriage, and is of continental provenance; it seems certain that the author was

---

[1] The filiation between the two collections can be briefly summarized as follows:

Claud.		Bridl.	Claud.		Bridl.
1–22	=	1–22	47	=	60
23	=	189–93	49–52	=	68–71
25	=	179	53:7d	=	7d
26–31	=	23–8	54–9	=	73–8
32	=	174.181	61–71	=	79–88
33–5	=	29–31	72	=	52
36	=	50	73–8	=	89–94
37	=	40	80–2	=	95–7
38	=	32	83	=	99
39	=	35	85	=	98
40–1	=	33–4	86	=	125
42	=	180	87–8	=	100–1
43	=	39	89	=	84
44–6	=	36–8	90–107	=	102–19

Claud. 24, 48, 60, 79 and 84 are not included in *Bridl.* Otherwise all items in *Claud.* 1–107 are found in both collections.

[2] *Claud.* 4, 6, 12, 27–31, 38–43, 50, 52–3, 56–7, 63, 72, 83, 95, 98–100, 113, 115, 123–52 and 180. The lists provided here and in the following footnotes are not exhaustive; many decretals in the 'Bridlington' collections are undissected, and deal each with several different topics.

indebted here, either directly or indirectly, to a continental collection; and this is the clearest example of subject-matter grouping
in the whole collection. In the closing part of the completed work
(156–216) marriage questions are almost entirely absent. To sum
up: the archetype had no significant concentration of decretals
concerned with marriage, but the supplement incorporated a book
of marriage decretals derived from a continental source.

Procedural and judicial problems:[1] at least eighty-three decretals
touch on these questions, and are fairly evenly distributed throughout the collection (except for the sequence 123–52 discussed
above). Procedural topics figure prominently at various stages in
the collection, but without being the exclusive subject of interest.

Churches:[2] at least ninety decretals touch on matters involving the
rights or interests of churches, but in the longer sequences other
topics are intermingled with them.

Clerical status:[3] this topic is closely related with the previous one,
and many decretals could be placed under either heading. At
least forty-seven decretals deal with the rights and status of clerks.
Again, they are widely distributed throughout the work.

Religious Orders:[4] the discussion of this subject is much slighter,
but at least thirty-one decretals touch on the interests of religious
houses. In contrast with this, the Bridlington Collection ends with
a sequence of decretals relating to religious houses (174–85) and
the canons of the Council of Tours.

Thus, apart from comparatively small groups, there is no
obvious arrangement of subject-matter, except in one or two un-
typical instances. The most notable integrated sequence of
letters occurs where the Claudian Collection is not dependent
on the Bridlington archetype: the thirty-one chapters 123–53
deal exclusively with marriage questions, and the great majority
of these decretals were received in the first instance by continen-

---

[1] *Claud.* 1, 6–9, 11–13, 17, 19, 26, 29, 33, 34, 37, 38, 40, 41, 51, 54–6, 59, 61, 62,
64, 67, 68, 70, 74, 76–82, 85, 88, 89, 91–4, 96, 97, 101–6, 108, 111, 114, 117, 153–62,
170, 187, 189, 192, 194 and 206–16.

[2] *Claud.* 2, 3, 7, 10, 12–16, 18, 20–2, 25, 26, 28–30, 32, 34–6, 40–2, 45–9, 52, 59,
60, 62, 65–7, 69–71, 73, 75, 78–80, 89, 90, 106, 107, 109, 112, 116, 120–2, 162–6,
171–6, 178, 179, 181, 182, 185–90, 192–99, 201–5 and 213.

[3] *Claud.* 1, 3, 4, 7, 12, 14, 22, 26, 28, 33–5, 39, 43, 48–51, 56, 58, 65, 66, 73–5, 78,
86, 90, 104, 109, 118, 119, 122, 123, 127, 162, 167–9, 181–6 and 200–1.

[4] *Claud.* 2, 7, 10, 15, 19, 25, 32, 33, 42, 46, 53, 54, 60, 69, 70, 79, 87, 110, 118, 124,
126, 160, 163–6, 172, 191, 198, 199, 203 and 210.

tal bishops;[1] and the Bridlington Collection (again where it is not dependent on the archetype) includes one sequence of letters, chapters 174–85, dealing mainly with religious orders.[2]

The 'Bridlington' archetype was completed about the year 1181; the Bridlington Collection was completed a year or two later, in 1182–3 or shortly after; the Claudian Collection was completed in 1185 at the earliest and hardly much later than 1187. The family archetype included no decretals later than the death of Alexander III, and it is no longer possible to determine whether or not it included the decrees of the Third Lateran Council: the Claudian Collection has them within its archetypal material, but the Bridlington Collection makes no reference to them in the corresponding position.[3] The inscriptions in the Bridlington Collection itself mention no pope later than Alexander, but its 134th chapter (which was not in the archetype) is correctly ascribed elsewhere to Lucius III: there is in fact a marginal rubric 'Lucius III' placed by the 132nd chapter (which is certainly incorrect), and there is little doubt that the rubric was intended as a correction to the 134th chapter but was misplaced in scribal error.[4] The Claudian Collection has no post-Alexandrian decretals in its first one hundred and forty-three items, but in the remaining section six letters of Lucius III and three of Urban III (1185–7)

---

[1] *Claud.* MS., fols. 207ra–210rb: Gran and Kolocsa, Pisa, Palermo, Lucca, Norwich, St Albans, Tours, Cassino, Bordeaux, Poitiers, Canterbury, Ancient canon, Poitiers, Toul, Bordeaux, Exeter, Worcester, Exeter and Worcester, Toulouse, Vicenza (MS.: Vicentino), Beauvais, Le Mans, Veroli, Exeter, St. Agatha, Amiens, Christian captives, Florence, Amiens, Salzburg and Chartres.

[2] *Bridl.* MS., fols. 128v–31v: York, Rievaulx, York-Lincoln-Chester, Canterbury, Canterbury, Dioceses with Savigniac houses, St. Laurence and Newbattle. These items are not numbered in the *Bridl.* MS. Excepting nn.177, 182 and 183, the sequence *Bridl.* 174–85 is included also in *Wig.* II in the following order: 13, 20, 21, 36, 17, 35, 13, 16 and 18. Cf. Rievaulx cartulary: J. C. Atkinson, ed., *Cartularium Abbathiae de Rievalle*, Surtees Society, LXXXIII (1887), pp. 199 and 378.

[3] The Lateran canons are *Claud.* 84.1–28, but they are not found in *Bridl.* The canons of the Council of Tours are included in both collections, but were not derived from their common source: *Claud.* 23a–g, fol. 191rb; *Bridl.* 186–93, fols. 131v–133v.

[4] *Bridl.* MS., fol. 118v: *Bridl.* 134 (MS.: 135), without inscription. Cf. *Claud.* MS., fol. 210va: *Claud.* 155: 'Lucius tertius Norwicensi episcopo', J-L 15185, 1181–5. *Claud.* 155 has two chapters, of which *Bridl.* 134 is the second. Through scribal error the numeration in the *Bridl.* MS. is sometimes slightly inaccurate: in all cases the correct number is cited here. The marginal rubric 'Lucius III' appears on *Bridl.* MS., fol. 118r; cf. *Claud.* 175, J-L 13953, 1159–81.

are included.[1] The collection was transcribed as an entity, and so could not have been completed in its present form before 1185-7.

The provenance of the family archetype was characteristically English. Assuming it to be represented by *Claudiana* 1–107 (as explained above), it seems likely that a continental source was responsible for only a very few of its concluding items: chapters 95–107.[2] Excluding these, only ten of the first ninety-four chapters have non-English inscriptions, in contrast with eight of the concluding thirteen.[3] Among the English decretals, the diocesan groupings are discovered similar to those already discussed in the 'English' collections: at least twenty letters were received at Exeter, sixteen at Worcester, and twenty at Canterbury.[4] The Canterbury grouping is once again particularly striking: seventeen letters to Canterbury are found in sequence between chapters 43 and 66 inclusive.[5] Only three of the first fifty decretals have non-English inscriptions, and these are French.[6] Dependence, whether directly or indirectly, on the records of Canterbury, Worcester and Exeter seems once more to be the only feasible explanation. In addition, the Claudian Collection has as its 24th item a list of brief chapters under the rubricated heading: 'Concilium Ricardi Cantuariensis'; these chapters can hardly be the actual decrees of Richard's 1175 provincial council, but they are further valuable evidence of the Canterbury origins of the manuscript, being discovered in this way in no other primitive collection.[7]

---

[1] For Lucius III, see *Claud.* 149, 155, 157, 162, 174 and 188; for Urban III, see *Claud.* 144, 150 and 216. Only *Claud.* 155b is found also in *Bridl.*; cf. p. 91, n.4, above.

[2] *Claud.* MS., fols. 203vb–205va: only five of the final thirteen decretals were received by English bishops, and only two in the sequence of ten from 95 to 104 inclusive.

[3] *Claud.* 1–95, fols. 189r–203v: ten decretals have certain continental inscriptions: 11, 41, 50, 52, 67, 71, 72, 82, 86 and 92: to Rouen, Reims, Limoges, Salerno, Lisieux, Tours, Bayeux, Rouen, Andria and Piacenza; four items are canons: 23, 24, 83 and 84. It is especially remarkable that only three of the first fifty items were addressed to continental bishops, while seven of the first eight continental decretals were received by French bishops.

[4] To Exeter: *Claud.* 4–6, 12, 16, 20–1, (22), 31, 33, 37, 59, 63–4, (67), 68–9, 76, 85, 89–90 and 107; To Worcester: *Claud.* 1, 3, 9, 16–17, 19, 22, 28–30, (34), 36, 74, 76, 81 and 90–1; To Canterbury: *Claud.* 15, 43–9, 51, 54–60, 65–6, 74 and 97.

[5] *Claud.* MS., fols. 196ra–198rb.

[6] *Claud.* 11, 41 and 50: to Rouen, Reims and Limoges.

[7] *Claud.* MS., fols. 191vb–192ra. Cheney, 'Legislation in the Medieval English

The parts of the Bridlington Collection independent of the archetype present a somewhat contrasting picture. Its chapters 41–67 are an assorted collection, predominantly English but with some admixture of continental (mostly French) decretals;[1] and chapters 120–73 reflect a similar arrangement (except that in this instance the continental decretals are mostly Italian).[2] These are followed by a group of twelve decretals including several to Cistercian abbeys, or involving their interests; and the collection is completed with the canons of the Council of Tours.[3] The chapters 120–85, which were not in the archetype, have very different ratios among their English decretals than either the archetype itself or the Claudian supplements. In this instance there are no decretals received at Exeter (a most unusual feature), but no less than thirteen received in the northern province.[4] The additions to the archetype in the Claudian Collection are different in provenance from those in the Bridlington Collection, and fall into three main parts: its chapters 108–22 are letters of varied but mainly English provenance;[5]

Church', *EHR*, L (1935), pp. 208, 219 and 385–8; D. Wilkins, ed., *Concilia Magnae Britanniae et Hiberniae*, London (1737), I, p. 474; Stubbs, ed., *Gesta Regis Henrici Secundi Benedicti Abbatis*, Rolls Series, I, p. 84; Brooke, *Canons of English Church Councils*, pp. 471–80. There is a possibility that these headings are connected with the canons promulgated at the 1175 Council of Westminster; Wilkins transcribed the headings from *Claud.*, and placed them under the year 1173, but that is impossible: Richard of Dover was not consecrated until 1174.

[1] *Bridl.* MS., fols. 94r–100r: this sequence of twenty-six decretals includes at least eight of continental provenance: *Bridl.* 42, 43, 45, 46, 47, 51, 52 and 66: to Chartres, Ascoli, Evreux, St. Pierre-sur-Dive, one uncertain (MS.: Maturiensis), Reims, Bayeux and Châlons.

[2] *Bridl.* MS., fols. 114v–128r: this sequence of fifty-four decretals includes at least twenty of continental provenance: *Bridl.* 123–6, 130, 133, 135, 138, 148, 150, 153–9, 163, 167, 172: to Bisceglie, Toul or Toledo, Andria, Bordeaux, Conza, Genoa, Chartres, Reims, Padua, Amantea, Fidenza, Trois-Fontaines or Trefontane (MS.: Trium Fontium), Lucca, Genoa, Cassino, Cosenza, Pisa, Cosenza, Grado and Florence. There can be little doubt of an Italian or curial influence here, presumably through acquaintance with a continental collection. The inscriptions are not always included in the *Bridl.* MS.

[3] For decretals concerning religious houses: *Bridl.* MS., fols. 128v–131v; cf. p. 91, n.2, above. For conciliar canons: *ibid.*, fols. 131v–133v.

[4] For decretals to York province or Scotland: *Bridl.* 145, 146, 149, 152, 160–2, 166, 174–6, 179 and 185. Decretals with more general inscriptions are also included: e.g., *Bridl.* 180–1: to Cistercians.

[5] *Claud.* MS., fols. 205vb–207ra: this sequence of fifteen decretals includes five of continental provenance: *Claud.* 112, 113, 114, 118 and 120. The inscriptions are not certain in all cases, but at least four of the five are Italian.

the chapters 123-52 are a book of marriage decretals of continental origin, discussed above;[1] and chapters 153-216 are a further group of letters similar in provenance to the archetype itself, and so with a marked emphasis on decretals received in the Canterbury province, intermingled with eight letters of later date issued by Popes Lucius and Urban between 1181 and 1187.[2] There is no suggestion, therefore, either in the Bridlington archetype or in the Claudian Collection of any connexion with the province of York.

To summarize these conclusions briefly: both 'Bridlington' collections stem from an archetype made in the Canterbury province not much later than 1181, and are dependent chiefly on its provincial records. There is clear evidence of derivation, whether direct or indirect, from the archives of the provincial see itself. Building on this basis, the Bridlington Collection added decretals from English and continental sources, concluding with a further sequence of letters relating to religious houses in the island. The Claudian Collection, in contrast, while preserving their common material more faithfully, added a group of marriage decretals derived from a contemporary continental source, and completed the whole with further letters of Canterbury provincial provenance, received in some cases as late as 1185-7. The Canterbury, Exeter and Worcester dominance, noticed already in the 'English' collections, is once more strikingly apparent in the 'Bridlington' collections, except in those brief supplementary sections clearly dependent on continental collections.

The principal features of the 'Bridlington' collections underline the conclusions already reached in considering the 'English' collections: an interest in decretal codification provided in the work of three distinguished English bishops: Roger of Worcester, Bartholomew of Exeter and Richard of Canterbury; a basic derivation of decretals from the diocesan records in the province of Canterbury, supplemented in the later stages by decretals from continental collections. Almost invariably the

---

[1] See pp. 89-90, above.

[2] *Claud.* MS., fols. 210va-216ra: roughly one quarter of all these decretals have continental inscriptions. For details of the decretals of Lucius and Urban, cf. p. 92, n.1, above.

collecting stimulus is in the province of Canterbury; and, even when a collection has been transcribed or expanded in the north, the basic component is an earlier collection completed in the south. Occasionally, the insertion of small groups of decretals received in the province of York proves that the appropriate materials existed in northern archives also, if canonists saw fit to use them in their professional collections (and indeed this is borne out by the monastic and cathedral achives preserved quite independently of canonical traditions). The fact that, generally speaking, the northern ecclesiastics have left little trace of their judicial activities in the decretal collections supports the theory that the greater initiative and enthusiasm resided elsewhere. This is a conclusion not altogether surprising in view of the personalities of the bishops involved, but nevertheless of the utmost historical significance, as will be shown in the chapter to follow.[1]

4. THE 'WORCESTER' FAMILY

The third and final group of English collections is the so-called 'Worcester' family, unique among English primitive families, since it alone reveals a clear pattern of technical development, the pattern already briefly described above as the 'Worcester' tradition. Six members of the family have been rediscovered so far, and may be listed conveniently with their manuscript references as follows:

(1) The Trinity Collection: *Trinitatis*: Trinity College Cambridge MS. R. 14.9, fols. 82–8.

(2) The Worcester Collection: *Wigorniensis*: Royal MS. 10 A. II, fols. 5–62.

(3) The Klosterneuburg Collection: *Claustroneoburgensis*: Klosterneuburg Stbl. MS. XXXII. 19, fols. 36–87.

(4) The 'Cheltenham' Collection: *Cheltenhamensis*: Egerton MS. 2819, fols. 11–102.

(5) The Cottonian Collection: *Cottoniana*: Cotton MS. Vitellius E. XIII, fols. 204–88.

(6) The Peterhouse Collection: *Peterhusensis*: Peterhouse Cambridge MSS. 114, 180, 193 and 203, first and final quires.

[1] This problem is discussed in Chapter V, Parts 1 and 4, below.

All six collections are technically primitive, and fall into three distinct though related categories. The first three take their names from Trinity College, Worcester and Klosterneuburg respectively, according to the conventions already made clear. They were completed in that order not earlier than 1181, but also not much later, and represent the earliest technical phase of family development. The remaining works stemmed from the same primary group, but in two quite different strands of evolution. The 'Cheltenham' Collection, so-named from its place in the Egerton Collection, was devised in several stages between 1181 and 1193 or shortly after: it is in part a direct descendant (and a very early one) from the 'Worcester' archetype, but in part also derived from the great Bamberg/Leipzig connexion of continental systematic collections. The Cottonian and Peterhouse Collections, though remaining closely within the 'Worcester' tradition, carried it to its logical and final conclusion by setting out their contents in an orderly and schematic arrangement of books and titles; but these were also influenced to some extent by the systematic traditions. The Cottonian Collection was designed about the year 1191, but not completed before 1193; and the Peterhouse Collection was completed in 1194 at the earliest. But neither collection includes letters later than 1193 in date of issue.

The Worcester and Klosterneuburg Collections are already available in printed analyses, and with the Trinity Collection reveal the earliest phase of 'Worcester' technical tradition. Their schematic arrangement is clearest in the Worcester Collection, since the Trinity manuscript is now merely a fragment, and the Klosterneuburg Collection is seriously defective in technical and historical details. The Worcester Collection includes two hundred and seventy-four decretals, comprising four hundred and twenty-nine chapters in all, distributed under the following seven headings:[1]

   I. De statu et iure coniugii sive contracti sive contrahendi.
  II. De statu religiosorum et eorundem privilegio.
 III. De statu clericorum.
 IV. De statu et iure ecclesiarum.
  V. De casibus, in quibus non est deferendum appellationi.

[1] Lohmann, *loc. cit.*, pp. 39–40.

VI. De casibus, in quibus deferendum est appellationi etiam si causa sit appellatione remota commissa.

VII. Ad informandum iudices in diversis casibus quandoque emergentibus.

The seven books are neatly arranged, and carefully distinguished in the manuscript format: each book begins on a fresh folio, and there is ample space at the end of each for the appropriate placing of later letters acquired after the first transcription.[1] All letters are numbered in sequence throughout the books, and there are frequent rubrics both for decretals and their component chapters. Nevertheless, the collection is primitive in conventional classification, since there is no formal division of books into titles (though there is certainly some arrangement of topics within the books), and there is no dissection of the separate decretals.[2] The Trinity fragment, transcribed in a characteristic English pointed hand, conforms substantially with this description in its few surviving folios, except that the books follow on one another without intermission, and there is no formal numeration of the individual letters. The Klosterneuburg manuscript, in contrast, is much less satisfactory, providing no outward indication of its underlying pattern of composition, omitting its decretal inscriptions, and providing extremely inaccurate historical details within the letters.[3] But the basic structure is the same in all three works.

It is evident from their collation that all three collections sprang from a common source (now lost), which was the fountain-head of the 'Worcester' family, and may be described conveniently as the 'Worcester' archetype. Each derivative collection can be broken down analytically into two major sources: firstly, the archetypal or common basis; and, secondly, an appendix or series of appendices peculiar to each work. In both the Trinity and Worcester Collections the supplementary decretals are themselves classified, according to subject-matter, and distributed as appendices to the component books or parts; whereas, in the Klosterneuburg version they appear in a single

[1] Cf. *ibid.*, p. 100, at *Wig.* II, 37; but Lohmann's analysis is incomplete at this point. See also Plates V and VI, below.

[2] See Chapter III, pp. 49–51 and 58–9, above.

[3] The inaccuracy of the *Claustr.* MS. in historical details is discussed and illustrated at the conclusion of this chapter.

undivided sequence at the end of the complete transcription.[1] It might be supposed at first sight that the latter preserves the oldest derivation within the group since it reflects most directly the contents of the family archetype as an entity. But Lohmann, when comparing the Worcester and Klosterneuburg Collections, demonstrated quite conclusively that the Worcester Collection preserves the earlier version of the two.[2] And now it can be further shown that the Trinity manuscript, which was unknown to Lohmann, records the earliest version of all three, and is in all probability the oldest 'Worcester' collection now surviving.[3] This latest conclusion calls into question the whole basis of the conventional description of the 'Worcester' family, but once again the established name must now be retained to avoid confusion. All three collections, as well as the archetype itself, must be dated in 1181 or shortly after, since their common stock included one decretal of that year, but nothing later.[4]

The 'Cheltenham' Collection was first described by Hampe

---

[1] For a detailed comparison of *Claustr.* and *Wig.*, cf. Lohmann, *loc. cit.*, pp. 43–8, and 164–87.

[2] *Ibid.*, p. 48.

[3] Trinity College MS. R. 14.9, fols. 82r–87v preserves only a fragment of the original collection, extending from *Trin.* II, 21 to *Trin.* IV, 7. Accepting Lohmann's analysis of *Wig.* as a basis of comparison, the relationship between the three collections can be summarized as follows: (*a*) Book II: The three collections correspond in this book as far as *Wig.* II, 24, at which point *Claustr.* passes to Book III, but *Trin.* and *Wig.* continue their parallel arrangement down to *Wig.* II, 30. At that stage, *Trin.* also passes to Book III, and *Wig.* continues alone to II, 37. (*b*) Book III: Full correspondence between all three works is resumed in this part, and is maintained down to *Wig.* III, 25b, at which point both *Claustr.* and *Trin.* pass to Book IV, but *Wig.* again continues alone to III, 40. (*c*) Book IV: Once more the full correspondence is resumed between all three collections, but collation is possible only as far as *Wig.* IV, 7, at which point the *Trin.* MS. is abruptly concluded. In this way it can be shown that *Trin.* is earlier in derivation than *Wig.*; and Lohmann had already demonstrated on independent reasoning that *Wig.* is earlier than *Claustr.*; therefore *Trin.* preserves the most original derivation of all three. At the same time there is no textual interdependence between any two of these three collections, but there is a greater affinity between *Trin.* and *Wig.* than that between either of them and *Claustr.*; and they are both members of a single tradition of development. These matters are now more fully discussed in my article: *Trinity Collection*, pp. 506–26.

[4] The family archetype included one decretal issued on 23 January 1181: *Wig.* VII. 59 = *Claustr.* 291, J-L 14365. Both *Wig.* and *Claustr.* also included decretals issued in the period 1179–81 within their supplementary sections: *Wig.* III, 40; and *Claustr.* 334. Strictly on internal evidence, the limits for *Trin.* are 1178–81, but in or after 1181 must be accepted in this case also.

over sixty years ago, later cursorily analysed by Seckel, and more recently referred to by Kuttner and Holtzmann.[1] On the basis of Seckel's incomplete analysis, it was formerly described as a dependent of the Bamberg family, related most closely to the Leipzig Collection, though Hampe noticed some affinity with the Worcester and Cottonian Collections. Now Holtzmann has classified it as a member of the primitive 'Worcester' family.[2] And both descriptions are in part correct. It is a direct descendant of the 'Worcester' archetype, supplemented from sources in the systematic tradition, including a Bamberg-Leipzig derivative. The opening decretals follow the *Lipsiensis* arrangement very closely, and together with an appendix of variously acquired decretals tend to obscure the 'Worcester' influence pervading the greater part of the work as a whole. Interpretation is complicated by the unusual format of the manuscript which, in contrast with all other members of the 'Worcester' family, appears divided into sixteen titles, or groups of titles, rather than into six or seven books; and there is a prefatory list of fifteen headings corresponding roughly with those found within the body of the collection itself. Superficially, therefore, the 'Cheltenham' Collection seems more like a systematic compilation in the *Appendix* tradition than a member of the primitive 'Worcester' group. But this impression is rather misleading, as may soon be seen by examining its 'titles' more closely:[3]

[1] K. Hampe. 'Reise nach England', *Neues Archiv*, xxiii (1897), pp. 388 ff.; E. Seckel, 'Ueber drei Canonessammlungen des ausgehenden 12. Jahrhunderts', *Neues Archiv*, xxv (1900), pp. 523–5 and 529–31; Kuttner, *Repertorium*, pp. 346 ff.; Holtzmann, *Nachrichten*, p. 22; L. R. Misserey, 'Collection de Cheltenham', *DDC*, iii (1942), cols. 682–3; Rathbone, *Bishops and Cathedral Bodies in England, 1066–1215*, London University Ph.D. Thesis (1935), pp. 509 ff.

[2] Holtzmann, *Sammlung Tanner*, pp. 92–4; *idem* and Kemp, *op. cit.*, p. xii; Misserey, *art.cit.*, col. 682: 'une collection systématique, satellite du groupe de la collection de Bamberg'.

[3] The subject titles are sometimes inadequate or even seriously misleading: thus the rubric 'De coniugiis' has been omitted from *Chelt.* MS. fol. 43r, where a long sequence of marriage decretals begins, remaining under the rubric 'De patronatu secundo' on fol. 40r. Other similar examples could be cited. The sixteen titles listed below appear respectively on fols.: 17v, 22v, 29v, 31r, 36r, 40r, 58v, 63r, 66r, 67v, 73r, 75v, 81v, 86v, 91r and 96r. The prefatory list of titles is found on fol. iv. The following folios include, among other matters, an incomplete transcription of the canons of the 1179 Lateran Council, fols. 11r–16r; and further decretals, beginning with a letter of Innocent III, transcribed in a different hand, fols. 16r–17v. The first folio bears the medieval inscription: 'Noverit universitas vestra quod ego Robertus Parvus dedi et concessi Petro Ruffo.' See also Plate VII, below.

I. De simoniacis et indebitis exactionibus, tam in ecclesiasticis, quam castris et scolis regendis. De transactionibus et patronatu in quibus quandoque notatur simonia.

II. De transactionibus et iure patronatus.

III. De iuramento calumpnie, et ut clerici non iurent.

IV. De responsis diffinitivis et interpretatione rescriptorum. De absolvendis excommunicatis et suspectis purgandis. De suspectis iudicibus. De foro et testibus.

V. De occupantibus ecclesias. Quod ecclesia iure minorum utitur. In quo foro agitur et respondere debetur. De sententia delegatorum iudicum a diocesano confirmanda.

VI. De patronatu secundo. De violatoribus ecclesiarum. De ordine edicti peremptorii (*MS.*: pereptorii). De auctoritate rei iudicate. De renunciatione et testium qualitate.

VII. De hospitalariis ceterisque religiosis, eorumque privilegiis et decimis. De electionibus.

VIII. De statu ecclesiarum, ne viventibus personis alii conferantur, ne novi census eis imponantur nec a laicis donentur, nec tradantur parvulis nec sacerdotum filiis.

IX. De clericis uxoratis, ut delinquentes post appellationem nichilominus puniantur. De sacerdote falsario et sacerdotum vicariis, ne concubinas abiurare compellantur.

X. De spoliatis. Quod ecclesia, vivente persona, loco religioso conferri potest. De litteris posterius impetratis. De bis baptizato. De mortuo ad non suam ecclesiam delato.

XI. De usuris. De violatoribus sacramenti vel fidei. De testibus. Ne pro spiritualibus homagium fiat. De bonis defunctorum. De testamentis clericorum.

XII. De appellationibus. Qualiter iudex delegatus coherceat ordinarium. De appellatione super omni gravamine. De excommunicatis offerentibus se ad iustitiam absolvendis, licet contra appelletur. Ut corpus debitoris non tradatur sepulture post appellationem. De remissionibus que fiunt in dedicationibus ecclesiarum. Quod delegatus potest delegare. De appellatione super suggestione falsi.

XIII. De decimis. De purgandis ob infamiam. De monachato clerico timore mortis. De sacerdotum filiis. Ne Judei Christiana habeant mancipia. De diacono alium vulnerante, et aliquo ordinem furtive suscipiente.

XIV. De clericis comam nutrientibus et tanquam laici conversantibus. Ne procuratores laicorum fiant. De accolitis uxoratis. De clericorum iudiciis. De testibus coactis.

XV. De Judeis. Ne monachi a laicis vel clericis firmam teneant. Ne archidiaconi curam animarum committant. Ne professos ordinis Cisterciensis (*MS.*: Cistrensis) quisquam suscipiat.

XVI. De penitentia.

This is a most impressive list, which seems at first sight a marked improvement compared with the earliest members of the 'Worcester' tradition. The divisions are now more numerous, and the rubricated headings touch more precisely on the various points of law. The 'Cheltenham' arrangement is certainly influenced by the systematic conventions, and the finished collection is in parts authentically systematic.[1] At the same time there are serious limitations in its application of the systematic concepts. The redistribution of chapters to suit a more logical pattern of composition has not been taken to its full conclusion; and many varied topics are still frequently discovered under a single heading and within a single section: Jews, monks, archdeacons and Cistercians, to mention a typical example. Still more significant, the essential device of individual decretal dissection is applied only in certain parts of the collection as a whole.[2] This is a very different picture from the accurate definition of topics and unity of subject-interest within the titles of properly systematic compilations. Moreover, collation quickly reveals a close identity in textual details and a correspondence in the sequence of items, for a substantial part of their contents, between the 'Cheltenham' Collection and the early members of the 'Worcester' family already described: the basic division of the latter into books and the sequence of their individual decretals are reflected very faithfully in the former also. The seven-fold division is abandoned, and different parts of a single book are sometimes distributed in several independent positions, so that the 'Cheltenham' manuscript presents a quite contrasting appearance. But, wherever a sequence of 'Worcester' decretals is found also in the 'Cheltenham' Collection, the original arrangement and grouping are quite frequently repeated.[3] Despite its

[1] Most obviously in the opening folios dependent on the Bamberg and Leipzig tradition: *Chelt.* MS., fols. 17vb–21; etc.

[2] Numerous decretals remain undissected in many parts of the collection, including the final folios.

[3] A few examples will suffice: *Chelt.* MS., fols. 25v–27v = *Wig.* VII, 73 and 76–9;

later completion and more mature arrangement, the collection retains a very accurate and early derivation from the family archetype, and is accordingly of the greatest value for its authentic textual details.[1]

Since the collection was built up in several quite separate stages, no single date of composition can be suggested for the whole. The 'Worcester' component was originally first devised not much later than 1181; but the 'Cheltenham' version even of that component must be later in transcription, since seven decretals of Lucius III (1181–5) are intermingled with the original 'Worcester' material, and one of these can be dated 1183–4.[2] The completion of this part cannot, therefore, be placed earlier than 1183. Moreover, the systematic derivative, transcribed on the opening folios, was also composed during the pontificate of Lucius III or shortly after.[3] But the concluding decretals (themselves collected in several separate stages) include letters not only of Lucius III, but also of Urban III (1185–7) and Clement III (1188–91); so that in part at least this final section is unlikely to be earlier than 1191 in date of completion.[4] The final letter (transcribed independently) was

fols. 63r–64v= *Wig.* IV, 1, 2, 8, 9, 10, 11, 30, 13 and 23; fols. 84r–86v= *Wig.* III, 1–3, 5–8, 19, 21–3, 26, 29, 32, 35 and 36.

[1] Collation of *Trin.*, *Wig.*, *Claustr.* and *Chelt.* proves that *Chelt.* is not later in derivation than *Wig.* and *Claustr.*, and is not textually dependent on any of the early 'Worcester' collections now surviving. Cf. Rathbone, *Bishops and Cathedral Bodies*, pp. 509 ff; Ullmann, *Forgotten Dispute at Bridlington Priory*, p. 460; and Duggan, *Trinity Collection*, pp. 511–13.

[2] Decretals of Lucius III: *Chelt.* MS., fol. 29vb: to the bishop of Worcester and the abbot of Evesham, *Ex transmissa conquestione*; fol. 37rb: to Baldwin of Worcester, *Ex conquestione*, J-L 15205; fol. 37rb: to the bishop and archdeacon of Hereford, *Dilectus filius*; fol. 37vb: to the dean and archdeacon of London, *Significaverunt nobis*; fol. 57vb: two letters, or two chapters of one letter, to the bishop of Lincoln, *Requisivit a nobis* and *Postremo fraternitati*, J-L 14966, 1183–4; fol. 73vb: to the bishop of Hereford, the dean of London and the abbot of Evesham, *Retulit nobis*, J-L 15177. Except where noted, these letters can be dated only by the pontifical years of Lucius III (1181–5); and J-L references are given whenever identified.

[3] Friedberg, *Canonessammlungen*, p. 127: the Leipzig Collection included several decretals of Lucius III, and one late acquisition from the decretals of Celestine III: *Lips.* VII, 14, J-L 17642, 1191–8. See also Friedberg, *Quinque Compilationes*, pp. 115–30.

[4] Decretals of Lucius III: *Chelt.* MS., fol. 97ra: to the bishop of Norwich, *Tua nos duxit*; fol. 97rb: to the same, *Quesitum est*, J-L 15185; fol. 99rb: to the archbishop of Canterbury, *Relatum est nobis*, J-L 15443, 26 June 1185; fol. 99vb: to the bishop of Winchester, *Constitutus in presentia*; fol. 100va: to the archbishop of Canterbury, *Quoniam ex plenitudine*, J-L 15164; fol. 101vb: to the patriarch of Jerusalem, *In*

issued in 1193 by Celestine III.[1] Thus, the collection was assembled from various sources, and completed between 1181 and 1193 or later.

In technical classification, the collection is primitive for the greater part of its contents, both in its 'Worcester' components and in various later acquisitions; but it is also systematic in parts, most notably where dependent on the more mature continental traditions. The systematic devices of decretal dissection, abbreviation of common-form phrases and excision of non-juridical matter are revealed at different stages in its composition. Thus, the conventional abbreviations are found occasionally at the beginning, fairly frequently towards the end, and seldom in the middle: these variations agreeing with the different sources already described.[2]

The final members of the primitive 'Worcester' family are the Cottonian and Peterhouse Collections, both completed later than *Compilatio Prima* (c. 1191), but preceding it for the most part in technical style. Unfortunately neither collection is now preserved intact: the Cottonian manuscript was heavily damaged in the fire which ravaged the Cotton Library in 1731; and the Peterhouse manuscript has suffered scarcely less severely but in a different way, being deliberately dismantled so that the resulting fragments might be used for binding purposes in several of the Dyngley volumes in the Peterhouse Library. At least a fragment of each folio has been preserved in the Cotton manuscript, though a large proportion of its total contents is no longer legible; and, in contrast, seven quires of the Peterhouse Collection have been rediscovered in excellent condition, but the rest of the work is entirely missing. The Peterhouse fragments

---

concessionibus. Decretals of Urban III: fol. 96vb: to the abbots of Welbeck and Old Leiston, *Gratum gerimus,* J-L 15751, 1185–7; fol. 100vb: to the bishop of Le Mans, *Cum in apostolica,* J-L 15729; fol. 101vb: inscription corrupt: to the abbot of 'Pessen' (? uncertain), *Sicut J. subdiaconi;* fol. 101rb: to Baldwin of Canterbury, *Veniens ad apostolicam,* J-L 15727, 1185–7. Decretal of Clement III: *Chelt.* MS., fol. 101rb: to the bishop of Worcester, the abbot of Tewkesbury and the prior of the Holy Sepulchre at Warwick, *Referentibus canonicis,* J-L 16181, 1187–91.

[1] *Chelt.* MS., fol. 102ra: to the prior and chapter of Huntingdon, *Bone memorie Alanus,* J-L 17055 and 17675, 1193.

[2] Conventional abbreviations (et cetera, et infra, etc et infra) occur on *Chelt.* MS., fols. 23r, 25r, 87v, 88r, 95r, 99v and 100v. The frequency of such abbreviations is particularly striking in the concluding folios. Abbreviations of common-form phrases in commissions to judges delegate are found on fols. 26r and 52v.

when fitted together reveal an uninterrupted sequence of the first fifty-six folios of the original collection, except where the double centre folio in each of two gatherings has become detached and is now lost.[1] The two collections are extremely closely interrelated, and it is a happy chance that the surviving material in each supplements to some extent that of the other, so that by combining the evidence of both their total material content and structure can be largely deduced.

Each collection follows the 'Worcester' convention in dividing the whole into six or seven books or major parts. As far as can be checked, each includes the vast majority of the archetypal decretals together with many later letters unknown in the earlier collections.[2] The concluding phase of the 'Worcester' tradition is achieved by a reorganization of the items in each book, and the subdivision of the books into numerous titles.[3] Through scribal neglect the actual rubricated headings for the books and titles do not appear in the extant manuscripts, except for the single instance of the second book in the Peterhouse Collection. The parallel arrangement of the two works is made clear in the following skeleton analysis:

Cottoniana:[4]

Fol. 204r: Preface of Conciliar Canons.
Fol. 210v: Marriage questions.

---

[1] Holtzmann, *Nachrichten*, p. 22; L. Falletti, 'Collectio Cottoniana', *DDC*, IV (1949), cols. 725–6; Holtzmann and Kemp. *op. cit.*, p. xiii; Kuttner, *Projected Corpus*, p. 348; *idem* and Rathbone, *art.cit.*, p. 283, n.14; C. Lefebvre, 'Collection de Peterhouse', *DDC.*, VI (1957), col. 1438. The seven fragments in the Peterhouse Library fit together in this order: MS. 193 (final quire), MS. 114 (first and final quires), MS. 193 (first quire), MS. 203 (final quire) and MS. 180 (first and final quires). Cf. M. R. James, *Descriptive Catalogue of the Manuscripts in the Library of Peterhouse*, Cambridge (1899): James was mistaken in describing these fragments as part of a volume of Cistercian Ordinances.

[2] This is made clear in the Comparative Tables in Appendices V–VII, below. For this purpose *Pet.* I is provisionally analysed in 95 chapters: it is a book of marriage decretals beginning on MS. 193 (final quire), fol. 6r, continuing through MS. 114 (first quire) and into MS. 114 (final quire). Appendix V collates *Claustr.*, *Wig.*, *Chelt.*, *Cott.* and *Pet.*; Appendix VI collates *Pet.*, *Appendix*, *Bamb.*, *Brug.*, *Lips.*, *Cass.* and *Comp. I*; Appendix VII collates *Cantab.*, *Trin.* and *Cott.*

[3] Appendices V and VI, below.

[4] Each collection opens with the canons of the Council of Tours and the Third Lateran Council. Cf. Holtzmann, *Sammlung Tanner*, pp. 105–7, and Kuttner and Rathbone, *art.cit.*, pp. 340–1. The conciliar canons provide a *prooemium* to the decretal collection, and were not considered as part of Book I: this theory is confirmed

Fol. 225v: Jurisdiction and procedure.
Fol. 242r: Religious Orders, tithes etc.
Fol. 254r: Simony, clerical status etc.
Fol. 263v: Rights of churches etc.
Fol. 276r: An extremely damaged section including decretals on:
prescription, spoliation, abjuration etc; Alexander's
'Golden Rose' decretal, etc.

Peterhusensis:[1]

Fol. 1r: Preface of Conciliar Canons.
Fol. 6r: Marriage questions.
Fol. 27v: Jurisdiction and procedure.
Fol. 36–7: (Double folio missing) Religious Orders, tithes etc.
(Fragment only remaining:) Simony, presentations
etc.

Thus, although the Peterhouse manuscript breaks off in the
fourth book, their common structure is clear enough to that point,
and may be assumed to have continued for the rest of the work
except in one respect: the concluding folios of the Cottonian
manuscript (extremely heavily damaged) provide not so much
an integrated book with a unity of interest, as an appendix of
decretals of varied subject-matter acquired too late for inclusion in the appropriate parts of the composition. As far as collation is now possible, these letters do not appear in a corresponding position in the Peterhouse manuscript, but are more
accurately redistributed on a subject-matter basis.[2] The Peterhouse Collection is, therefore, the later and more finished work.
Apart from this, and apart also from other later letters included
in the Peterhouse Collection, a parallel arrangement is closely
maintained between the two.[3]

by the system of references used by the English glossators in the Caius College MS.
676. It is evident that these English canonists used *Tanner* or some other closely
related collection as a basis of decretal reference. Holtzmann's numeration of books
in *Sammlung Tanner* should therefore be adjusted in the light of this evidence. The
'Golden Rose' decretal is *Ex antiqua Romanorum*: Alexander III to Louis VII, J-L
10826, 3 March 1163.
[1] The foliation given here represents the original sequence before the collection
was broken up. For the present order and position of the fragments, see p. 104,
n.1, above.
[2] E.g., *Cott.* MS., fols 286v–287r=*Pet.* MS. 203 (final quire), fols. 2rb–3rb:
Celestine III to John, dean of Rouen, *Prudentiam tuam*, J-L 17019, 17 June 1193,
etc.
[3] Appendix V, below.

The accurate redistribution of letters in this phase of the 'Worcester' tradition, to conform with a logical sequence of special aspects within the major topics, is seen most clearly in the second book of the Peterhouse Collection, where the rubricator has inserted the following headings:[1]

1. Quando liceat appellare et intra quod tempus appellatio sit prosequenda.
2. Non valent littere ante terminum appellationis fraudulenter impetrate.
3. Quotiens in eadem causa liceat appellare.
4. Officium eius qui appellat.
5. Officium eius a quo appellatum est.
6. De officio ad quem appellatur.
7. Quorum appellationes non recipiuntur.
8. Appellans contra disciplinam ecclesiasticam non exauditur.
9. Appellans ad fovendum errorem suum non auditur. (twice)
11. De appellatione super re modica.
12. Nimis generaliter appellans non auditur.
13. Ante citationem maliciose appellans non auditur. (At this point three rubrics are now illegible.)
17. De incidentibus questionibus.
18. Appellatione utrique partium inhibita, tertius cuius interest appellans, processum cause suspendit.
19. De absolutione excommunicatorum.
20. De sententia excommunicationis.
21. De communicantibus excommunicatis cuius auctoritate ligentur, et a quo absolvi debeant.
22. Num excommunicatus possit conveniri.
23. De potestate iudicum delegatorum et officio.
24. De officio iudicis ordinarii.
25. Quando morte mandantis expirat iurisdictio.
26. Que littere sunt revocatorie.
27. Que taciturnitas litteras impetratas viribus evacuet.
28. De interpretatione rescriptorum.
29. De rasura litterarum.
30. De suspectis iudicibus.

By these means the original appearance and sequence of decretals in the archetype have now been lost, but the individual letters have almost invariably been retained in one title or

---

[1] *Pet.* MSS. 114 (final quire), 193 (first quire) and 203 (final quire).

another. Thus, in support of this conclusion: the first forty-nine decretals in the Worcester Collection (with only two exceptions) are also found in the first book of the Peterhouse Collection, but with a radical readjustment in their order.[1] Moreover, the letters which were added to the archetype in the Worcester Collection are very frequently found also in the Cottonian and Peterhouse Collections, even where they were not received in certain earlier 'Worcester' compositions, such as (for example) the 'Cheltenham' Collection. In this and various other similar ways it can soon be shown that the two later collections follow the Trinity–Worcester branch of the family, as described above.[2]

The Cottonian manuscript was not completed earlier than 1193–4, though its first five books include nothing later than 1191. It appears that a first recension of the collection was made c. 1191, and that the extant version was completed two or three years later.[3] But, as explained already, the whole of the Peter-house Collection is somewhat later in its overall construction, including material as late as November 1193 in date of issue; and, therefore, it is extremely unlikely that this work was com-pleted in any part before 1194.[4] On the other hand, the absence

---

[1] Appendix V, below.

[2] The close textual agreement between *Wig.*, *Cott.* and *Pet.* is typified by the following example: cf. *Decretales* V, 3, 11: 'Alexander III Toletano archiepiscopo. De hoc, autem, quod rex et principes sui a Bernardo quondam Oxomensi episcopo *etc.*' The historical details of this decretal involving Toledo and Osma caused the 'Worcester' scribes considerabe trouble: *Claustr.* MS., fol. 63r–v has the version: 'Hec autem, quod rex et princeps Anglie H. quondam Eximse episcopo . . . ecclesie Eirm̄si *etc*'; *Chelt.* MS., fol. 18r has 'De hoc autem, quod rex et principes sui a B. Examensi *etc.*,' the original transcription being 'Exoniensi', later altered to 'Exa-mensi'; but a single identical version is found in *Wig.* MS., fol. 39r, *Cott.* MS., fol. 226v and *Pet.* MS. 114 (final quire), fol. 6ra–b: 'De hoc autem, quod rex et prin-cipes sui a B. quondam Exim̄se episcopo *etc*'.

[3] Falletti, *art.cit.*, cols. 725–6, dates *Cott.* by the pontificate of Clement III (1188–1191), but at least two decretals in the closing folios were issued by Celestine III in 1193, though their inscriptions are no longer legible in the damaged MS.: *Cott* MS., fol. 287v: to the prior and chapter of Huntingdon, *Bone memorie Alanus*, J-L 17055 and 17675, 1193: *ibid.*, fol. 286v: to John, dean of Rouen, *Prudentiam tuam*, J-L 17019, 17 June 1193: cf. *Pet.* MS. 203 (first quire), fol. 2rb.

[4] Lefebvre, *art.cit.*, col. 1438, dates *Pet.* at least five years too early in 1188. Cf. *Pet.* MS. 193 (first quire), fol. 2vb: 'Celestinus papa J(ohanni) Rothomagensi de-cano. A nobis fuit *etc.* Dat. Lat. XIX. Kl. Decembris, pontificatus nostri anno tertio.' The *Pet.* version provides two corrections to the J-L 17053 details: 'Cui-dam', 1193; the recipient is now identified as John of Rouen, and the date is

of decretals of Innocent III makes it most improbable that either
collection was completed as late as 1198. By a curious coincidence the Peterhouse scribe refers in one instance to 'Innocent III', where 'Innocent II' was correctly intended; but it
would be unwise to build too much on a typical scribal error of
this kind.

In the technical sense, both collections are primitive, despite
their advanced development. Their authors did not apply to
the individual letters the systematic device of decretal dissection, so that the letters received from the family archetype
still preserve the same unbroken form as in the earlier period.
This is a most surprising fact considering their maturity and
date of composition, and considering too the decisive influence
which the systematic traditions had already exerted widely
through the schools.[1] Nevertheless, the care and skill of the
authors should not be undervalued, and a single extract from
the Peterhouse manuscript will sufficiently summarize the extent
of their technical achievement. It is a group of cross-references
inserted integrally within the body of the collection, composing
in this way a complete and separate title:[2]

> *Rubric:* Que taciturnitas litteras impetratas viribus evacuet.
>
> Supra cap. Non valent littere. Significavit nobis.
> Supra cap. De potestate iudicum. Quamvis.
> Infra. Ceterum etc. Quesitum. Infra. Si autem aliquis.
> Infra cap. De suspectis. Ad aures.
> Infra cap. De auctoritate rei iud. Scripsimus.
> In libro III. De decimis monachorum. Mandamus etc. Cum
> ordinem.
> In libro IIII. De flamenariis. Veniens ad apostolice.

13 November 1193 (though there is perhaps a scribal slip in the MS. since XIX
Kal.Decemb.=Idus Novemb.). Among other decretals of Celestine III in *Pet.*, at
least one was sent to Hubert Walter as archbishop of Canterbury, its earliest possible date being that of Hubert's elevation in 1193: *Pet.* MS. 193 (first quire), fol.
11a.

[1] Appendices V-VII, below. A good example of the undissected decretal in
Cott. and *Pet.* is Alexander III's *Licet praeter*, to Salerno, J-L 14091: *Pet.* MS. 193
(final quire), fols. 6rb–7ra.

[2] *Pet.* MS. 203 (final quire), fol. 1va. The very curious reference: 'In libro IIII.
De flamenariis. Veniens ad apostolice' must be a scribal error; the title should be
'De transactionibus'. The word 'flamenariis' seems to be a misapplication of a
place-name included in the decretal *Veniens ad apostolice*: the name appears in various MSS. as Flavill, Flavilla, Flamevil, etc, and is perhaps Flavell (Pershore).

In libro V. Ne plures dignit. Cum tenemur.
In libro VI. De transactione. Ex litteris.
Causa XXV, Questio II, Dicenti.

In fact, the general structure of the 'Worcester' collections had now reached a point of development comparable with that of the systematic collections, as may readily be seen if they are collated with some of the more famous continental collections. A collation reveals that the order and grouping of individual decretals in the Peterhouse Collection corresponds quite often with that in the titles of the systematic collections. Even more striking is the fact that the agreement is sometimes very close indeed: thus several groups of letters in *Compilatio Prima* occur in substantially the same arrangement in the Peterhouse Collection;[1] and similar points of identity can be established between the latter and the great collections named after Bamberg, Leipzig, Cassel, Bruges and so forth, not to mention the seminal *Appendix Concilii Lateranensis*.[2] Exactly how this relationship was achieved cannot be explained at present without further research into the many collections involved, yet it is clearly significant. At the same time, many chapters in the Cottonian and Peterhouse Collections have been so far discovered in no other manuscripts, and so the collections have an individuality of their own.[3] Nevertheless, it appears quite certain that these final members of the 'Worcester' family were influenced by systematic traditions very close to the main line of development which led at last to *Compilatio Prima*, and thence to the Gregorian *Decretales*. The rubricated titles preserved in the second book of the Peterhouse Collection confirm this judgement when compared with those in the major systematic compilations.[4] In view of these substantial technical developments, the retention of the primitive style of undissected decretal letters is rather astonishing. And yet the undissected letter is entirely characteristic of both these works.

The logically derived stages in composition and the clear

---

[1] Appendix VI: *Pet.* I, 2–5=*Comp. I*, IV. 4, 4,3,7 and 6; *Pet.* I, 45–7=*Comp. I*, III. 28, 5,6,4 and 3; *Pet.* I, 76–81=*Comp. I*, IV. 18, 6,1,2,3,5 and 7; etc.

[2] Appendix VI: *Pet.* I, 50–53 = *App.* 12.5, 7, 4 and 3; *Pet.* I, 76–80 = *Bamb.* 53.8, 3, 4, 5 and 7; etc.

[3] Appendix VI: *Pet.* I, 12 and 30; and other similar examples in the later books.

[4] Cf. Friedberg, *Canonessammlungen*, pp. 187–91; and pp. 51–7, above.

expression given to them in successive phases of the 'Worcester' tradition contrast sharply with the style and technique of almost all other English collections in their period. When compared with the systematic compilations stemming from the *Appendix* even the most mature 'Worcester' collections must seem very deficient from a professional point of view. The successive division of material into books, and of books into titles, produced a style of composition superficially very much akin to that of the best works in the systematic tradition. But the juristic maturity of the latter, especially in the handling of the separate decretals, was immeasurably superior. For this reason the 'Worcester' collections were without permanent influence, technically speaking, in the history of medieval canon law. In respect of substance, however, their influence was very great indeed. The 'Worcester' collections played their part in serving as quarries from which the systematic collectors drew much of their raw material: the earliest 'Worcester' collections transmitted their contents into a generally accepted body of decretal law for the whole Church. This was their contribution of most lasting importance as will be explained in the concluding chapter.

5. BALDWIN OF FORD AND THE WORCESTER COLLECTION

It was made clear at the outset that the 'Worcester' collections are of interest chiefly for their part in the technical development of decretal collections in the hands of English canonists. For this reason, and also because their more mature style of composition tends to obscure the local, regional and personal factors so obvious in members of the 'English' and 'Bridlington' families, no attempt has been made so far to analyse statistically their contents from a provenance point of view. Furthermore, to a greater extent than in the other groups, the 'Worcester' collections synthesize many varied sources: the familiarity of their authors with existing continental collections is perfectly clear. But in many ways these collections also reveal no less obviously the work of English canonists, composing collections based very largely on English sources. And perhaps their most striking evidence of this kind is provided by the Worcester Collection, which will now be examined more closely from this point of view.

It is well known that distinguished schools of canon lawyers flourished at Exeter and Worcester in the later-twelfth century;[1] and it is only to be expected that the canonists of those dioceses were closely interested in the judicial work of their own respective bishops. Bartholomew of Exeter and Roger of Worcester were among the most famous ecclesiastical judges and papal judges delegate in England at that time, and their work has left an unsurpassed impression on the material contents of the primitive English collections.[2] Two associations of Exeter and Worcester help to explain the use and intermingling of their decretal records in canonical collections. Firstly, there was the well-known collaboration of the two bishops in legal cases: they were not only the most frequently appointed judges delegate in England during Alexander III's pontificate, but they were sometimes jointly commissioned by the pope to deal with particular problems.[3] And, secondly, there was the no less significant link between the sees provided by Baldwin, a friend of both bishops and a member of Bartholomew's *familia*.

Baldwin first emerges clearly in English history as archdeacon of Totnes (c. 1161–70), member of the cathedral school of Exeter, and a friend and confidant of Bartholomew and John of Salisbury.[4] There is little doubt that his sympathies were with the archbishop, Thomas Becket, in the great politico-ecclesiastical struggle of the period; and at the height of the bitter controversy he retired (c. 1169) to the Cistercian abbey at Ford, where he was abbot by 1175 at the latest.[5] As abbot of

[1] For law schools and other centres of learning in twelfth-century England, see Stubbs, *Seventeen Lectures on the Study of Medieval and Modern History*, Oxford (1900 ed.), pp. 132 ff.; H. G. Richardson, 'The Schools of Northampton in the Twelfth Century', *EHR*, LVI (1941), pp. 595–605; *idem*, 'The Oxford Law School under John', *LQR.*, LVII (1941), pp. 319–38; K. Edwards, *English Secular Cathedrals in the Middle Ages*, Manchester (1949), pp. 189 ff.; Rathbone, *Bishops and Cathedral Bodies*, Chapter on Canon Law; *idem* and Kuttner, *art.cit.*; for medieval libraries including decretal collections, Brooke, *English Church and the Papacy*, pp. 106 ff., and N. R. Ker, *Medieval Libraries of Great Britain*; for bishops and chancery developments, Cheney, *Bishops' Chanceries*, pp. 1–43; for Worcester, Hall, *Roger Bishop of Worcester*; and for Exeter, Morey, *op. cit.*, esp. pp. 100 ff.

[2] Cf. p. 70, n.3, above.

[3] In *Wig.* alone the following decretals were received jointly by Worcester and Exeter: I, 31, J-L 14167; III, 22, J-L 14224; IV, 4, J-L 13928; IV, 44; IV, 47, J-L 13923; IV, 50; VII, 22; VII, 70.

[4] For Baldwin at Exeter and Ford, see Morey, *op. cit.*, pp. 23–9 and 105–9.

[5] On the alignment of English bishops during the Becket controversy, see D.

Ford he was commissioned as papal judge delegate by Alexander III on several occasions.[1] Already well-acquainted with both Bartholomew and Roger in the political and judicial affairs of the English Church, he was promoted to the bishopric of Worcester in 1180, following Roger's death in 1179.[2] Four years later, on the death of Archbishop Richard, Becket's successor, he was elected to the archbishopric of Canterbury, and died on Crusade at Acre in 1190.[3] These principal stages of Baldwin's career provide a remarkable commentary on the provenance of a manuscript volume now in the British Museum. This volume is the Royal MS. 10 A. II, which incorporates the Worcester Collection as its major item.[4] Both in the decretal collection itself, and in the various later papal letters transcribed on the end folios and bound up with it in the single volume, the phases of Baldwin's career seem accurately reflected.

It was explained above that the Worcester Collection can be broken down analytically into two principal components: the 'Worcester' archetype, and a series of appendices to its several component books. In each of these principal elements more decretals are found addressed to the bishops of Exeter and Worcester than to any other bishops: some of these letters were sent to Exeter or Worcester individually, and others jointly to both.[5] This striking feature is not in fact unusual in the English primitive collections, as already made clear above. But, whereas the

Knowles, *The Episcopal Colleagues of Archbishop Thomas Becket*, Cambridge (1951), pp. 1–52.

[1] Maitland, *Roman Canon Law*, p. 128: Maitland noticed the large number of decretals sent by Alexander III to the abbot of Ford, but was unaware of the significance of their inclusion in the collections. Cf. Kuttner and Rathbone, *art.cit.*, pp. 282–3. It cannot be assumed that all decretals addressed to the abbot of Ford were received by Baldwin: cf. Ullmann, *Forgotten Dispute at Bridlington Priory*, p. 465.

[2] Lohmann, *loc. cit.*, p. 53, n.1; Foreville, *op. cit.*, pp. 384–7. Roger died on 9 August 1179; Baldwin succeeded him on 10 August 1180.

[3] Foreville, *op. cit.*, pp. 533–4. Baldwin was promoted to Canterbury on 16 December 1184, and died at Acre on 19 November 1190.

[4] For the decretal collection, see fols. 5r–62v. Further letters are transcribed independently on fols. 1r–3r and 62v–63v, the latter group breaking off abruptly due to the loss of one or more folios. For details of these letters, see P. M. Baumgarten, 'Papal Letters relating to England', *EHR*, IX (1894), pp. 531–41.

[5] It is well known that decretal inscriptions are not always reliable in any given manuscript, but the margin of possible errors of this kind in *Wig.* could not invalidate the general conclusions suggested here.

decretals to Exeter and Worcester provide only a minority, however significant, of the total number in the 'Worcester' archetype, they form a remarkably large proportion of the letters in
the supplementary appendices.[1] Moreover, whereas the decretals to Exeter outnumber those to Worcester in the archetype,
the reverse is true in the later additions.[2] Both Exeter and Worcester decretals are significantly present in each of the major
sources of the completed work, and the abbot of Ford is named
no less than eight times in decretal inscriptions: five times in the
archetype, and three times in the supplements.[3] There can be
little doubt that Baldwin was the abbot who received the decretals addressed to Ford, but that Roger was the bishop who received those addressed to Worcester. Roger died in August 1179,
and Baldwin succeeded him in 1180. The archetype in its
earliest known form was assembled c. 1181 or slightly later. The
Worcester Collection itself, though necessarily completed later
than its source, contains no decretals later than 1181 in date of
issue.[4] It must be assumed, therefore, that the Worcester Collection was completed at Worcester after Baldwin's arrival, and
that in its composition the 'Worcester' archetype (or rather a
derivative from the archetype) was supplemented with further
decretals drawn from the episcopal records of Baldwin's pre-
decessor, and to some lesser extent from the recent similar
records of the Exeter diocese from which he had recently been
promoted. Exactly how these resources were brought together can
no longer be determined with any certainty, though Baldwin's

[1] Lohmann, *loc. cit.*: notice especially the concluding items in Books III, IV and
VII. Cf. Duggan, *Trinity Collection*, pp. 525–6.

[2] Cf. *ibid.*, I, 2–47 and IV, 35–50. Many of the supplementary decretals received
at Worcester were previously unknown when Lohmann analysed *Wig.* in 1933: cf.
Wig. I, 48, II, 34, III, 38 and 40; IV, 39, 44, 45, 48, 49 and 50; VII, 70, 72, 73,
79 and 80. It is significant that none of these items was included in the 'Worcester'
archetype.

[3] *Ibid.*, I, 43, VII, 2, 14, 15, 26, 65, 77 and 78. It is possible that VII, 11 was also
received by Baldwin, being addressed to the archdeacon of Exeter.

[4] Since Baldwin became bishop of Worcester in August 1180, and the latest definite
date in both the 'Worcester' archetype and *Wig.* is 23 January 1181 (*Wig.* VII, 58),
it is most unlikely that any decretals of Worcester provenance in *Wig.* were sent to
Baldwin, as bishop of Worcester. Since Roger died in August 1179, and the
earliest possible date of composition of *Wig.* must be after 23 January 1181, the
absence of so many of Roger's decretals from the archetype itself, and their massive
supplementation of the archetype in *Wig.* strongly support the conclusion that the
archetype was not itself of Worcester provenance.

I

own career suggests an obvious explanation. On internal evidence alone it could not be assumed that the 'Worcester' archetype was made in fact at Worcester, but there is every reason to believe in the Worcester provenance of the extant collection. This conclusion accords entirely with Lohmann's theory that the Worcester Collection was completed where its archetype was not accessible.[1] The known details of Baldwin's career, and the contrasting emphasis in the provenance of the two principal sources of the Worcester Collection, thus jointly support the conclusion that his influence may be traced in either part.

But if this conclusion, based solely on internal evidence within the decretal collection, falls short of full conviction, there can be no reasonable doubt about Baldwin's connexion with the completion of the manuscript volume as a whole. Letters of later popes, received in England between 1181 and 1187, are transcribed on the folios at either end of the volume, bound up with the Worcester Collection, but independent of it in composition and transcription. Five letters of Lucius III are entered on the closing folios: three to Baldwin as bishop of Worcester, one to Rapallo and one further fragment of English provenance but without inscription.[2] Five letters of Urban III are transcribed on the opening folios: three to Baldwin as archbishop of Canterbury, one to the Canterbury clergy to advise them of Baldwin's legatine status, and one letter to Henry II on the same subject.[3] Finally, one letter of Clement III, issued in 1187 on the subject of his own election, is found on the closing folios, addressed in this transcription to the English bishops generally.[4] These varied letters were written by different hands and at different times. At least six, and almost certainly seven, were received by Baldwin personally as bishop of Worcester or archbishop of Canterbury between 1181 and 1187; and two further letters are

[1] Lohmann, *loc. cit.*, pp. 45–8 and 51–3.

[2] Royal MS. 10 A. II: the letters of Lucius III to Baldwin: fol 63va, *Ex conquestione*, J-L 15205, 13 December 1181; fol. 62va, *Fraternitati tue*, J-L 15204, 1181–3; fol. 63vb, *Significavit nobis*, J-L 14964, 5 June 1182–3. Cf. Plate VI, below.

[3] *Ibid.*: the letters of Urban III to Baldwin: fol. 1r, *Celestis altitudo*, J-L 15518, 12 January 1186; fol. 2va–b, *Sinceritas devotionis*, 13 December 1185; fol. 3rb, *Sicut tue littere*, 23 June 1186–7. To the Canterbury clergy: fols 2vb–3ra, *Divine sapientie*, 18 December 1185. To Henry II: fol. 2r, *Ab oculis Romane*, 17 December 1185.

[4] *Ibid.*: fol. 62v, *Illud operata*, December 1187.

concerned with his legatine status. The personal factors here are obvious: the parallel stages in his own career and the gradual completion of the manuscript volume are too close for mere coincidence. If not his personal possession, the Royal MS. 10 A. II, must surely have belonged to a member of his circle.

The Klosterneuburg Collection presents a quite contrasting picture. All additions to the 'Worcester' archetype in this work were made in a single concluding appendix, and are in provenance quite different individually from those in the Worcester Collection examined above. The manuscript itself includes no decretal inscriptions, though many of these can be supplied from other sources. As far as such identification is now possible for the decretals supplementary to the archetype, it reveals no particular emphasis either of regional or personal influence, in striking contrast therefore with the additions in the Worcester Collection. And, thus, there is no evidence of the provenance of the Klosterneuburg appendix as an entity: it has no English diocesan emphasis in its individual letters, and many of these were received originally by continental bishops.[1] Considering Lohmann's theory that the Klosterneuburg Collection was composed where the family archetype was itself available (whereas the Worcester Collection was not), this evidence is of the utmost significance: revealing, firstly, the way in which English canonists expanded their own collections from both continental and insular sources; and, secondly, arguing once more against an authentic Worcester origin for the family which takes its name.

Yet, despite their undisputed family connexions, the Klosterneuburg Collection stands apart from all other members of the 'Worcester' family in textual details. Except perhaps for a brief fragment, of uncertain origin, among the manuscripts of Oslo University, this is the only English primitive collection now found in a continental library. Its rendering of English placenames is often extremely individualistic, and no other English primitive collection can be compared with it for unreliability in historical references. Nor is this defect due to the well-known scribal misinterpretation of abbreviations, for details of persons and places usually appear here in full though inaccurate versions. Thus, the Devon town of Ralegh appears as 'Taleg.'; the

[1] Schönsteiner, *loc. cit.*, *Claustr.* 298, 303, 306, 316, 322, 327, 334b, 335, 344, etc.

dean of Chichester as 'Cisterciensis'; Rufford as 'Ronforde' and 'Ruforde'; Ulfketel as 'Bultekel'; Horton as 'Barrona'; St. Edmund's as 'Sancti Ethemundi'; Harwood as 'Harvalt', 'Harwalde' and 'Harwalt' within a single letter; St. Frideswide as 'Sancte Frederende' or 'Freneside'; and, most startling of all, Henry of Winchester appears as 'heretico (!) quondam Wintoniensi episcopo'.[1] Such misreadings could just conceivably be due in some cases to the unfamiliarity of a continental scribe with English names and places. If this were in fact the true explanation, the manuscript at Klosterneuburg would provide a remarkable proof of English influence on the continent at a very early stage in the primitive period, for the work is undoubtedly a 'Worcester' composition. But such a solution is extremely unlikely, in view both of the nature of the errors cited above, and of further evidence of English provenance within the collection.[2] Too little is known at present of the practices in twelfth-century scriptoria to suggest a confident explanation of these curious textual details, though they could be explained (for example) by a dependence on oral transmission at some stage in the collection's history. The presence of the manuscript now in Klosterneuburg, and it has every appearance of being an original English transcription, is doubtless due to a movement of the work some time after its completion.

One final brief example will typify the numerous instances of provenance evidence with which the 'Worcester' collections abound. The Cottonian and Peterhouse Collections include in common several decretals received by Norwegian bishops in the pontificate of Alexander III, received in some cases by the archbishop of Trondhjem; and they appear in these English manuscripts in full and accurate versions. Now, these decretals are otherwise known in no other sources, in no other manuscripts either of English or continental origin. The question arises: how did these typically English collections acquire such unique and outlandish material? Dependence on the papal registers is quite inconceivable in this case. But it so happens that Archbishop Eystein of Trondhjem visited England in the early 1180s, and stayed at Bury St. Edmunds from August 1181 until

---

[1] *Ibid., Claustr.* 66, 104, 110, 135, 145, 197, 290 and 224.
[2] See p. 107, n.2, above, *Claustr.* MS., fol. 63r–v.

February 1182, as we know from various references in contemporary English chronicles.[1] And his presence there at that time could easily explain the inclusion of these otherwise unknown decretals in the later English collections.

[1] Holtzmann, 'Krone und Kirche in Norwegen', *Deutsches Archiv*, II (1938), pp. 375–6; H. E. Butler, ed., *The Chronicle of Jocelin of Brakelond*, Nelson's Medieval Classics (1949), pp. 15–16; Stubbs, ed., *Gesta Regis Henrici Secundi*, I, p. 269 and n.1; etc.

CHAPTER V

The Importance of the Decretal Investigation in English History

1. English Canonists and the Primitive Decretal Collections

IT remains only to fit these technical conclusions into the wider context of English history, and more particularly into the pattern of papal legislative policy in England in the light of the dramatic clash of jurisdictions in the conflict between Henry II and Becket. For this purpose it is best first to examine more closely the work of those English ecclesiastical judges whose influence was so decisive in the development of canonistic studies in the island. The primitive phase of decretal collecting is pre-eminently the 'English Period' in the history of canon law, when English or Anglo-Norman lawyers made their greatest and most lasting contribution to the law of the entire Christian community of Western Europe. The enthusiasm of English canonists in accumulating the most recent papal rescripts reached previously unheard-of proportions in the years immediately following the Avranches Settlement (1172): unprecedented in the island and unparalleled in Europe; and by these means they provided a corpus of decretal law of permanent value, though they were less skilled in its presentation than their continental colleagues. We have noticed the outstanding importance in this work of the English judges delegate in general and of four distinguished bishops in particular: Bartholomew of Exeter, Roger of Worcester, Richard of Canterbury and (combining in himself associations with all three) Baldwin, archdeacon of the Exeter diocese, abbot of Ford, bishop of Worcester and archbishop of Canterbury in turn.

Baldwin was perhaps less important than the others in his actual judicial assignments, but he is far more interesting in the technical aspects of the history of canon law. In the story of decretal collections as developed in England his is the clearest and most decisive personality.[1]

Now, many influences are apparent at various stages in the development of the English collections, but transcending all others and generally pervading the entire range of collections is an association with the canonists and ecclesiastical judges at Exeter, Worcester and Canterbury. It is this quite extraordinary phenomenon which, through misunderstanding, has vitiated so much research into the canonical history of the period. It has been suggested, for example, that Alexander III sent more decretal letters to Bartholomew of Exeter than to any other ecclesiastical judge in Europe;[2] and more generally that the Alexandrian decretals received in England were roughly half his total issue to the whole Church.[3] But these are in fact insubstantial conclusions, which spring from an uncritical use of the sources available. The essential point to grasp is this: the decretals of Alexander III as found in the Gregorian *Decretales* (and therefore also in the generally accepted body of decretal law from that time) derived through a complicated network of generations from the private and primitive collections assembled in his own pontificate. In other words, they depend ultimately on the English primitive collections discussed in the previous chapter, and on the contemporary continental collections, which are less individualistic than their English counterparts.[4] It is obvious from an understanding of these factors that the proportions of decretals received by individual bishops, or in particular districts, bear no necessary relationship with the proportions recorded in the canonical collections, which are

---

[1] Cf. Kuttner and Rathbone, *art. cit.*, pp. 282–3.

[2] Holtzmann, *Nachrichten*, p. 16; Morey, *op. cit.*, p. 44.

[3] Maitland, *Roman Canon Law*, pp. 122 ff.; Brooke, *Effect of Becket's Murder*, pp. 213–28; *idem, English Church and the Papacy*, pp. 211–14; S. E. Thorne, 'Le Droit Canonique en Angleterre', *RHD*, 4th Ser., XIII (1934), pp. 499–513; Holtzmann and Kemp, *op. cit.*, pp. xvi–xvii.

[4] The most recent discussions of continental primitive collections and their connexions with the papal Curia are by Holtzmann, 'La "Collectio Seguntina" et les décrétales de Clément III et de Célestin III', *Revue d'histoire ecclésiastique*, L (1955), pp. 400–53; and Vetulani, *Collections primitives*, pp. 64–72.

arbitrarily selective. Since, therefore, a significant proportion of these primitive collections was made in England, and since also these reflect the interests and influence of the most active ecclesiastical judges in the country, the high percentage of decretals received by them and recorded in the Gregorian collection, need excite no further comment than this present explanation. To express the matter most succinctly: there can be no valid grounds *a priori* for interpreting the course of decretal legislation in general on a basis of the statistical evidence provided by the professional collections. This argument overthrows the thesis of Maitland and Brooke quite decisively.

It is unfortunately true that a final or complete analysis of Alexander III's decretals is no longer possible, since the papal registers have not survived from his period. But fragments of the official records have left their traces in individual decretal collections; and whenever this has occurred there is positive evidence that the ratios of letters in the canonical collections as a whole are not a true indication of papal legislative activities relative to the various countries of Western Europe generally. Perhaps the most striking evidence for this conclusion is found in the 50th Title of the vulgate edition of the *Appendix*. This familiar version is based on the sixteenth-century edition by P. Laurens of a manuscript now lost. But it can easily be shown that the so-called '50th Title' had no place in the original scheme of composition, and is in fact a derivative from the lost registers of Alexander III. The register fragment is composed of sixty-seven chapters, and its most striking feature is that the proportion of English decretals contained within it is quite different from that in the primitive decretal collections in general, as well as from that in the earlier titles of the *Appendix* itself. Statistically, about one sixth of the register fragment is English in provenance, or eleven decretals in a total of sixty-seven, which seems a much more probable reflection of the overall trends in papal policies.[1] And this conclusion agrees entirely with what has been noticed already when analysing the contents of the English primitive collections: wherever a collection is known to

---

[1] For the register fragment, see Holtzmann, *Register Papst Alexanders*, pp. 13 ff.; see also Kuttner, *Projected Corpus*, p. 346; Cheney, *art. cit.*, p. 182, n.3. The matter is discussed more fully later in this chapter.

be partly derived from non-English sources, there is evidence that earlier theories concerning the ratios of decretals issued by Alexander III to the various countries in Europe are inaccurate and misleading. A single example from the many collections discussed in the previous chapter will serve as a reminder: when discussing the Claudian Collection, in the 'Bridlington' family, a group of marriage decretals was found intruded into a collection of general English provenance. The decretals were derived from an unknown source of continental origin, and the proportion of decretals received in England which they contain is strikingly different from that elsewhere in the same collection: there are in fact only seven English inscriptions in a total of thirty decretals.[1] Therefore, even within the decretal collections, there are good grounds for questioning the arguments which have been based on a statistical analysis of their contents.

But there is still more conclusive evidence in the non-professional archives of the period: in the records of monastic houses and in cathedral cartularies. Although the source material of this kind is exceedingly rich and relevant, very little has been done so far to correlate the evidence for the various countries. It must be remembered that no satisfactory explanation of ecclesiastical developments in the twelfth century is possible except in their European framework. And it is necessary to realize in our present context that there was a gradual acceleration in the issue of decretal letters throughout the century and in every direction: it is particularly clear under Eugenius III, Adrian IV and above all Alexander III. In the total bulk of surviving Papsturkunden there is little to distinguish the English records from those for the rest of Europe. The records in Italy, France and Spain are especially rich in papal documents of all kinds, including *privilegia* and decretal letters.[2] So we are led to the conclusion that if the canon lawyers

---

[1] See Chapter IV, pp. 89–90, above.

[2] For Spanish documents, see Kehr, *Papsturkunden in Spanien: Katalanien; idem, Navarre und Aragon.* For England, see Holtzmann, *Papsturkunden in England,* Vols. I–III. Many other similar volumes deal with the various parts of the Western Church. Papal documents from the twelfth century are printed in chronological order in these volumes: the majority are *privilegia* and *littera mandatoria,* but many decretal letters are also included, letters which could be fittingly included in decretal collections. For Italy, see Holtzmann, *Ergänzungen zur Italia Pontificia* (1957 and 1958).

had referred only to central or curial records for their material (as the continental canonists undoubtedly did in some instances),[1] the resulting regional or 'national' proportions would have been very different from those which are in fact discovered in their collections.

Not only does this explanation satisfactorily account for the high proportion of decretals of English provenance in the Gregorian *Decretales*, it explains equally well the large number of those decretals received originally by the small group of English bishops mentioned above. The comparatively infrequent references to certain English bishops are no less significant than the repeated references to others. Why are so few letters received by northern English bishops found in the decretal collections: why so few received by Roger of York or Hugh of Durham? Among bishops of the southern province, why are so few decretals received by Gilbert Foliot discovered in these works? It is admittedly extremely likely that Bartholomew of Exeter and Roger of Worcester received in fact a larger number of papal mandates and commissions than any other English bishops.[2] They were recognized by their contemporaries as the most distinguished judges delegate in England at that time. Therefore, their greater influence on the substance of the English decretal collections is not surprising. But the archbishop of York and the bishop of Durham are known to have received more decretals than the proportion addressed to them in the collections would suggest. It is clear enough from the independent, non-professional, archives that numerous decretals were received by these and many other English bishops; and many such letters are found in fact in the canonical collections. But they are seldom incorporated in so significant a way as the decretals of Canterbury, Worcester and Exeter. They are rarely grouped together in a manner suggesting some immediate dependence on local or diocesan records. The northern archives are rich in papal letters of all kinds; but the northern archives and the judicial business of the northern prelates seem not to have influenced the development of the English collections as directly as did those of Canterbury, Worcester and Exeter.

---

[1] See p. 119, n.4, above.
[2] Cf. Hall, *Roger of Worcester*, p. 100.

Again, considering the position of Gilbert Foliot at London: it is well known that Foliot was a canonist of some repute who received many papal mandates, and was frequently commissioned by Alexander III as a papal judge delegate.[1] But there is little evidence that he exercised any direct influence on the growth of the professional decretal collections. Even that part of the Belvoir Collection which was undoubtedly connected in some way with Foliot's London archives was entirely without influence on later canonical works.[2]

The striking impression of the archbishop of Canterbury and the bishops of Worcester and Exeter on the substance of the English primitive collections is a measure of their livelier interest in the most recent papal rescripts, resulting from their frequent commissions as papal judges delegate. These bishops, or more probably the canonists in their circles, gathered together the latest decretals passing through their hands, to form handbooks of reference to guide them in their judicial careers. The essential material was most readily available in the commissions and mandates which they themselves received from the pope. Such access to local records fully explains the provenance of the constituent letters in the most primitive English collections. Later, the local resources were supplemented from similar records in other districts, especially from the records of associated judges delegate; and this development explains satisfactorily the intermingling of Exeter and Worcester decretals. Finally, as skill and knowledge grew, the collections were greatly expanded by derivation from other, already-existing, collections: firstly from elsewhere in England, and secondly from the continent. This is the explanation of the genesis of the primitive collections assembled in England. But above all there was the association of the bishops of Exeter and Worcester. It was the judicial work of these two bishops and their circles, together with that of Richard of Canterbury, which moulded the contents of the primitive collections composed in England, and, therefore, ultimately of a significant part of the Alex-

[1] For the northern prelates, see Holtzmann, *Papsturkunden in England*, I, epp. 106, 107, 132, 133, 157, 158, 191–5, etc. For Gilbert Foliot, see Hall, *Roger of Worcester*, pp. 49–50 and 92.
[2] Appendix II: *Belver*, II. 1–9: with the exceptions of items 1 and 4, these decretals are not found elsewhere in the 'English' family.

andrian letters in the Gregorian *Decretales.*[1] This is the key to a true interpretation of the evidence. Problems arising in the course of litigation and the increase in the actual number of decretals issued by the popes, together provided the stimuli for the earliest English collectors. But this was less true in the later and systematic collections, whose authors were trained jurists, concerned primarily with an integrated and scientific exposition of ecclesiastical jurisprudence. And in this way we are reminded once again of the practical emphasis in the work of the English canon lawyers.

2. CONNEXIONS WITH THE CONTINENTAL PRIMITIVE COLLECTIONS

If the typical features of English decretal collections, as described above, were merely a local expression of general trends in the Western Church, the collections made elsewhere in Europe (in France or Italy, or in Spain, for example) would reflect local traditions and local resources in a comparable way. But there is little evidence to suggest that this is true in fact. Simply on a numerical basis the English share of surviving primitive collections is astonishing. In the whole of Europe twenty-seven collections of this kind have so far been rediscovered, and fifteen of these are English.[2] It would be rash to assume without independent evidence that the surviving ratios of manuscripts necessarily reflect the true relative contributions of the various countries to the original development. The surviving evidence could be simply accidental and subject to the varying fortunes of English and continental libraries in the course of so many centuries. But if chance were the true explanation of the English predominance among the surviving primitive collections, it is most remarkable that quite the reverse phenomenon is observed among the systematic decretal collections, which are for the most part French or Italian. It is in fact most likely that both phenomena reflect the true course of develop-

---

[1] Morey, *op. cit.*, pp. 44–5; Knowles, *Episcopal Colleagues*, pp. 51–2; Cheney, *Bishops' Chanceries*, p. 82.

[2] Holtzmann, *Nachrichten*, pp. 22–3: the English collections are items 12–26; Kuttner, *Projected Corpus*, p. 348. The Oslo Collection (a fragment among the MSS. of Oslo University) was at first thought to be a member of the 'Worcester' family, but this view is now rejected: Holtzmann and Kemp, *op. cit.*, p. xiii; Ch. Lefebvre, 'Fragment d'Oslo'. *DDC*, VI (1957), col. 1180.

ments: the English collectors were widely influential in the earliest phases of decretal collecting; but the continental jurists surpassed them later and brought the movement to its full maturity. It should be remembered that after the publication of *Compilatio Prima*, and still more after that of the Gregorian *Decretales*, all earlier collections (primitive and systematic alike) became redundant. There was no reason why one type of collection rather than another should have received preferential treatment later. But if this argument of widespread English influence in the earliest phases is somewhat conjectural, it is confirmed by evidence within the decretal collections. Not only do these reveal very clearly the great enthusiasm of English canonists in compilation, but they show no less clearly the influence of English collections in the mainstream of European developments. A study of the most primitive continental collections now surviving reveals in significant cases the evidence of English influence.

All continental primitive collections composed primarily of Alexander III's decretals can be grouped into three 'national' streams or families, identified as Roman or Spanish, French, or Italian. It would be impossible to discuss here all these continental works as closely as their English counterparts have been examined in the previous chapters, but at least one member of each family has been analysed from the viewpoint of its structure and source material. In each instance there is evidence of a knowledge of English sources, gained directly or indirectly from an English collection already existing. In this respect also an English influence could not be assumed simply on the basis of the large number of letters of English provenance included in the collections, for that deduction would evade the basic question in the present investigation. It is the manner in which the English material was incorporated that is chiefly remarkable, faithfully reflecting the structure and contents of English archetypal collections.[1]

---

[1] For continental primitive collections: Holtzmann, *Nachrichten*, pp. 21-2, items 1-11. The classification of continental families in this chapter is provisionally accepted from Holtzmann's list. For brevity, the Roman or Spanish family is referred to as 'Tortosa', but it is realized that this description is not entirely satisfactory in all cases; cf. the discussion on *Eberbacensis*, below. There is certainly an Italian or Curial element in the group.

(a) The Roman or 'Tortosa' Family

The Roman or 'Tortosa' group is composed of three collections known as *Eberbacensis, Dertusensis* and *Alcobacensis*.[1] The precise origin of these works is by no means established beyond dispute, but two at least were almost certainly transcribed in the Spanish peninsula. *Eberbacensis* was once owned by the Cistercian abbey at Eberbach, though it is now in the British Museum; *Dertusensis* is now at Tortosa; and *Alcobacensis* belonged originally to the Cistercian abbey at Alcobaça, though it is now in Lisbon. The Tortosa manuscript is a perfect illustration of the argument advanced above concerning English influence on continental collections. There is little doubt that the manuscript was transcribed in the Spanish peninsula, and the writer was unfamiliar with the commonest of English place-names: thus, the bishop of Winchester appears in one inscription as 'W. Itoniensi', and the bishop of Hereford as 'Berofordensi' in another.[2] Such transliteration is perfectly understandable in the work of a scribe unacquainted with these famous English bishoprics, but quite inexplicable in the work of an English transcriber. And yet the opening forty-one decretals were clearly obtained from an English collection: twenty-eight have English inscriptions, and are grouped together in the same significant fashion as in the authentic English manuscripts.[3] But following the forty-first item no further decretals to England (except for an isolated item) are included in the rest of the collection.[4] The letters in this latter part were derived in two further stages: firstly, from a source in which French and Italian decretals are intermingled; and, secondly, from a group of Spanish and Hungarian decretals discovered in no other collection.[5] Therefore, the Tortosa Collection was built up in three separate stages: the

---

[1] Kuttner, *Projected Corpus*, p. 346; Holtzmann, *Nachrichten*, p. 21: items 1–3. *idem*, 'Beiträge zu den Dekretalensammlungen', *ZRG, Kan.Abt.*, XVI (1927), pp. 37 ff: *Dertus.*, pp. 39–77; *idem*, 'Papst Alexander III und Ungarn', *Ungarische Jahrbücher*, VI (1926), pp. 397–426; *idem*, 'Collectio Eberbacensis', *ZRG, Kan. Abt.*, XVII (1928), pp. 548–55. *Alcobac.* has not yet been analysed.

[2] Holtzmann, *Beiträge*, p. 55: *Dertus.* 3 and 4.

[3] *Ibid.*, pp. 54–61: *Dertus.* 12, 21, 25–32, 35–9, etc.

[4] *Ibid.*, pp. 62–72: *Dertus.* 42–74; the exception is *Dertus.* 72, to Canterbury; *Dertus.* 58 is the letter *Redolet Anglia* announcing the canonization of Becket, but not received exclusively in England.

[5] *Ibid.*, pp. 65–72: *Dertus.* 62–74.

first and basic element was an English collection of Canterbury provincial provenance; the second was a contemporary continental work, possibly Italian or Curial in origin; and the third was an appendix composed mainly of Spanish and Hungarian material. Except in this brief appendix, there is no evidence of Spanish influence on the composition of the collection as a whole, and there is only one decretal of Spanish provenance elsewhere in the entire work.[1] But the cathedral and monastic records of the period show clearly enough that large numbers of papal decretals were reaching the Spanish peninsula in the same period.[2] If Spanish canonists had been equally enthusiastic in decretal compilation as their English counterparts, or had shown comparable initiative in exploiting their own resources, the decretals which they themselves received would surely have been included in their 'national' collections in more fitting proportions.

The Eberbach Collection is no less revealing, following the Tortosa Collection closely both in matter and arrangement, except that its author had no knowledge of the Spanish and Hungarian decretals at the end of the latter. Therefore, it reveals no connexion with Spanish collectors (though in a single letter its Spanish references are unusually accurate[3]), and is derived from other continental and English sources. The Eberbach Collection is divided into twenty-five sections, comprising one hundred and eleven chapters in all, of which the final twenty-seven are canons of the 1179 Lateran Council.[4] At least thirty-two of the first forty-seven decretal chapters were received by English ecclesiastics, and no less than twenty have Canterbury inscriptions, including one unbroken sequence of twelve items. But in the rest of the collection about nine-tenths of the decretals are addressed to non-English prelates. Thus, an English archetype appears as the basic component, and this is expanded from continental, possibly Italian, sources. A comparison with the Tortosa Collection establishes the membership

---

[1] *Ibid.*, p. 62: *Dertus.* 44: to Toledo.

[2] See p. 121, n.2, above; and Chapter II, p. 39 and n.4, above.

[3] B.M. Arundel MS. 490, fol. 216vb: Alexander III to the archbishop of Toledo, *De hoc autem*; cf. Chapter IV, p. 107, n.2, above. The decretal refers to the former bishop of Osma; English scribes almost invariably erred when writing 'Oxomensis'; but the correct form is found in the Eberbach MS.

[4] Holtzmann, *Eberbac.*, pp. 551–5.

of this work in the Roman or 'Tortosa' group, though its place of transcription must remain at present conjectural, and it is quite certain that the manuscript was owned at one period by the monks of Eberbach. Yet, whatever conclusion is reached on the difficult question of its origin, the Eberbach manuscript provides clear evidence of widespread English influence. No other explanation will account so satisfactorily for the disposition of English material either in this collection or in the Tortosa manuscript. Equally interesting is their early date of composition: neither work has any decretals later in issue than the 1179 Lateran Council, though the Eberbach manuscript has the conciliar canons included as an appendix. The third 'Tortosa' collection is now at Lisbon, but has yet to be analysed. Its special importance in our present context lies in the evidence which it contains of English influence. Particularly significant are its letters to Exeter, several of which were previously unknown when Morey published his study on Bartholomew of Exeter, to whom these decretals were addressed.[1]

(b) *The French Family*

Four manuscripts now survive to illustrate the primitive phase of the French decretal collections. Two of these are now in the Bibliothèque Nationale in Paris, and are known as *Parisiensis I* and *Victorina*; a third is in Luxemburg, and is therefore identified as *Aureaevallensis*; and the fourth is in the library of Trinity College Cambridge, and is named simply *Cantabrigiensis*. All except the Victorine Collection have already been published, and they show no less clearly than the 'Tortosa' collections an influence from England.[2] To such a marked degree is the provenance of their individual letters English that the Cambridge Collection was itself described as English when its manuscript was first investigated.[3] The very large proportion of English decretals in the collection (at least thirty-seven in a total of ninety-nine items), together with the discovery of the manu-

[1] Morey, *op. cit.*, pp. 133–5.

[2] Holtzmann, *Nachrichten*, pp. 21–2, items 4–7. For *Cantab.*: Friedberg, *Canonessammlungen*, pp. 5–21; *Victorina* has not yet been analysed, but see Holtzmann, *Register Papst Alexanders*, p. 70; for *Paris. I*, see Friedberg, *Canonessammlungen*, pp. 45–63; and for *Aureaev.*, see Holtzmann, *Beiträge*, pp. 77–115.

[3] As recently as Van Hove, *Prolegomena*, p. 351: 'confecta in Anglia'. Likewise, van Hove describes *Paris. I* as an English collection: *ibid.*, pp. 351–2.

script in an English college library, created the natural assumption that its composition was originally English; but this opinion receives little current acceptance. In assessing the nature of the English influence on this work, the most remarkable feature is not so much the ratios of English and continental letters included, but the manner of their insertion (and this also has been noticed in the 'Tortosa' collections discussed above). The now-familiar sequences of decretals addressed to English bishops are once again discovered. The most notable single derivative in this instance is from the Canterbury provincial records; and in one position a group of nine decretals, all with Canterbury inscriptions, appears in unbroken sequence.[1] But the evidence in *Parisiensis I* is even more conclusive. Its first one hundred and eight chapters (in a total of one hundred and eighty-five) are overwhelmingly English in provenance, transcribed in ordered sequence according to diocesan origins. The first seven items (with only one exception) were sent to Canterbury; and these are followed in turn by blocks of decretals received at York, London, Winchester, Worcester, Exeter, Norwich and St. Albans.[2] Only occasionally are continental decretals inserted among these English groupings. But the provenance of the letters changes significantly after this long opening sequence, and there is no further evidence of dependence on English sources. It seems obvious that the author drew first on an English collection and later on a continental work, though without any predominantly regional emphasis in the latter. This extraordinary relative arrangement of English and continental decretals in the Paris Collection touches the central interest of our present study, for it reveals a material arrangement difficult to explain except on the basis of a reliance on English archetypes. It would be quite absurd to suppose that any canonist would trouble to arrange his decretals according

---

[1] For decretals with Canterbury inscriptions, see Friedberg, *Canonessammlungen*, pp. 12–14: *Cantab.* 20–8. The dating limits of this collection are 1177–c.1179, the earlier limit being fixed by the inclusion of the decretal *Cum Christus*, to Henry of Reims, J-L 12785, 1177.

[2] Friedberg, *Canonessammlungen*, pp. 52 ff.: *Paris. I*, 1 and 3–7: to Canterbury; 8–20, 31 and 32: to York; 33–6: to London; 45–55: to Winchester; 56–72: to Worcester; 73–83, 91 and 92: to Exeter; 93–6 and 98: to Norwich; 99–105 and 107: to St. Albans. Cf. Lefebvre, 'Parisiensis Prima', *DDC*, VI (1957), cols. 1222–9, esp. 1228.

K

to so juristically irrelevant a pattern; it is equally impossible to suggest that the disposition of decretals could reflect the order of their transcription from the papal registers. But it would be an entirely natural result if the collection were dependent in some way on an existing English collection, assembled in stages from the records of the various bishops mentioned. This rather obvious solution is also the most satisfactory, and there is little purpose in contriving a more subtle explanation. In general, the problem of interpretation in the French family remains much the same as that in the 'Tortosa' group: the French archives were rich enough in records of decretals received by French bishops, as particular collections such as the systematic *Brugensis* make very clear.[1] But there was little apparent use of this material in the French collections of the most primitive kind. Even where these are not clearly indebted to English source material, they reveal no 'national' emphasis in the selection of decretals to suggest or underline the provenance of the work as a whole. And this also was a feature of the 'Tortosa' collections, as explained above.

(c) *The Italian Family*

Third and most important of the continental primitive families is an Italian group of collections known respectively as *Beroli-nensis*, *Cusana*, *Duacensis* and *Florianensis*, these names being derived from the present location of the manuscripts at Berlin, Cues, Douai and St. Florian.[2] Unfortunately, not enough is known at present of the Italian family, and its general importance must be determined largely by inference: the Douai manuscript is merely a fragment, and the Berlin manuscript alone has been made available in a published analysis.[3] The Berlin Collection is a superior type of composition, compared with most collections discussed so far, but it is correctly classified by

---

[1]Friedberg, *Canonessammlungen*, pp. 140–70; P. Le Mercier, 'Collection de Bruges', *DDC*, II (1937), cols. 1118–20; see also pp. 145–6, below.

[2] Holtzmann, *Nachrichten*, p. 22: items 8–11; Kuttner, *Repertorium*, pp. 279, 281 and 291; Holtzmann and Kemp, *op. cit.*, pp. xi–xii.

[3] J. Juncker, 'Die Collectio Berolinensis', *ZRG, Kan.Abt.* XIII (1924), pp. 284–426; Lefebvre, 'Collectio Duacensis', *DDC*, V (1953), col. 1; *idem*, 'Collection de St Florian', *DDC*, V, col. 856; Le Mercier, 'Collection de Berlin', *DDC*, II (1937), cols. 766–70. See also *Ambrosiana*: Kuttner, *Projected Corpus*, p. 348.

Holtzmann as primitive.[1] The author was certainly familiar
with the systematic technique of decretal dissection and with the
desirability of a convenient pattern of subject-matter arrangement. In fact there is little doubt that the collection is related
in some way to the great systematic line of development which
reached its most mature realization in *Compilatio Prima*. The
systematic conventions are not applied in it completely or consistently, but it was through such collections that a transition
was gradually made to a more satisfactory plan of composition.
As might be expected in a more mature collection of this kind,
there is little clear evidence of the sources from which it was
derived: the various source strata, so obvious in many of the
most primitive collections, are no longer readily distinguished
in this work. Therefore, it is much more difficult to identify
the various regional or personal influences which contributed to
its final development. Yet, whenever a sequence of decretals,
received originally in a single country, appear compactly
grouped together in the Berlin manuscript, their provenance is
English. At least nine items in one sequence of twelve chapters
were received in England; a second group of five chapters is
exclusively English in provenance; and other similar instances
could easily be cited.[2] The evidence of English influence is
admittedly less striking in the Berlin Collection than in the
'Tortosa' and French families discussed above, but its limited
concentration of letters of English provenance assumes a
heightened significance in view of the widespread English influence already established elsewhere. There is evidence also
that the Italian collection now in St. Florian was subject to
English influence at some stage in its development.[3] Therefore,
even in the homeland of the most mature canonists in Europe
the English collections played their part in producing a
generally accepted corpus of decretal law. It is not strictly
necessary to analyse here in detail the varied sources and composition of the Italian and curial collections, which raise

[1] For correspondence between *Berol.* and the great systematic collections, see
tables of correlation supplied by Juncker, *loc. cit.*, pp. 412–19, at *Berol.* 49–52, 65–
67, 105–7, etc. For the use of decretal abbreviation in *Berol.*, see *ibid.*, 34, 42, 48, 51,
58, etc. Cf. Holtzmann, *Nachrichten*, p. 22; *idem* and Kemp, *op. cit.*, p. xi.

[2] Juncker, *loc. cit.*, pp. 364–95; *Berol.* 37–48, 100–5, etc.

[3] I am indebted to Professor Holtzmann for this reference.

important problems outside the scope of our immediate interest: these problems involve the question of access to the papal registers and the dissemination of archetypal collections derived from the central records. These are crucial questions in a total investigation of the origins of the primitive decretal collections, but are familiar enough already in the works of Holtzmann and more recently of Vetulani.[1] But this at least seems clear: only the Italian collections rivalled their English contemporaries in the extent of their influence throughout Europe generally in the earliest phases of decretal compilation. The body of decretal law which survived from Alexander III's pontificate was due in large measure to a fusion of these two prolific traditions.

(d) *General Conclusions*

The following points emerge in general conclusion: the English and Italian canonists displayed the most striking initiative in constructing the earliest decretal collections now surviving, and their work was roughly parallel in time. The schools of canon lawyers elsewhere in Western Europe appear to have relied very largely on the supply of decretals amassed in their different ways by English and Italian collectors; and in this manner the decretals gathered together by these two schools governed the substance of decretal law for Alexander III's pontificate as discovered in the professional collections. This factor explains the phenomena already discussed concerning the relative ratios of 'national' rescripts in the Gregorian *Decretales*.

The principal purpose of this section has been to explain the presence of so many English decretals in the continental collections. It was realized at the outset that their presence did not necessarily imply a direct infusion of English source material into the continental works. The proportions might reflect the true ratios of letters sent out from the chancery, though this appeared unlikely. An analytical survey of the contents and structure of both English and continental collections now establishes beyond all reasonable doubt that English decretals were directly transmitted to the continent through collections assembled first in the island, and chiefly based on the records of

[1] Cf. p. 119, n.4, above.

English ecclesiastical judges. It was the disposition of the decretals and the manner of their inclusion which justified this interpretation; and therefore it could be assumed that the continental families were indebted at some stage in their development to English collections already existing. This was most obviously true in the French and 'Tortosa' families. It was less true in the Italian family, but even in these collections there were good grounds for assuming some measure of English influence. The following point is no less significant: wherever the French or 'Tortosa' collections are palpably indebted to English sources, the English material appears as the opening part of the completed composition, and is never supplementary to the continental sources by appearing as an appendix. But, if we consider the English collections of comparable structure and composite origins, wherever these are partly indebted to continental sources, exactly the reverse is true relative to place of origin, since the local or English material is transcribed first in these works also, followed by the accessions from collections made on the continent. In other words, in all the primitive collections examined so far, except the Italian, the English decretals appear as a major or basic component.[1] From this it seems certain that not only were the English primitive collections extensively used on the continent, but in the critical opening phases they provided the bases on which all but the Italian collections were constructed.

The argument may now be carried one stage further. The role of the Italian collections in the total development of the decretal collections was very considerable, but it was different in nature from the English contribution. There is no emphasis in the Italian works comparable in any way with the personal and local selections of materials so characteristic of the English primitive collections, reflecting in some cases the influence of identifiable English judges delegate. The decretals in the Italian collections are much more general in provenance, and there is little evidence that they were dependent at any stage on the personal archives of Italian bishops or ecclesiastical judges. They seem much more likely to reflect the influence of central or

---

[1] In some instances, as in *Cantabrigiensis*, the sources are intermingled, but even there the English decretals do not appear as an appendix.

curial registers.[1] And only comparatively minor groups of decretals, in the Italian collections, suggest a relationship between regional or provincial archives and the sequence of letters in the canonical manuscripts. The private collections and family traditions as they developed in England reveal, in contrast, the work of ecclesiastical judges making effective the latest decretal law as it became known to them in the papal mandates which they themselves received. The Italian collectors were much more selective and much less personal in the choice of their material; and much more likely to record the interests of canonists in juristic exposition. They are perhaps the products of the legal schools rather than local records of case-law as it accumulated in the hands of practising lawyers and judges in the ecclesiastical courts. But the distinction suggested here has less validity when the English canonists also began to arrange and analyse their material within a mature and juristic framework. It helps also to explain how the continental lawyers outstripped their English counterparts in juristic evolution. The importance of the English collections lapsed once the primitive phases had been superseded, but they had left their traces in the mainstream of canonical development.

Once the very primitive phases were left behind, it is increasingly difficult to disentangle the individual threads which contributed to the completion of a given collection. A reciprocal stream of interconnexions swiftly developed, and the works of each school intermingled freely with those of the others. From the viewpoint of technical developments in decretal codification, the French and Italian collections were to prove in the long run more progressive; but the English collections had made a decisive contribution to the general developments. The systematic collections depended on the primitive collections, both English and continental, for their Alexandrian decretals; that is how

---

[1] Cf. Holtzmann, *Beiträge*, pp. 60 ff.: *Dertus.* 42–61: to Arras, Bisceglie, Toledo, Cosenza, Neus (uncertain), Andria, the Duke of Venice, Le Mans, Bari, Mainz, the King of France, Trefontane or Trois Fontaines, Prester John, Lucca, Clermont, one uncertain, Becket's canonization, Bisceglie, Trani and Rouen. This arrangement is characteristic of continental archetypes, the letters being much more varied in provenance than those in the typical English primitive collections, except where these are clearly indebted to continental sources of this kind. Local influences appear at times in continental collections also, but not so characteristically.

the records of the English judges delegate found their way at last into the Gregorian *Decretales*. And that is why the decretal legislation of Alexander III for the English Church seems, in the most famous compilations, so disproportionately high compared with the rest of Europe. But whether the problem is considered from the viewpoint of English influence on collections made in other parts of Europe, or *vice versa*, the rapidity of intercommunication between the various schools in England and on the continent and the swift passage of decretals from one group to another are astonishing. All the collections discussed in this section were completed between 1178 and 1181, and some within the narrower limits of 1178 and 1179: which is an illuminating reflection on the extent of professional consciousness and unity among English and continental canonists in the era of the Third Lateran Council of 1179.[1]

3. English Influence on the Systematic Families: the *Appendix Concilii Lateranensis*

The English decretals passed into the mainstream of canon law through two main channels. The first of these, as explained above, was by their reception into the primitive continental collections which formed part of the raw material from which later canon lawyers assembled their systematic collections. In this way the English primitive collections transmitted their contents into a widely accepted corpus of decretal law, and there is reason to believe that the English collections associated with Canterbury itself were most decisive in this connexion.[2] The second channel, which was related to the first but by far the more significant, was through their reception into the great systematic collections, and especially into the *Appendix* a fountain-head of the entire systematic tradition.[3] The origin of this collection has been much discussed, but its English provenance is suggested by several considerations. In view of its decisive influence on the whole course of later systematic developments, the question of its authorship is clearly of crucial

---

[1] *Cantab.* was completed c. 1178–9, *Paris. I* c. 1179–81, *Aureaev.* c. 1181, *Dertus.* post 1179, *Eberbac.* c. 1179–81, *Berol.* c. 1179–81, and so forth. These dates are determined by internal evidence, and refer to composition, not to transcription.

[2] Cf. Brooke, *Canons of English Church Councils*, p. 476.

[3] See Chapter II, pp. 51–5, above.

importance. From the *Appendix* sprang the great Bamberg Collection, of French provenance, together with its derivatives the
Cassel and Leipzig Collections, the Amiens, Compiègne, Erlan-
gen and Oriel I manuscripts; the Tanner and St. Germain
compilations; the epoch-making Italian collection of Bernard
of Pavia: the *Breviarium*, more famous as *Compilatio Prima*;
through the latter a single central tradition can be traced from
the *Appendix* to the Gregorian *Decretales* of 1234.[1] The formative
influence of the *Appendix* is therefore self-evident, and its provenance and authorship are of the utmost historical interest.

Among recent scholars, van Hove and Holtzmann have suggested an Italian or continental origin for this collection.[2] But a
counter-theory of English or Anglo-Norman authorship has
been argued still more persuasively by Kuttner. The justification
for this later theory lies in the use made of the *Appendix* by
English canonists in their canonical commentaries in contrast
with its seemingly total neglect by canonists in other schools:
whereas the former cited the *Appendix* as a decretal source-book
in such commentaries as the *Summa In Nomine* and *Summa de
Iure Canonico tractaturus*, the latter referred in similar contexts to
the derivative Bamberg Collection or to even later generations.[3]
Nevertheless, the evidence of English influence at some vital
stage in the development of the *Appendix* tradition could not be
established solely by this argument, and it is worth stating
briefly the various circumstantial features which lend further
support to the theory, bearing in mind that a work of such complex ancestry as the *Appendix* was not narrowly based on either
English or continental sources alone, since it was clearly dependent on both. Among famous earlier works of continental
provenance, the systematic Italian collection *Parisiensis II* was
one obvious source of influence;[4] and among early English
collections, the primitive 'Worcester' family reveals a comparable relationship. Thus, the Worcester Collection itself can be

---

[1] Amanieu, *art.cit.*, cols. 833–41; Naz, 'Quinque Compilationes Antiquae',
DDC, III (1942), cols. 1239–41; G. Le Bras, 'Bernard de Pavie', *DDC*, II (1937),
cols. 782–9; G. Mollat, 'Les Décrétales de Grégoire IX', *DDC*, IV (1949), cols.
627–32. For transmission from *App.*, see Holtzmann and Kemp, *op. cit.*, pp.
xiii–xv.

[2] Van Hove, *Prolegomena*, p. 352; Holtzmann and Kemp, *op. cit.*, p. xiii.

[3] Kuttner, *Projected Corpus*, p. 349; *idem* and Rathbone, *art.cit.*, pp. 283–4.

[4] Friedberg, *Canonessammlungen*, pp. 21–6 and 71–84.

broken down analytically, as already explained, into two main components: an archetypal basis devised in seven books on a broad subject-matter classification; and a series of additions inserted as appendices to each of the several parts. Of the very large number of decretals composing the first five books of the 'Worcester' archetype, all but a small minority are also found in the printed editions of the *Appendix*, though parts of the seventh book were unknown to the author of the latter.[1] As far as the supplementary decretals in the Worcester Collection are concerned, some of these also are found in the *Appendix*, but not the most recent acquisitions.[2] Both the Worcester Collection and the *Appendix* include decretals which were unknown to the authors of all other primitive collections, whether English or continental, reviewed by Lohmann in his meticulous analysis of the former.[3] Therefore, while it is clear that no immediate interdependence existed between these two collections, there is ample evidence to suggest that both were partly dependent on a common source of supply.

A further point of circumstantial interest is provided by the 44th Title in the *Appendix*, appearing under the heading 'De pre-eminentia Lundonensis et Eboracensis.'[4] This manifestly English emphasis is derived from the famous letter of Gregory I to St. Augustine of Canterbury in 601, advising him on the future provincial structure of the English Church. It was Gregory's intention that the Church should be organised in due course under the jurisdiction of two archbishops at London and York respectively. But, for various well-known historical reasons, Canterbury in the event retained the primacy of the south, and the papal plan was never fulfilled in a strictly literal way. In

---

[1] Decretals in the 'Worcester' archetype but not in *Appendix*: *Wig.* I, 12, 40, 42 and 43; II, 3, 6, 19 and 21; III, 6, 13 and 19; IV, 5, 8, 12, 13, 17 and 24; V, 2; VII, 1–8, 14, 15, 18, 20–3, 25–6, 59 and 61. Cf. also p. 138, n.2, below.

[2] Decretals supplementary to the archetype in *Wig.* but not in *Appendix*: I, 45 and 48; II, 32, 33, 34 and 36; III, 34, 38 and 40; IV, 34, 39, 41–6 and 48–50; VII, 55, 64, 66, 67 and 70–81.

[3] *Wig.* II, 30 and 37; III, 26, 27, 30, 32, 33 and 35; IV, 28, 29, 31, 32, 36–8, 40 and 47; VII, 65. It must be remembered that the earliest known members of the 'Worcester' family were themselves of complex and varied origins; the family archetype, in the earliest form now deducible had already blended sources of English and continental origin.

[4] Friedberg, *Canonessammlungen*, p. 65.

view of the revival of interest in this question in the course of the twelfth century, and of the bitter disputes which arose through the triangular rivalry between Canterbury, London and York, while Becket was archbishop, the selection of this heading in the *Appendix* creates a presumption in favour of English authorship —the more so considering the insertion of a corresponding title in the Bamberg Collection, referring with similar regional emphasis to the comparable rivalry between Tours and Dol.[1] It is to say the least very interesting that the importance attached by Gregory I to London was still reflected in the chosen title, which the English authors of the later Tanner Collection and the English decretists in the Caius MS. 676 diplomatically altered to 'De pre-eminentia Eboracensis et Cantuariensis.'[2]

On the other hand, the *Appendix* is completed in the printed edition with a 50th Title, which Holtzmann has identified as a derivative from an excerpt from the papal register.[3] Since the register fragment is clearly not of English origin, its presence in the completed collection appears at first sight an argument against the English authorship of the work as a whole. But the final title in the vulgate *Appendix* was not included in the original composition. It is not discovered in the extant manuscripts, except in a related section in *Orielensis I*, a member of the Bamberg group, and must have appeared as a supplement in the manuscript on which Laurens based his edition. Therefore, this title provides no evidence on the provenance of the *Appendix* archetype. The point is exemplified by the Lincoln MS. 121, one of the three main surviving *Appendix* texts. The Lincoln version includes in place of the 50th Title other decretals corresponding with late acquisitions in the Cottonian and Peterhouse Collections in the 'Worcester' family, completed in or after 1193-4, and in the Anglo-Norman systematic *Tanner*, composed at the

---

[1] For the general background of the English dispute, see Foreville, *op. cit.*, pp. 27 ff. and 64 ff.; Knowles, *Episcopal Colleagues*, p. 48. In Friedberg the letter to Augustine appears under the title: 'De penitentia', *Bamb.* XLVII; this is immediately followed by the title 'De discordia Turonensis ecclesiae cum Dolensi', *Bamb.* XLVIII; Friedberg, *Canonessammlungen*, p. 110 and n.1. The titles referring to London and Tours respectively are found adjacent to one another in some manuscripts.

[2] Caius College MS. 676, fol. 173rb; Tanner MS. 8, p. 688b.

[3] For the text of *Appendix*, see Crabbe, *ed.cit.*, pp. 836-944; cf. Holtzmann, *Register Papst Alexanders*, pp. 13 ff.

close of the century.[1] Such evidence as this could not establish that the *Appendix* was originally an English work. The Lincoln manuscript may preserve an English copy of a continental collection already existing: a theory supported by the location of other major *Appendix* manuscripts in continental libraries. But the Lincoln manuscript preserves a textually interesting transcription, and certainly records a continuation of the *Appendix* in English hands.[2] Now another, previously unknown, fragment has been identified in the St. John's College Cambridge MS. 148.[3] This fragment is in part related to the *Appendix*, though its evidence is too slight to allow the investigation of authorship to be pursued much further. But it does throw fresh light on the formation of the collection at an early stage of development. The preservation of these manuscripts in Lincoln and Cambridge, in volumes of legal matter of possible English provenance, lends circumstantial support to a theory of English authorship, though this is counterbalanced by the location of other related works elsewhere.[4]

Considered together, all these factors suggest a reasonable presumption that the *Appendix* was of English origin, or at least of English connexions, and reveal the second main link between the English collections and the great systematic tradition on the continent. By these means many decretals which Alexander III addressed to the Church in England were incorporated in the permanent law of the Universal Church.

---

[1] Lincoln Cathedral MS. 121 (A. 5.11), fols. 1–61. For examples of decretals at the conclusion of this version of *Appendix*, unknown to the author of Crabbe's version, but included also in *Chelt.*, *Cott.* or *Pet.*: Lincoln MS., fol. 58v: Celestine III to John, dean of Rouen, *Prudentiam tuam*, J-L 17019, 17 June 1193 (cf. *Cott.* MS., fol. 286v, and *Pet.* MS. 203, final quire, fol. 2rb); Linc. MS., fol. 59v: *Bone memorie Alanus*, J-L 17055 and 17675, 1193 (cf. *Cott.* MS., fol. 287v, and *Chelt.* MS., fol. 102ra): in this case the Linc. MS. provides the exact date, hitherto unknown: 'Dat. Lat. VIII Kal. Augusti pontificatus nostri anno III'=25 July 1193. See also *Tanner*, App. I; Holtzmann, *Sammlung Tanner*, p. 143.

[2] *Appendix*, II, 3, 4, and 5, etc.: cf. Linc. MS., fols. 3r–4r; Mansi, *ed.cit.*, cols. 279–81; Crabbe, *ed.cit.*, pp. 847–8.

[3] St. John's College Cambridge MS. 148/F.11, fols. 82v–84v. For this MS., see my forth-coming article: 'English Canonists and the *Appendix Concilii Lateranensis*; with an Analysis of the St. John's College, Cambridge, MS. 148', *Traditio*, XVII (1962).

[4] Thus the Lincoln MS. includes the procedural work *Ulpianus de edendo*, once attributed to Vacarius; cf. Kuttner and Rathbone, *art.cit.*, p. 290. The Oriel fragment is *Orielensis II*, Oriel College MS. 53, fols. 253–4; there are also MSS. at Leipzig and Vienna: see Holtzmann and Kemp, *op. cit.*, p. xiii.

4. THE IMPORTANCE OF THE INVESTIGATION IN ENGLISH HISTORY

The interest of English historians in papal decretal legislation dates from Maitland's famous refutation of Stubbs's thesis that the 'Roman' canon law was not considered binding by the medieval Church in England.[1] We are not concerned here with the central issue of that controversy, and it is enough to note that Maitland's vindication of the contrary opinion has held the field until the present day, and is nowhere seriously called into question. But in the course of his enquiry into the part played by the English Church in the development of ecclesiastical law, he was misled into a position which has vitiated most of the later study of the subject. The nature of his misunderstanding was pointed out briefly in the introductory chapter above, and the broad course of development in decretal legislation and the evolution of the decretal collections have been described in the central chapters, revealing the true pattern of the phenomena which Maitland so grievously misinterpreted. It remains now to draw together these threads and see precisely what modifications must be made to his opinions. Noticing that the Gregorian *Decretales* contained an astonishingly high number of decretals of Alexander III with English inscriptions, more in fact than to any other single part of Europe, Maitland accepted this evidence at its face value, and consulted no earlier sources for confirmation or explanation.[2] It must be admitted that, in the state of historical knowledge of decretal developments then existing, he had no reason to suspect the apparent evidence in a famous official book of law made in Italy with papal authorization. And, therefore, he assumed that Alexander III had in fact sent more decretals to England than to any other part of Christendom:[3]

---

[1] Maitland, *Roman Canon Law, passim*. Maitland's thesis was mainly based on the evidence in the fifteenth-century *Provinciale* of William Lyndwood, Official Principal to Archbishop Chichele, on the decretals, and on the concept of the pope as Universal Ordinary for all Christians. In refuting the arguments advanced by Stubbs, he drew the essential and basic distinction between what the English Church recognized as legally binding and what it was permitted by the secular power to put into practice.

[2] Maitland, *Roman Canon Law*, p. 123.

[3] *Ibid.*, p. 122.

Just at that moment England seems to have demanded, or at any rate to have received a far larger number of papal mandates than would have fallen to her lot, had the supply that was exported from Rome been equally distributed among the importing countries according to their populations.

Armed with this assumption he advanced to the conclusion that more than a third of the permanently important Alexandrian decretals had English cases for their subjects:[1]

Which is or ought to be one of the most prominent facts in the history of the English Church.

Now, in its strictly literal meaning, this final conclusion was perfectly accurate, but not in the meaning which Maitland intended. The astonishing number of permanently important decretals which were originally received by English bishops was due directly to the formative influence of English canon lawyers in the crucial early phases of decretal codification. There was nothing intrinsically more important or more significant in the decretals received at that time in England than those received elsewhere, and their striking presence in the decretal collections is easily explained in the light of the technical development of the latter. But Maitland's argument was developed still more forcefully by Zachary Brooke who carried the investigation back into the *Quinque Compilationes Antiquae.* It is obvious enough, however, from an understanding of the history of the decretal collections and their technical development that the earlier collections naturally reveal an even higher English content than the Gregorian collection. Brooke raised the proportion of English decretals from one third to one half for Alexander III's pontificate, and to two-thirds for that of his successor Lucius III, with a sharp decline thereafter.[2] Maitland's argument appeared to have been triumphantly vindicated. But let us examine the details of Brooke's analysis more closely: Why, he asked, did the bishops of England more than those of any other country in Europe put so many questions to the pope on points of law at that moment; and why did the

---

[1] *Ibid.*, p. 124.

[2] Brooke, *English Church and the Papacy*, pp. 211–14; *idem, Effect of Becket's Murder,* pp. 216–22.

appeals from England alone require so many legal rulings? The following explanation appeared to him the most convincing: the canon law was fully valid in England only after Henry II's submission at Avranches in 1172, and the English bishops were in need of papal guidance both in matters of law and on points of procedure. Their continental contemporaries, on the other hand, were well abreast of the most recent developments, so that their appeals did not provoke such interesting decisions, and naturally the latter were not incorporated in the decretal collections. But by the end of Lucius III's pontificate this necessary work of instructing the English was completed, and that factor explains the decline in English interest after that date.[1]

At least two major defects in this line of argumentation come instantly to mind: if the continental canonists and ecclesiastical judges were so conversant with the law that they had no need to question the pope in the same way as their English colleagues, why did they also assiduously gather together the resulting papal rescripts, as was certainly their practice even where they had not taken the original initiative in composing the archetypes? And, secondly, if the English ecclesiastics alone in some particular way were in need of such guidance, through lagging behind their continental contemporaries, how is it that later decretals of a similar nature were sent predominantly to European rather than English recipients, once this necessary task of instructing the English had been completed? For this is the conclusion which must be reached if the evidence in the decretal collections is taken consistently at its face value. And, lastly, if the decretals addressed to England were designed simply to bring the regional church into line with the state of law already existing elsewhere in Europe, why did these very letters form so important a part of the great Gregorian collection, a work of universal importance assembled by Raymond of Peñaforte half a century later in Italy?

The answer to these questions has become evident as a knowledge of the history of decretal codification has increased, chiefly through the identification of the sources on which both the most primitive and the later systematic collections ultimately depended. It is clearly misleading to build historical

[1] *Ibid.*, pp. 220–2.

theories on the regional ratios of decretals received into the Gregorian *Decretales*, since this collection depended chiefly on the *Quinque Compilationes Antiquae; Compilatio Prima* in turn was the fruit of the systematic tradition which can be traced still further back through such works as *Lipsiensis* and *Bambergensis* to the *Appendix*; the latter derived its Alexandrian letters from primitive collections such as those examined in the chapters above; the decretals in the primitive collections were drawn more frequently from English sources than from those of any other country, though the influence of the Italian collections was also vital. We have shown above that many of the most primitive of the continental collections were largely indebted to earlier English archetypes for much of their raw material; and that, even where they were not so indebted, they reveal no personal or regional interests in their composition comparable with those so very evident in English collections. Therefore, it is not altogether surprising if more letters of English provenance were ultimately recorded in the most famous decretal collections than those which were sent to any other part of Europe. But this conclusion bears no relationship with the numbers of decretals sent out from the papal chancery. Whenever dependence on a non-English or curial source can be proved in a given collection, the proportion of English decretals contained in it is decidedly different and much less remarkable than that in the decretal collections as a whole. Thus, to revert once again to the register fragment appearing as the 50th Title in the edited version of the *Appendix*: this sequence has only eleven English inscriptions in a total of sixty-seven chapters, which is one sixth of its total contents, compared with one half in *Compilatio Prima* or with nine-tenths in some of the most primitive collections now surviving.[1] The proportion of English decretals increases as the examination is carried back into the primitive period, so that even a non-English work may reveal a third or a half of its total contents with English inscriptions. Thus, the Cambridge Collection in the French family has not less than thirty-seven English items in a total complement of ninety-nine.[2]

---

[1] This has been shown in various collections discussed in Chapter IV, above. Thus, only three decretals with continental inscriptions are found in the first fifty items in *Claud.*: 11, 41 and 50: to Rouen, Reims and Limoges.

[2] Friedberg, *Canonessammlungen*, pp. 5–21.

It is a paradox of the decretal investigation that the further back the examination is retraced in time, and the larger the number of collections analysed, the more convincing does the thesis advanced by Maitland and Brooke appear at first to be: precisely because, in so doing, one approaches more closely that period in which the infusion of English material was at its greatest. The apparent cessation of papal legislative interest in England about the year 1185, if the evidence in the decretal collections were taken at its face value, marks in reality not a change in papal policy but the decisive supremacy which the continental jurists and collectors had by then achieved over the whole range of decretal codification. With this development, the accumulation of rescripts in England, although it continued much as before, ceased to leave any decisive impression on the general corpus of decretals still amassing in the rest of Europe. Therefore, from an examination of the systematic collections composed after that time, it appears as if the stream of papal mandates and commissions flowing into England was suddenly halted. Whereas in fact the change in decretal provenance reflects merely the closure of a widespread dependence on English archetypes and decretal records, and a more general reliance on decretals addressed to all parts of Europe. In a total of at least one thousand and fifty-five decretals now known from the collections preceding *Compilatio Prima*, seven hundred and thirteen were issued by Alexander III; and of these no less than three hundred and fifty-nine were dispatched to England. Including all Anglo-Norman territories, together with Scotland and Ireland, three hundred and ninety-nine of these Alexandrian letters were received in regions subject to English influence. But, in the same general total, one hundred decretals were received in France, eighty-nine in Italy, twenty-one in Spain and Portugal, and only three in Germany. Finally, in a total of almost four hundred decretals sent by Alexander III to the British Isles, no more than three or four were addressed to Ireland. These proportions merely reflect the relative influence of the canonists in the various countries in providing the raw material for the professional collections. They can have no relationship with the numbers of decretals sent out. To cite one final but most significant example: considering the vital developments in the Irish Church in the period, it would be absurd to suppose that the pitifully small number of Irish decretals preserved in the professional collections reflects in any way the extent of papal legislative interest in the island. Numerous decretals must undoubtedly have been received there, but they have left no traces in the canonical collections.[1]

The raw material suitable for inclusion in the decretal collections existed in fact in most districts if local canonists saw fit to use it, as the systematic Bruges Collection confirms very strikingly. Based largely on the central systematic tradition which included the *Appendix* and the Bamberg Collection, this great compilation was made in France about the same time as *Compilatio Prima* was published in Italy; but it was unknown to the author of that epoch-making Italian collection, and its individual contribution of decretals found no place in the generally accepted corpus of decretals on which the Gregorian *Decretales* ultimately depended. The chief interest of the Bruges Collection in the present context lies in its large number of decretals derived from the regional archives in the province of Reims, relating especially to Reims itself, Amiens, Arras, Châlons, Epernay and other central or northern French districts. Most of these letters were sent out by Alexander III and are found in no other collection so far published, and provide a convincing refutation of the thesis that the large number of decretals to English bishops in most decretal collections suggests that the English were in fact in need of particular instruction. If Brooke's argument were valid as applied by him to the Church in England, then the Bruges Collection provides equally acceptable evidence that the great archbishopric of Reims was similarly out of touch with the latest state of canonical opinion. The theory is of course invalid in either case. At least thirty-five decretals, or parts of decretals, received by French ecclesiastics, or of special interest to them, are found in the Bruges Collection, but are otherwise unknown. So interesting and significant are these examples that it is worth citing a few of their inscriptions in illustration:[2]

[1] Holtzmann, *Nachrichten*, p. 34.
[2] Friedberg, *Canonessammlungen*, pp. 140–70. For other examples, see *Brug.* XXVI, 2; XXVII, 4; XXXI, 2; XXXII, 3; XXXVI, 2 and 6; XXXIX, 2; XL,

L

Brugensis:

IV, 6.	To the archbishop of Reims.
VIII, 3.	To the bishop of Beauvais and the dean of Reims.
XIII, 5.	To the abbot and chapter of St. Bartholomew's at Noyon.
XIV, 18.	To the prior and others of Reims.
XVII, 7.	To the dean and chapter of Reims.
XIX, 19.	To the bishop of Amiens and the abbot of St. Quentin's at Lille.
XX, 3.	To the archbishop of Reims.
XXIV, 1.	To the archbishop of Reims.
4.	To the bishop of Arras.
5.	To the bishop of Amiens.
XXVI, 1.	To the bishop of Amiens.

And there are many other examples of this kind.

One final consideration now remains. What explanation can be offered for this remarkable English interest in papal decretal legislation, far surpassing in its earliest stages that of all other parts of Western Europe? And, within this wider problem, why was it governed so largely by so few of the English bishops? The classical solution of the first of these problems has been sought in the failure of Henry II's policy to limit the jurisdictional independence of the *ecclesia Anglicana* vis-à-vis the secular government, and in the resulting inrush of decretal letters which signalized the papal victory. The barriers which the Conqueror had raised in his relations with the English Church and the Papacy, to prevent bishops leaving England without his permission and papal legates coming in, had been largely overthrown in the turbulent reign of Stephen; and it was Henry's intention that these should be re-erected as opportunity provided. The early years of Henry's reign witnessed a further advance in the Church's concern for its liberties and jurisdictional freedom, under the guidance of Theobald, and reflected in the increasing reception and study of canon law. But the situation was no longer as favourable to the Church, as it had been during the years of Stephen's weakness; and the parallel growth of secular law and royal administration increasingly now provoked a conflict of ecclesiastical and secular

14 and 15; XLIV, 3; XLV, 8 and 9; XLVI, 6; XLVII, 26; XLIX, 16 and 23; LI, 2 and 5; LIII, 1, 2 and 14; LIV, 3; LVIII, 1 and LIX, 1.

interests.[1] In these circumstances, the right of appeal from the English ecclesiastical courts to the papal Curia, and the growing practice of referring to the pope on all sorts of questions as a judge of first instance, in his capacity as Universal Ordinary, raised the problems of church-state relations in an unusually acute form. The actual clash between Henry II and Becket arose over the vexed question of clerical immunity from secular judgement in criminal cases, ending for Thomas in violent death in his own cathedral, and for Henry in humiliation and in the concession at Avranches (1172) of most of what the archbishop had demanded. It is suggested that the 'flood-gates' were thereby thrown wide open to full-scale papal intervention after a long period of isolation, in which the English Church had been cut off from developments taking place elsewhere in Europe. According to this theory, the English bishops were through their former isolation in need of special guidance, and the legally-minded Alexander seized the opportunity to work out in these ideal circumstances the latest legal theories and principles, thus explaining his seeming preoccupation with the English Church. But it is obvious enough from the history of the decretal collections, as outlined briefly in the preceding chapters, that such an interpretation is quite misleading in many particulars. It is defective both in respect of fact and in appreciation of the sources available.[2]

As to the question of fact: the independent records of papal letters being now made increasingly available from monastic and cathedral archives provide two major conclusions: the acceleration of papal legislation through decretal letters, in the Western Church as a whole, has no necessary connexion with the peculiar course of developments within the Church in England. Its origin is independent in motive, and prior in initiation, to the struggle between Henry II and Becket; and so to consider the apparent inrush of decretal letters which

---

[1] A. Saltman, *Theobald, Archbishop of Canterbury*, Athlone Press: University of London Historical Studies, 2 (1956); Cheney, *From Becket to Langton: English Church Government, 1170–1213*, Manchester (1956).

[2] This is not to deny the importance of the studies by Maitland and Brooke on the history of the English Church in the period. Much of their work is valid and of permanent value. Even within the present context some of their conclusions could be supported, but not on a basis of the evidence which they cited.

followed the Avranches settlement as a novel departure in papal policy is to misunderstand completely its European context. The new decretal era in papal legislation was an expression of the centralizing tendencies which had increasingly characterized ecclesiastical government from the time of the Hildebrandine Reform in the previous century; and, in its canonistic setting, must be interpreted in the light of the closure of *ius antiquum* and the emergence of a true science of canon law with the publication of Gratian's *Decretum*.

What imparts an aura of peculiar importance to the 1172 settlement for England is its coincidence in time with the flood-tide of decretal legislation under Alexander III, coming after a period of confused church-state relations in Europe generally and in England in particular. Still more important is its coincidence in time with the emergence of a novel interest in the professional collecting of papal decretal letters, which is quite a different matter from a change in papal legislative policies. The origin and development of this new canonistic interest have been the main theme of this study, so little further need now be said about it. It was precisely in the period of the Avranches settlement and the years immediately following it that canonists began for the first time to assemble their own collections of contemporary decretal letters. And it seems indisputable from the evidence discussed above that the most striking enthusiasm in the earliest phases of the movement was displayed in England. For these reasons, the large number of decretals then received in England and taken into the professional collections need excite no particular attention in considering the course of central papal policy. Nevertheless, the fact that so many of the earliest collections were devised by English canonists is a matter of the utmost importance for English ecclesiastical historians, illustrating the one phase above all in which English initiative exercised a crucial influence on the development of canon law for the Universal Church.

Herein lies the true importance of the 1172 agreement.[1] If the policy of Henry II had proved successful, the various expressions of papal jurisdictional authority would have been ex-

---

[1] *Ibid.*, p. 108: 'The so-called compromise of Avranches settled nothing; but the next generation was a period of effective adjustment.'

cluded (at least to some extent) from England, and the introduction of decretal letters and commissions to judges delegate
gravely diminished. This could scarcely have influenced the
course of papal legislation in Europe generally, but it would
have effectively prevented that striking contribution which
English bishops and canonists made in the event to the development of the decretal collections. For this reason, it is fitting to
claim for the settlement a place of permanent importance in the
history of the English Church, but even more in the history of
the Church as a whole.

A final word must be said of the personal role of the English
bishops and canonists who had the greatest share in the application of decretal law in England, and the greatest influence
on the development of the English collections. Bartholomew of
Exeter, Roger of Worcester, Baldwin of Ford and Richard of
Canterbury: these are the names which have recurred most
significantly above; these are the men who left their indelible
mark on the English collections. It is scarcely a matter of simple
coincidence that these are also the men who most clearly represent the Becket position or party in the dramatic struggle which
had recently been concluded.[1] Above all other bishops in
England, Bartholomew and Roger are known to have sym-
pathized with the exiled and martyred archbishop: Roger
actually shared his exile (together with John of Salisbury, Her-
bert of Bosham and others), and finally incurred with Bartholomew the anger of Henry II on this account. Baldwin, too,
maintained close correspondence with the exiled party, and
retired to Ford at the height of the conflict. Richard of Canterbury was not a participant in the conflict, and indeed was sometimes regarded later as too lukewarm in his defence of the rights
for which Thomas had died, yet he may be considered involved
in the Becket position through right of succession in the primatial
see.[2] But, in contrast with this, the famous English bishops
whose share in the systematic extension of papal jurisdiction in
England appears very much slighter than that of these, are

[1] Morey, *op. cit.*, pp. 15–30.
[2] On one occasion Alexander III reproached Richard for endangering the rights
of the Church for which Becket had shed his blood: see the decretal *Qua fronte*,
J-L 14312, 1174–81.

known for the most part as ecclesiastically indifferent or more typically as Becket's opponents: Hugh of Durham, Roger of York, Gilbert of London. It is not unreasonable to suggest a relationship between these phenomena, and to conclude that the pro-Becket bishops played the decisive part after the settlement in clinching the victory through a rapid extension of papal jurisdictional authority. And this is all the more likely since they were naturally more acceptable to Pope Alexander, and were involved personally in what may be called the papalist position in the recent controversy. The prelates of the north and Gilbert Foliot in the south were by no means excluded from the receipt of decretal letters, but it seems that in practice they showed little interest in their professional accumulation. These factors, together with the frequency with which Bartholomew, Roger and Baldwin were commissioned as judges delegate, firmly support our thesis that the chief instruments in the application of decretal legislation in England, as well as in the accumulation of decretal letters in professional collections, were found most conveniently as well as most naturally in the supporters of the late archbishop. By what means precisely the fruits of this English enthusiasm were transmitted into the main streams of contemporary continental developments cannot be established with certainty in the present state of historical knowledge. But we shall end with this speculation: an ideal instrument for their propagation may be seen in the widespread dominions and the numerous diplomatic missions of the Angevin king, exceeding those of any other secular ruler in Western Europe at that time. From Scotland in the north to the Pyrenees in the south, and to the Atlantic coast of Brittany in the west, the Angevin king held direct sway; while, as a result of the political marriages of his daughters, he numbered among his relations King William II of Sicily, King Alphonso of Castile and Duke Henry the Lion of Saxony. The ceaseless and restless diplomatic exchanges and journeyings between England and almost every part of western Europe, conducted for the most part by English clerics, and the councils and arbitrations held under the presidency of the English ruler, afforded an ideal opportunity for the dissemination of material and ideas. The career of John of Salisbury, and his connexions with the schools of

France and with southern Italy and Sicily; the council con-
vened at Westminster in 1177 to arbitrate between the Kings of
Navarre and Castile (at which both Bartholomew of Exeter and
Roger of Worcester were present, together with Spanish prelates): these are but a few random examples of the numberless
points of contact between English bishops and canonists and
their continental colleagues.[1] By such means the Angevin
Empire played its part in facilitating the spread of English
decretal collections throughout the west of Europe. And this is a
striking reflection of the failure of Henry II's ecclesiastical
policy.

[1] Morey, *op. cit.*, p. 41; Hall, *Roger of Worcester*, p. 47. See also Chapter IV, pp.
116–17, above. The conclusions summarized in this final chapter do not imply
that the work of the English collectors ceased after the mid-1180s, but simply that
their influence declined in the overall development of decretal codification
throughout the Western Church. The Tanner, St Germain and Avranches Collections record later channels of transmission of English or Anglo-Norman influence
on collections made elsewhere, and lend further support to the arguments developed above in connexion with the *Appendix*. It is hoped in future studies to trace
more closely the interconnexions between the English and continental schools of
canonists. See my forthcoming 'Primitive Decretal Collections in the British
Museum', *Studies in Ecclesiastical History*, I, Nelson (1963).

APPENDICES

THE following appendices are merely a selection from the analyses provided in the second volume of my unpublished Cambridge thesis: *Twelfth-Century Decretal Collections and their Importance in English History* (1954). All members of the 'English' family are analysed in that volume, together with select parts of the 'Bridlington' and 'Worcester' collections. Pending the publication of Professor Holtzmann's reconstruction of the authentic texts of all decretal letters surviving in the twelfth-century canonical collections, it is clearly desirable to avoid as far as possible conflicting systems of reference and numeration in the analysis of decretal manuscripts. In these circumstances, the examples supplied below provide simply a sufficient insight into the provenance and technical construction of the earliest English collections, and afford a convenient basis of reference for discussions in the present volume. Analyses of the Worcester II, Belvoir, Canterbury and Rochester Collections, together with tables revealing their interconnexions, are found in Appendices I–IV respectively, while Appendices V–VII provide comparative tables to illustrate the interrelations between various other collections referred to in the chapters and footnotes above. My thanks are due to Professor Holtzmann for generous advice on the identification of decretals and conciliar canons.

I

Wigorniensis Altera: The Worcester II Collection
British Museum Royal MS. II B. II, fols. 97r–102

ANALYSIS

1. A(lexander) episcopus servus servorum Dei venerabili fratri
   B(artholomeo) Exoniensi episcopo, salutem et apostolicam
   benedictionem.   *F.97r.*
   Sicut dignum est et omni consentaneum .   . immunis.
       (a) Sicut dignum   .   .   .   . coerceri.

(b) Super eo vero . . . . immunis.
Dat.Tuscul. II Kal.Febr.
J-L 12180 and 13771: 31 January 1171–2.

2. (Alexander III Rogerio Wigorniensi episcopo.)   *F.98r.*
   Inter cetera, sollicitudinis tue . . . nuncupandum.
   See c.3, below.

3. (Alexander III Rogerio Wigorniensi episcopo.)
   Presentium etiam auctoritate . . . spoliare.
   (a) Presentium etiam . . . . amovere.
   (b) De sacerdotibus vero . . . spoliare.
   Dat.Senon. VI Kal.Decembr.
   Wig.Altera 2 and 3: J-L 12254: 26 November 1164.

4. (Alexander III Rogerio Wigorniensi episcopo.)
   Super eo, quod a nobis tua sollicitudo . . efficere.
   (a) Super eo, quod a nobis . . . inhibeatur.
   (b) De appellationibus vero . . . compellas.
   (c) Ceterum, cum aliquam causam . . expirare.
   (d) De monachis autem, qui . . . efficere.
   See c.5, below.

5. (Alexander III Rogerio Wigorniensi episcopo.)   *F.98v.*
   Meminimus nos ex parte tua . . . habere.
   (a) Meminimus nos . . . . rescindere.
   (b) Quod si aliquis . . . . iniungenda.
   (c) Ceterum, si abbatem . . . iudicandum.
   (d) Verum, cum alicui ecclesie . . deberet.
   (e) Scripta vero autentica . . . habere.
   Wig.Altera 4 and 5: J-L 13162: 1164–79.

6. (Alexander III Rogerio Wigorniensi episcopo.)   *F.99r.*
   Ad aures nostras perlatum fuisse . . . conferri.
   (a) Ad aures nostras . . . . constringas.
   (b) Illas vero terras . . . . conferri.
   J-L 13163 and 14132: 1164–79.

7. Alexander episcopus servus servorum Dei Willelmo Norwicensi episcopo, salutem. *F.99v.*
   Personas ecclesiarum in tua . . . mandatum.
   (a) Personas ecclesiarum . . . recipiantur.
   (b) Ad hec, de sacerdote . . . mandatum.
   J-L 12253 and 14146: 1159–17 January 1174.

8. (Alexander III Gaufrido Lincolnensi archidiacono.)
   Ad presentiam nostram accedens R. presbiter . amoveas.
   *J-L 13982: c.1173. To Geoffrey Plantagenet, archdeacon of Lincoln
   c.1173, elected bishop of Lincoln 1173, resigned unconsecrated 1182.*

9. (Alexander III Rogerio Wigorniensi episcopo.)   *F.100r.*
   Cum nos tibi iampridem si bene . . . habuisset.
   J-L 13164: 1164–79.

10. (Alexander III Rogerio Eboracensi archiepiscopo.)

Fraternitatem tuam scire volumus . . . permaneat.

    (a) Fraternitatem tuam . . . . teneremur.

    (b) Cautum siquidem . . . . postulares.

    (c) I. Ex privilegio Alexandri (*Wig. II, 13:* Adriani) pape

        Sane laborum . . . . presumat.

        Hoc idem etiam ex privilegiis aliorum Romanorum pontificum.

      II. Decreta pontificis Pascalis pape secundi.

        Decimas a populo . . . . debeant.

      III. Unde beatus Gregorius ait:

        Communi vita . . . . sunt vobis.

      IV. Item Magociense (*Correctly:* Cabilonense) concilium.

        Decrevit sacer iste . . . audiunt.

      V. Item Gregorius papa:

        Statuimus ut monasteria . . . se subdunt.

      VI. Item Pascalis secundus:

        Novum exactionis . . . . accipiunt.

      VII. Item ex privilegio Alexandri pape:

        Statuimus ut, si super decimis . . permaneat.

    Wig.Altera 10a–b: J-L 13873: 1159–81.

11. (Alexander III Henrico Remensi archiepiscopo.)   *F.100v.*

Cum sacrosancta Romana ecclesia . . . credimus.

Dat.Tuscul. XI Kal.Aprilis.

J-L 12020: 22 March 1171–2.

12. (Alexander III Rogerio Eboracensi archiepiscopo.)   *F.101r.*

Sicut Romana ecclesia omnium . . . ducere.

Dat.Signie (*Elsewhere:* Anagnie.)

J-L 12293: 2 June 1173–4.

COMPARATIVE TABLE

COLLATING THE WORCESTER II, BELVOIR, CANTERBURY AND ROCHESTER COLLECTIONS.

Wig.Alt.	Belver.	Cantuar.	Roff.
1a-b	I.12a-l	I.23a-b	48
2 ⎱	I.9a-b.I-III	–	–
3 ⎰		II.4	–
4 ⎱	I.10	I.22	112
5 ⎰			
6	I.13	–	–
7	I.14	III.6	–
8	I.15	I.51	64
9	I.16	–	–
10a-c.I-VII	I.11a-c.I-VII	–	–
11	–	I.42a-d	46a-d
12	I.18	I.41	42

II
Belverensis: The Belvoir Collection
Oxford Bodleian MS. E. Mus. 249, fols. 121ra–135rb

ANALYSIS

PART I
Capitula concilii Alexandri III habiti Turonis.   *F.121r.*

1. Quoniam enormis quedam .   .   . non habetur.
   Tours, 1163: Mansi, c.5.

2. Non satis utiliter   .   .   .   . sed auget.
   Tours, 1163: Mansi, c.6.

3. Quia in quibusdam   .   .   .   . plectatur.
   Tours, 1163: Mansi, c.7.

4. Non magnopere   .   .   .   . amittat.
   Tours, 1163: Mansi, c.8.

5. Quamvis grave nimis .   .   . prostratus.
   Tours, 1163: Mansi, c.3.

6. Maioribus ecclesie .   .   .   . prohibemus.
   Tours, 1163: Mansi, c.1.

7. Plures clericorum   .   .   .   . videatur.
   Tours, 1163: Mansi, c.2.

8. In partibus Tholose .   .   . vetentur.
   Tours, 1163: Mansi, c.4.

9. Alexander tertius episcopus servus servorum Dei venerabili
   fratri R(ogerio) Wigorniensi episcopo, salutem et apostolicam
   benedictionem.   *F.122v.*
   Inter cetera sollicitudinis .   .   . spoliare.
      (a) Inter cetera .   .   .   . promoventur.
      (b) I. Quod quia indignum .   . nuncupandum.
         II. Presentium etiam .   .   . amovere.
         III. De sacerdotibus .   .   . spoliare.
   J-L 12254: 26 November 1164.

10. Alexander III episcopus servus servorum Dei venerabili
    fratri R(ogerio) Wigorniensi episcopo, salutem et apostolicam
    benedictionem.   *F.123r.*
    Meminimus nos ex parte .   .   . habere.
       (a) Meminimus nos .   .   . rescindere.
       (b) De monachis autem .   .   . habere.
       (c) Illis etiam   .   .   .   . respondere.
       (d) Preterea, illi .   .   .   . efficere.
       (e) Ceterum, cum aliquam .   .   . observandum.
       (f) Si autem lis infra .   .   . exspirare.
       (g) Super eo, quod .   .   . supersedeatur.

(h) Si autem adversa pars   .   .   . inhibeatur.
(i) De appellationibus .   .   .   . compellas.
(k) Si aliquis parrochianorum .   .   . permanere.
(l) Si autem id occultum   .   .   . iniungenda.
(m) Ceterum, si abbatem   .   .   . iudicandum.
(n) Verum cum alicui .   .   .   . deberet.
(o) Scripta vero autentica   .   .   . habere.
J-L 13162: 1167–9.

11. Alexander III episcopus servus servorum Dei venerabili fratri
R(ogerio) Eboracensi archiepiscopo, salutem et apostolicam
benedictionem.   *F.124r.*
Fraternitatem tuam   .   .   .   . consistat.
   (a) Fraternitatem tuam .   .   . immunes.
   (b) Sed pie recordationis Adrianus .   . postulares.
   (c) I. Ex privilegio Alexandri pape:
       Sane laborum   .   .   .   . presumat.
     II. Hoc etiam ex privilegiis aliorum Romanorum ponti-
         ficum. Decreta pontificis Paschalis pape secundi:
         Decimas a populo .   .   .   . debeant.
    III. Unde beatus Gregorius ait:
         Communi vita   .   .   .   . sunt vobis.
     IV. Item Magotiense concilium:
         Decrevit sacer   .   .   .   . audiunt.
      V. Item Gregorius papa:
         Statuimus ut   .   .   . subdunt.
     VI. Item Paschalis secundus:
         Novum exactionis .   .   .   . accipiunt.
    VII. Item ex privilegio Alexandri pape:
         Statuimus ut   .   .   .   . consistat.
J-L 13873: 1159–81.

12. Alexander III episcopus servus servorum Dei venerabili fratri
B(artholomeo) Exoniensi episcopo, salutem et apostolicam
benedictionem.
Sicut dignum est et omni .   .   .   . immunis.
   (a) Sicut dignum est   .   .   . obviare.
   (b) Illi vero, qui .   .   .   . provocassent.
   (c) Illi quoque non fuerunt   .   . prebuerunt.
   (d) Eos vero, qui se   .   .   . erogare.
   (e) Illi vero, qui sola   .   .   . indicenda.
   (f) Clericos autem, quos   .   . coherceri.
   (g) Super eo vero   .   .   . venire.
   (h) Monachi vero et canonici .   . adhibenda.
   (i) Si vero aliquis   .   .   . vulneraverit.
   (k) Officialis pro   .   .   . ledat.
   (l) Si clericum vero   .   .   . immunis.
J-L 12180 and 13771: 31 January 1171–2.

13. Alexander III episcopus servus servorum Dei venerabili
fratri R(ogerio) Wigorniensi episcopo, salutem et apostolicam
benedictionem.   *F.126v.*
Ad aures nostras perlatum fuisse . . . conferri.
   I. Ad aures nostras . . . . constringas.
   II. Illas vero terras . . . . conferri.
J-L 13163 and 14132: 1164–79.

14. Alexander III episcopus servus servorum Dei venerabili
fratri W(illelmo) Norwicensi episcopo, salutem et apostolicam
benedictionem.   *F.127r.*
Personas ecclesiarum . . . . mandatum.
   I. Personas ecclesiarum . . . non possit.
   II. Quod si aliquis . . . . constringas.
   III. Verum si coram te . . . recipiantur.
   IV. Ad hec, de sacerdote . . . mandatum.
J-L 12253 and 14146: 1159–17 January 1174.

15. Alexander III episcopus servus servorum Dei dilecto filio
G(aufrido) Lincolnensi archidiacono, salutem et apostolicam
benedictionem.   *F.127v.*
Ad presentiam nostram accedens R. . . amoveas.
J-L 13982: c.1173.

16. Alexander III episcopus servus servorum Dei venerabili
fratri R(ogerio) Wigorniensi episcopo, salutem et apostolicam
benedictionem.
Cum nos tibi iampridem . . . . habuisset.
J-L 13164: 1164–79

17. Alexander III episcopus servus servorum Dei venerabili
fratri B(artholomeo) Exoniensi episcopo et dilecto filio
Sy(moni) abbati Sancti Albani, salutem et apostolicam
benedictionem.   *F.128r.*
Robertus de Ber . . . . . postponatis.
J-L 13930 and 14228: 1162–81.

18. Alexander III episcopus servus servorum Dei venerabili
fratri R(ogerio) Eboracensi archiepiscopo, salutem et apostolicam benedictionem.   *F.129r.*
Sicut Romana ecclesia . . . . in uxorem.
J-L 12293: 2 June 1173–4.

PART II

1. Alexander III episcopus servus servorum Dei venerabili
fratri G(ilberto) Lundoniensi episcopo, salutem et aposto-
licam benedictionem.
Universalis ecclesie . . . . . poteris.
Dat.Tuscul.Kal.Mart.
J-L 14267: 1 March 1171–81.

2. Gualterus Dei gratia Albanensis episcopus et domini pape
   vicarius venerabili et in Christo fratri G(ilberto) eadem gratia
   Lundoniensi episcopo et dilectis in Domino filiis capitulo hun-
   dredi de Rocheford, salutem et omnium plenitudinem gau-
   diorum.
   Veniens ad apostolice sedis clementiam   .   . vexetis.
   1163–77; cf. J. A. Giles, ed., Letters of Gilbert Foliot, II, 204.

3. Alexander III episcopus servus servorum Dei venerabilibus
   fratribus universis episcopis per Angliam constitutis, salutem
   et apostolicam benedictionem.   *F.129v.*
   Ad audientiam nostram   .   .   .   . evitari.
   Dat.Benevent. XIII Kal.Junii.
   J-L 11398: 19 May 1168.

4. Alexander papa III Symoni abbati Sancti Albani, de quibus-
   dam questionibus.   *F.130r.*
   Consultationibus singulorum   .   .   . spoliari.
      (a) Consultationibus singulorum   .   . prorogare.
      (b) De cetero, si aliquis   .   .   . removeri.
      (c) Donationes vero   .   .   . spoliari.
   Dat.Anagn. VI Id.April.
   J-L 12636: 8 April 1173–6.

5. Alexander III episcopus servus servorum Dei venerabili
   fratri R(otrudo) Rothomagensi archiepiscopo, salutem et
   apostolicam benedictionem.   *F.130v.*
   Quoniam quesitum est a nobis   .   .   . remitti.
   Dat.Tuscul. V. Id.Octob.
   J-L 13583: 11 October 1171–80.

6. Alexander III episcopus servus servorum Dei venerabili
   fratri G(ilberto) Lundoniensi episcopo et dilecto filio
   R(adulfo) archidiacono Lundoniensi, salutem et apostolicam
   benedictionem.
   Significatum est nobis   .   .   .   . suspendatis.
   J-L 14222: 1163–81.

7. Alexander III episcopus servus servorum Dei venerabili
   fratri G(ilberto) Lundoniensi episcopo, salutem et apostolicam benedictionem.   *F.131r.*
   Ad audientiam nostram   .   .   .   . sustineatis.
   J-L 14223: 1163–81.

8. Alexander episcopus servus servorum Dei dilectis filiis priori
   et monachis Cantuariensis ecclesie, salutem et apostolicam
   benedictionem.
   Gaudendum est universitati   .   .   . impetrare.
   Dat.Signie IIII Id.Martii.
   J-L 12201: 12 March 1173.

9. Alexander episcopus servus servorum Dei venerabilibus
fratribus archiepiscopis, episcopis et dilectis filiis aliis ecclesiarum prelatis et universo clero et populo per Angliam constitutis, salutem et apostolicam benedictionem.   *F.131v.*
Redolet Anglia   .   .   .   .   . intercedat.
Dat.Signie III Id.Mar.
J-L 12203–4: 13 March 1173.

PART III: COUNCIL OF WESTMINSTER, 1175.

Mansi, XXII, cols. 145 ff.; C. N. L. Brooke, 'Canons of English Church
Councils in the Early Decretal Collections', *Traditio*, XIII (1957), pp.
471–9.
Prooemium: Ideo in ecclesia   .   .   . contraire.

1. Ex decretali epistola Alexandri pape III.   *F.132r.*
   Si quis sacerdos vel clericus   .   .   . relinquant.
   See c.2, below.

2. Decernimus etiam eiusdem epistole auctoritate ne filii sacerdotum   .   .   .   .   .   . obtineant.
   Belver. 1 and 2: Mansi, c.1. Cf. J-L 12254–5: 26 Nov. 1164.

3. Ex Carthaginensi (*MS.:* Cartag.) concilio tertio.
   Clerici in sacris ordinibus .   .   .   . deponantur.
   Mansi, c.2.

4. Ex concilio Toletano tertio.
   His qui in sacris ordinibus .   .   .   . loco.
   See c.5, below.

5. Inhibemus quoque   .   .   .   . secularis.
   Belver. 4 and 5: Mansi, c.3.

6. Ex concilio Agatensi.
   Clerici, qui comam   .   .   .   . subiaceat.
   Mansi, c.4.

7. Ex diversis decretis.
   Quia quidam clerici   .   .   .   . suspensum.
   Mansi, c.5: Ex diversis decretis Urbani, Innocentii, et concilii
   Chalcedonensis et Carthaginensis.

8. Cum ecclesia Dei secundum   .   .   . refugii.
   Mansi, c.6: Ibidem.

9. Ex concilio Triburiensi (*MS.:* T'ib.)
   Dictum est solere   .   .   .   .   . anathema sit.
   Mansi, c.7.

10. Ex decretis Urbani pape.
    Nullus prelatus in recipiendo   .   .   . anathema sit.
    Mansi, c.8.

11. Nulli liceat ecclesiam nomine   .   .   . statuimus.
    Mansi, c.9: Decretum novum.

12. Ex decretis diversorum patrum.
Secundum instituta patrum . . . suscipiant.
Mansi, c.10.

13. Alexander papa ad W(illelmum) Norwicensem episcopum. *F.133r.*
Illud etiam de vicariis . . . . admittantur.
Mansi, c.12. J-L 12252: 1160–74.

14. Ex concilio Rotomagensi.
Omnes decime terre . . . . subiacere.
Mansi, c.13.

15. Calumpniam et audaciam temere . . relinquimus.
Mansi, c.14: ibid.

16. Ex decreto Pelagii pape.
Invenimus decem prefationes . . . adiicere.
Mansi, c.15.

17. Ex decretis Julii pape.
Prohibemus ne quis, quasi . . . signaret.
Mansi, c.16: Inhibemus ne *etc.*

18. Ex concilio Remensi.
Precipimus ne consecretur . . . . interdicimus.
Mansi, c.17.

19. Ex decreto Hormisde (*MS.:* Ormisde) pape.
Nullus fidelis cuiuscunque . . . . suspendatur.
Mansi, c.18.

20. Ex decreto Nicholai pape.
Ubi non est consensus . . . . toleretur.
Mansi, c.19.

21. Ex concilio Spanensi. *F.133v.*
(U)t unicuique ecclesie mansus integre . . ecclesiasticum.
Cf. MGH., Capitularia, 1, p. 277, sub annis 818–9, cap. 10; and ibid., p. 407: Ansegisi cap. 85.

Part IV

1. Alexander papa III Cantuariensi archiepiscopo et eius suffra-
ganeis, salutem et apostolicam benedictionem.
Ex crebris querimoniis . . . . nihil inde.
J-L 13814: 1159–81.

2. Alexander papa III Cantuariensi archiepiscopo, salutem et
apostolicam benedictionem. *F.134r.*
Ad hoc, in beatorum . . . . compellas.
  (a) Ad hoc, in beatorum . . . exequaris.
  (b) Preterea, de his qui . . . . compellas.
Dat.Ferent. X Kal.Aprilis.
J-L 12448 and 14314: 23 March 1175.

3. Alexander episcopus Cantuariensi (archiepiscopo) et eius
suffraganeis.

Pervenit ad nos, quod   .   .   .   . persolvant.
J-L 13821: 1159–81.

4. Alexander papa III dilectis filiis abbatibus (et) fratribus
monasteriorum Cisterciensis ordinis, qui sunt in Anglia con-
stitutis, salutem et apostolicam benedictionem.
Relatum est auribus   .   .   .   . sinistri.
Dat.Ferent.
J-L 12412: 1161–75.

5. Alexander papa III Thome Cantuariensi archiepiscopo.   *F.134v.*
Commisse nobis a Deo   .   .   .   . persolvi.
J-L 11660: 1162–70.

6. Idem monachis Sancte Marie de Laurentio
Audivimus quod decimas .   .   .   . observaturi.
J-L 13978: 1159–81.

7. Idem abbati et fratribus de Neubothe.
Dilecti filii nostri   .   .   .   .   . extendere.
*J-L 14023: 1159–81. Addressed to the Cistercian house at New-
battle in Scotland.*

8. Alexander episcopus servus servorum Dei dilectis filiis univer-
sis monachis et canonicis regularibus per Cantuariensem
provinciam constitutis, salutem et apostolicam benedictionem. *F.135r.*
Cum deceat nos   .   .   .   .   . respondere.
Datum.
J-L 13829: 1159–81.

9. (Alexander III) abbati et monachis Sancti Andree.
Si de terra quam habetis   .   .   .   . surripiendis.
Val(ete).
J-L 13739: 1159–81.

COMPARATIVE TABLE

COLLATING THE BELVOIR, WORCESTER II, CANTERBURY AND
ROCHESTER COLLECTIONS

	Belver.	Wig.Alt.	Cantuar.	Roff.
Part I				
1–8: Canons of the Council of Tours, 1163.				
	9a-b.I-III	2, 3a	II.4	–
	10	{ 4a-c	I.22a-m	112a-l
		{ 5a-c		
	11a-c.I-VII	10a-c.I-VII	–	–
	12a-l	1a-b	I.23	48
	13	6	–	–
	14a-d	7a-b	III.6.I-v	–
	15	8	I.51	64
	16	9	–	–
	17	–	III.3	–
	18a-b	12	I.41a-e	42a-d

M

	Belver.	Wig.Alt.	Cantuar.	Roff.
Part II				
	1	–	I.15	92
	2	–	–	–
	3	–	–	–
	4a-c	–	I.37a-c	111a-c
	5	–	–	–
	6	–	–	–
	7	–	–	–
	8	–	–	–
	9	–	–	–

Part III
Canons of the Council of Westminster, 1175.

	Belver.	Wig.Alt.	Cantuar.	Roff.
Part IV				
	1	–	I.11	33
	2a-b	–	I.1a-b	76
	3	–	I.13	56
	4	–	I.8	35
	5	–	–	–
	6	–	–	–
	7	–	–	131
	8	–	I.7	28
	9	–	I.62	50

III

Cantuariensis: The Canterbury Collection

British Museum Royal MS. 10 B. IV, fols. 42–65v

in Holtzmann - Cheney
fols. 42-57v: 1 Cant
58r - v 2 Cant
59v-61v. 3 Cant

ANALYSIS

PART I

1. Alexander papa III R(icardo) Cantuariensi archiepiscopo.   *F.42v.*
   Ad hoc, in beatorum   .   .   .   . compellas.
      (a) Ad hoc, in beatorum   .   .   . exequaris
      (b) Preterea, de his   .   .   .   . compellas.
   J-L 12448 and 14314: 23 March 1175.

2. Alexander papa III Wigorniensi episcopo.   *F.43r.*
   Archidiaconis de ecclesiastica   .   .   . promulgare.
   J-L 13166: 1164-79.

3. (Alexander III Cantuariensi archiepiscopo.)
   Ex parte venerabilis fratris   .   .   . compellas.
   Dat. Ferent. XVII Kal.Aug.
   J-L 14317: 16 July 1174-81.

4. Idem ad eundem et suffraganeos eius.
   Ex frequentibus querelis . . . . presumatis.
   J-L 13817: 1174–81.

5. Idem ad eundem et suffraganeos eius. *F.43v.*
   Sicut ad extirpanda . . . . compellatis.
   J-L 13813: 1174–81.

6. Idem universis fratribus et sororibus monasteriorum et ecclesiarum regularium, que sunt in provincia Cant(uariensi) constitute, prelatorum provisione carentibus. *F.44r.*
   Cum ex defectu pastorum . . . compellat.
   Not in J-L: 1174–81; Lohmann, loc. cit., p. 95.

7. Idem universis monachis et canonicis regularibus per Cantuariensem provinciam constitutis.
   Cum deceat nos . . . . . respondere.
   J-L 13829: 1159–81.

8. Idem abbatibus et fratribus monasteriorum Cisterciensis (*MS.*: Cistern.) ordinis, qui sunt in Anglia constituti.
   Relatum est auribus nostris . . . sinistri.
   J-L 12412: 1161–75.

9. (Cantuariensi archiepiscopo et eius suffraganeis.) *F.44v.*
   Viris ecclesiasticis . . . . . extorquere.
   Not in J-L. Cf. Cantuar. I. 32; Lohmann, loc. cit., p. 114.

10. Idem Cantuariensi archiepiscopo et suffraganeis eius.
    Indecorum est admodum . . . . puniemus.
    J-L 13820: 1159–81.

11. Idem Cantuariensi (archiepiscopo) et suffraganeis eius.
    Ex crebris querimoniis . . . . compellatis.
    J-L 13814: 1159–81.

12. Idem eisdem.
    Cum vos plerumque . . . . reservare.
    J-L 13822: 1159–81.

13. Idem eisdem. *F.45r.*
    Pervenit ad nos quod, cum . . . persolvant.
    J-L 13821: 1159–81.
    Cf. Roff. 56: Londoniensi et Wigorniensi episcopis.

14. Eugenius papa Jocel(ino) episcopo Saresberiensi.
    Clerici, qui relicto habitu . . . . generari.
    J-L 8959: 26 Nov. 1146; cf. Berol. 57.

15. Idem Lundoniensi episcopo.
    Accepimus, quod plerique . . . poteris.
    J-L 14267: 1 March 1171–81.

16. Idem B(artholomeo) Exoniensi episcopo.
    Ex presentium latoris . . . . cohercere.
    J-L 13911: 1162–81.

17. Idem Wigorniensi et Exoniensi episcopis.   *F.45v.*
   Cum Simon clericus   .   .   .   . continere.
   J-L 13924: 1164–79.

18. Idem episcopo Wigorniensi et abbati de Evesham.
   Cum aliquibus adiudicata .   .   .   . corporali.
   J-L 14035: 1164–79. Cf. Cantuar. III. 7.

19. Alexander papa III J(ohanni) Norwicensi episcopo.
   Rediens ad nos Wi(llelmus)   .   . adherere.
   J-L 13902 and 14159: 1176–81.

20. Alexander papa III Wintoniensi episcopo.
   Quamvis simus negotiorum   .   . dampnandus.
      (a) Quamvis simus negotiorum .   . potest.
      (b) Porro, si aliquis   .   .   . puniri.
      (c) Super eo vero, quod .   .   . respondendum.
      (d) Quod si questio   .   .   . disponat.
      (e) Ceterum, si aliquis   .   . firmitatem.
      (f) Si vero in secundis   .   . debet.
      (g) Quemlibet autem   .   . consuevit.
      (h) Sententiam vero   .   . irritanda.
      (i) Ad hec, si persona   .   . dampnandus.
   Dat. Venet. in Rivo Alto XII Kal.Augusti.
   J-L 14152, 14154 and 14156: 21 July 1177.

21. Idem episcopo Lundoniensi.   *F.46v.*
   Cum tibi sit de benignitate   .   . terminandam.
   J-L 13991: 1159–81.

22. Alexander III Wigorniensi episcopo.
   Super eo, quod a nobis   .   .   . expirasse.
      (a) Super eo, quod   .   .   . supersedeatur.
      (b) Si autem adversa   .   .   . inhibeatur.
      (c) De appellationibus   .   .   . deferendum.
      (d) Quod si aliquis   .   .   . iniungenda.
      (e) Verum si appellantes   .   . compellas.
      (f) Ceterum, si abbatem   .   . iudicandum.
      (g) Verum, cum alicui .   .   . habere.
      (h) Meminimus nos ex parte   .   . rescindere.
      (i) Nemo monachos autem   .   . respondere.
      (k) Preterea, illi qui episcopo   .   . efficere.
      (l) Ceterum, cum aliquam   .   . observandum.
      (m) Si lis infra certum terminum   .   . expirasse.
   J-L 13162: 1164–79.

23. Idem W(illelmo) Norwicensi episcopo. (*Correctly:* Bartholomeo
   Exoniensi episcopo.)   *F.47v.*
   Sicut dignum est et omni consentaneum .   . immunis.
      (a) Sicut dignum est   .   .   . respondemus.
      (b) Quod si clerici infra   .   . immunis.

J-L 12180 and 13771: 31 January 1171–2.
Cf. Wig.Altera 1 and Belver. I. 12.

24. Idem B(artholomeo) Exoniensi (episcopo) et abbati (For-
densi).   *F.48v.*
Lator presentium R.   .   .   .   . decidat.
J-L 14218: 1162–81, Wigorn. VII. 26; Lohmann, loc. cit., p. 129.

25. R. Circel' episcopo.   *F.49r.*
Veniens P. lator presentium   .   .   . promovendum.
*J-L 13988: 1159–66. Corrupt inscription; addressed elsewhere to
Lincoln or Langres.*

26. Celestinus papa Florentine ecclesie.
Videtur nobis quod secunda   .   .   . recipiuntur.
    (a) Videtur nobis   .   .   .   . assumere.
    (b) Quod autem parentes   .   .   . recipiuntur.
*Uncertain origin: see J-K 384 (422–32); J-L 4920 (Gregory VII,
5 January 1075); Decretum Gratiani: Palea ad c. XXXV, qu. 6, c.2;
Gregorian Decretales, IV. 18, 3.*

27. Alexander papa III B(artholomeo) Exoniensi episcopo.   *F.49v.*
Significatum est nobis   .   .   .   . cogendi.
J-L 13094: 1162–81.

28. Idem eidem.
Super hoc, quod a nobis   .   .   .   . coniungant.
J-L 13903, 13907 and 13916: 1162–81.

29. Idem ad eundem.   *F.50r.*
Venit ad audientiam nostram   .   .   . terminare.
J-L 14214: 1162–81.

30. Idem (Rotomagensi archiepiscopo et abbati Gemetrensi).
Ex certa quorundam relatione   .   .   . parere.
J-L 14087: 1165–81. Cf. Cantuar. II. 2.

31. (Alexander III Bartholomeo Exoniensi episcopo.)
Ex presentium latoris confessione .   .   . procedas.
J-L 13900: 1162–81.

32. (Alexander III Cantuariensi archiepiscopo et eius suffra-
ganeis.)
Viris ecclesiasticis   .   .   .   .   . extorquere.
Cf. Cantuar. I. 9; Wig. IV. 34, 1159–81.

33. (Alexander III Cantuariensi archiepiscopo.)
Cum teneamur singulorum   .   .   . licebit.
J-L 13809: 1159–81.

34. (Alexander III Cantuariensi archiepiscopo et eius suffra-
ganeis.)
Relatum est auribus nostris   .   .   . incurrant.
J-L 13823: 1159–81. Cf. Cantuar. II. 3.

35. (Alexander III Cantuariensi archiepiscopo et eius suffra-
    ganeis.)   *F.51r.*
    Pervenit ad nos, quod   .   .   .   . astringatis.
    J-L 13794: 1159–81.

36. (Alexander III Herefordensi episcopo.)
    Intelleximus ex parte tue fraternitatis   .   . procedas.
    J-L 13950: 1159–81.

37. (Alexander III Simoni abbati Sancti Albani.)
    Quesitum est siquidem   .   .   .   . spoliari.
      (a) Quesitum est   .   .   .   . prorogare.
      (b) De cetero, si aliquis   removeri.
      (c) Donationes vero   .   .   .   . spoliari.
    J-L 12636: 8 April 1173–6. Cf. Belver. II. 4.

38. (Alexander III Eboracensi archiepiscopo.)   *F.51v.*
    Inter ceteras consultationes   .   .   . ordinare.
      (a) Inter ceteras .   .   .   .   . impediri.
      (b) De cetero, cum aliqua   .   .   . iniquitatem.
      (c) Ad hec, cum laici   .   .   .   . ordinare.
    J-L 13878 and 14346: 1179–81; Wig. VII. 40 and 49.

39. Alexander papa III Ric(ardo) Cantuariensi archiepiscopo. *F.52r.*
    Pervenit ad nos quod, cum presbiteri   .   . representent.
    J-L 14313: 1174–81.

40. Idem episcopo Exoniensi.
    In litteris, quas tua nobis .   .   .   . aboletur.
      (a) In litteris, quas   .   .   .   . functus.
      (b) Super videlicet quidem   .   .   . restituendus.
      (c) Item, si quis rei   .   .   .   . diffinire.
      (d) Item, cum quis dicit   .   .   . existere.
      (e) Ad hec, cum aliquis   .   .   . stare.
      (f) Preterea, licet ad personatum   .   . recipere.
      (g) De his sane, qui   .   .   .   . aboletur.
    J-L 13921, 13915 and 14219: 1177.

41. Alexander (III) papa abbati Ram(esie).   *F.52v.*
    Sicut Romana ecclesia   .   .   .   . ministrare.
      (a) Sicut Romana   .   .   .   . generali.
      (b) Super eo vero, quod .   .   .   . deferendum.
      (c) Si autem infra certum   .   .   . suscepisse.
      (d) Preterea, super hoc   .   .   . potestatem.
      (e) Si vero aliquis   .   .   .   . ministrare.
    J-L 12293: 1159–81. Cf. Wig. V. 9: Senonensi archiepiscopo;
    Wig. Altera 12 and Belver I. 18: Eboracensi archiepiscopo;
    2 June 1173–4.

42. Alexander papa III Remensi archiepiscopo.   *F.53r.*
    Cum sacrosancta Romana   .   .   . credimus.
      (a) Cum sacrosancta   .   .   . excommunicavit.

(b) Ad hec, si in una . . . . ordinarius sit.
(c) Item, si duobus . . . . appellasse.
(d) Denique, quod in fine . . . credimus.
J-L 12020: 22 March 1171–2.

43. Alexander papa III B(artholomeo) Exoniensi episcopo. *F.53v.*
Meminimus fraternitati tue . . . potuerunt.
J-L 13917: 1162–81.

44. Idem ad eundem.
Veniens ad nos R. lator . . . . iniungas.
J-L 14215: 1162–81.

45. Eidem *F.54r.*
Ad aures nostras perlatum esse . . . revoces.
Not in J-L. Cf. Wig. IV. 17 and Claud. 21.

46. Idem Rotom(agensi) archiepiscopo et Ambianensi episcopo. *F.54r.*
Sane si his exequendis . . . . exequatur.
Uncertain origin; common-form conclusion of commission to judges delegate. Cf. Cantuar. I. 49.

47. Idem Wigorniensi (episcopo).
Licet nuntius Hugonis . . . . temptetis.
J-L 14143: 1159–81.

48. Idem Exoniensi (episcopo).
Suggestum est auribus nostris . . . ammovere.
J-L 13913: 1162–81.

49. Alexander episcopus servus servorum Dei venerabili fratri J(ohanni) episcopo et dilecto filio T. archidiacono Norwicensi, salutem et apostolicam benedictionem. *F.54v.*
Querelam R. nobilis . . . . exequatur.
Not in J-L. Cf. Claustr. 320: 1175–81.

50. Idem R(icardo) archiepiscopo (*MS.*: archid.) Cantuariensi et episcopo Cicestrensi. *F.54v.*
Retulit nobis A. presbiter . . . . terminare.
(a) Retulit nobis . . . . potest.
(b) Quia vero sollicitudini . . . terminare.
J-L 13824: 1174–81.

51. Alexander papa III G(aufrido) Lincolnensi electo. *F.55r.*
Ad presentiam nostram . . . . ammoveas.
J-L 13982: c. 1173. Cf. Wig.Altera 8.

52. Alexander papa III Roberto Foliot episcopo Herefordensi.
Super eo quesitum fuit . . . . standi.
(a) Super eo quesitum . . . . venerunt.
(b) Sane super eo quod . . . . ordinare.
(c) Quesisti etiam utrum . . . promittat.
(d) Ad hec, cum contingat . . . standi.
J-L 13946, 13948 and 13949: October 1174–81.

53. (Alexander III abbatibus sancti Albani et Leicestrie.)
Cum episcopus quidam . . . . restituatis.
J-L 13729. Cf. Roff 58: 1159–81.

54. Idem Lundoniensi G(ilberto) et R(ogerio) Wigorniensi
episcopis. *F.55v.*
Pervenit ad nos ex parte . . . . imponere.
J-L 13160. Cf. Roff. 53: 1164–79.

55. Idem Wigorniensi (episcopo) et abbati Sancti Albani. *F.56r.*
Quia Will(elmus), qui violenter . . . iudicaretur.
J-L 14140: 1159–81.

56. Idem archiepiscopo Salernitano.
Licet preter solitum . . . . incurrit.
   (a) Licet preter . . . . . remanere.
   (b) Utrum autem filii . . . . intercedit.
   (c) Si vero vir . . . . patrocinari.
   (d) De cetero, laicos . . . . admitti.
   (e) Et si clerici . . . . videtur.
   (f) Si vero coram . . . . removendi.
   (g) De adulteriis et aliis . . . conterere.
   (h) Porro, si clericus . . . . subsecuta.
   (i) In causis vero ecclesiasticis . . . disputari.
   (k) De quarta vero decime . . . admittit.
   (l) De presbitero autem . . . . extitisset.
   (m) Presbiterum autem . . . . incurrit.
J-L 14091: 1174–6.

57. Idem Cantuariensi (archiepiscopo) et Wigorniensi (episcopo.) *F.57r.*
Precipimus ut N(icholao) ecclesia . . ammoveri.
J-L 13825: 1159–81.

58. Alexander papa III Sagiensi (episcopo).
Insinuatum est auribus . . . . formidare.
*Not in J-L. Cf. Roff. 30; Wig. IV. 14: Salesburiensi episcopo.
1159–81.*

59. (Alexander III Cantuariensi archiepiscopo et eius suffraganeis.)
Cum clerici vestre iurisdictionis . . . reportare.
   (a) Cum clerici . . . . . puniatis.
   (b) Ad hec, quia sunt . . . . reportare.
J-L 13816: 1159–81. Cf. Wig. IV. 30; Lohmann, loc. cit., p. 114.

60. Alexander papa III Placentino episcopo. *F.57v.*
Fraternitatis tue nos . . . . iuramentis.
J-L 14066: 1159–81.

61. Wigorniensi episcopo.
Causam, que vertitur inter fratres . . suscitare.
*J-L 13166: 1159–81; Wig. II. 11: Wigorniensi episcopo et
abbati de Evesham.*

62. Abbati et monachis sancti Andree.
Si de terra, quam habetis . . . . surripiendas.
J-L 13739: 1159–81.

PART II

1. (Alexander III Johanni Carnotensi episcopo.) *F.58r.*
   Cum sacrosancta Romana ecclesia . . celebrantur.
   (a) Cum sacrosancta . . . . supponat. ~~incl.~~ JL 1383S
   (b) De testibus . . . . . delictum. JL 1383S
   (c) Questioni vero, quam . . . observari. JL 1383S
   (d) Super eo autem, quod . . . violentas.
   (e) De his autem, qui . . . . probatur. incl. JL 13768 (*Mulieres*) *vel*
   (f) Item, quia quesitum . . . . cohercere. JL 13770
   (g) Terminum vero cause . . . coartare.
   (h) Subdiaconos autem . . . . habeant. JL 13769
   (i) Sabbato vero pentecostes . . . celebrantur.
   J-L 13768, 13769, 13770 and 13835: 1176–80.

   [margin annotations: L. Carnot. or Cantuar. { (a)(b)(c)(d); ep Bath (e); ep Bath or BaitEx (f); ep Bath (h)]

2. Alexander episcopus servus servorum Dei dilectis filiis B.
   (*Correctly:* Rotrudo) Rotomagensi archiepiscopo et R. abbati
   Gemetrensi (*MS.*: Gemecensi), salutem. *F.58v.*
   Ex certa quorundam . . . . equitati.
   Cf. Cantuar. I. 30: J-L 14087, 1165–81.

3. Cantuariensi archiepiscopo et eius suffraganeis.
   Relatum est auribus nostris . . . compellatis.
   Cf. Cantuar. I. 34: J-L 13823, 1159–81.

4. (Alexander III Wigorniensi episcopo.)
   Presentium (*MS.*: Presertim) auctoritate . . spoliare.
   *J-L 12254: 26 November 1164. Cf. Wig.Altera 2 and 3; Wig. II.
   8n–o, Lohmann, loc. cit., pp. 91–2.*

5. Lucensi episcopo.
   Consuluit nos tua discretio . . . dissolvit.
   J-L 14005: 1159–81.

PART III

1. Alexander III Bathoniensi episcopo. *F.59v.*
   De illis, qui infra annos . . . . negavit.
   J-L 13767: 1159–81.

2. (Alexander III Eboracensi archiepiscopo.) *F.60r.*
   Ea que honestatis . . . . . decernas.
   J-L 15171: 1159–81.

3. Idem Exoniensi (*MS.*: ex m̄) episcopo.
   Robertus de Ber (*MS.*: deber) nobis intimavit . postponatis.
   J-L 13930=14228: 1162–81.

4. Idem abbati Rivallensi et decano (*MS*.: Nec.) et archidiacono Lincolnensi.
   Dilecti filii nostri decanus . . . . noscuntur.
   J-L 14085: 1159–81.

5. Idem abbatibus, prioribus et aliis ecclesiasticis viris per Eboracensem archiepiscopatum constitutis.
   Cura pastorali constringimur . . . censemus.
   J-L 13893: 1159–81.

6. (Alexander III Willelmo Norwicensi episcopo.) *F.6or.*
   Ex tenore litterarum . . . . mandatum.
   J-L 12253 and 14146: 1159–17 January 1174.

7. Idem R(ogerio) Wigorniensi episcopo et abbati de Evesham. *F.6ov.*
   Scripsimus vobis ad suggestionem . . imponatis.
   J-L 14035: 1164–79. Cf. Cantuar. I. 18.

8. Idem Wigorniensi episcopo.
   Nosti sicut vir prudens . . . . revocare.
   J-L 12753: 1176.

9. (Alexander III Astionensi electo *or* abbati Sancti Albani.)
   Singulorum consultationibus . . . reportare.
   J-L 12636; cf. Wig. I. 15: 1159–81.

10. Idem R(icardo) Coventrensi episcopo.
    Querelam A. Panthus . . . . exequatur.
    Not in J-L. Cf. Wig. V. 2; Lohmann, loc. cit., p. 119, 1160–81.

11. (Alexander III Lincolnensi episcopo.)
    Ex insinuatione prioris et fratrum . . restituas.
    Not in J-L. Cf. Claustr. 133 and Chelt. MS., fol. 67r. 1159–66.

12. Idem T(home) Cantuariensi archiepiscopo. *F.6ir.*
    Helias iste ad nostram presentiam . . removeas.
    Not in J-L. Cf. Abrinc. II. 15.1 and Chelt. MS., fol. 9or. 1159–70.

13. Idem Wigorniensi episcopo.
    Abbas Sancti Edmundi . . . . restituas.
    J-L 14131: 1159–81.

14. Maioribus ecclesie beneficiis . . . prohibemus.
    Tours, 1163: Mansi, c.1.

15. Idem Saresberiensi (*MS*.: Sareb.) et Exoniensi episcopis.
    Suggestum est quod J. . . . . existat.
    J-L 14097: 1162–81.

16. Idem. *F.6ir.*
    Cum olim E. ad presentiam . . . astrictum.
    Not in J-L. Cf. Sang. VI. 1.22 and VI. 15.3: 1159–81.

17. Idem Urbanus papa. (*Correctly:* Eugenius III.)
    Quotiens aliqui separantur . . . et ita esse.
    J-L 9657: 1145–53. Cf. Font. MS., fol. 37v: Wigorniensi episcopo.

18. Alexander (III) G(ilberto) Londoniensi episcopo.   *F.61v.*
    Cum H. de Dive   .   .   .   .   . compellas.
    Not in J-L. Wig. VI. 4 and Abrinc. II. 7.4: 1163–81.

19. Idem abbati Rivallensi et priori de Bridlingt(on).
    Dilecti filii nostri abbas   .   .   .   . procedatis.
    Not in J-L. Cf. Wig. VII. 38; Lohmann, loc. cit., pp. 135–6. 1159–81.

20. Idem.
    Sicut ex tuarum tenore litterarum   .   . postponat.
    Unidentified chapter: 1159–81.

21. Alexander III Treverensi episcopo.
    Litteras tue (*MS.*: sue) fraternitati   .   . permittas.
    J-L 13947: 1159–81. Cf. Regal. MS., fol. 108r, and elsewhere:
    Herefordensi episcopo.

22. Alexander III Vigiliensi episcopo.
    Cum sancta Romana ecclesia. Si vero puella   . audiendi.
    J-L 14126: 1159–81.

PART IV

Canons of the Third Lateran Council, 1179.   *F.62r-65r.*

COMPARATIVE TABLE
COLLATING THE CANTERBURY, ROCHESTER, WORCESTER II AND BELVOIR COLLECTIONS

	Cantuar.	Roff.	Wig.Alt.	Belver.
Part I				
	1a-b	76	–	IV.2a-b
cf. I.61	2	67	–	–
	3	55	–	–
	4	34	–	–
	5	93	–	–
	6	–	–	–
	7	28	–	IV.8
	8	35	–	IV.4
cf. I.32	9	77	–	–
	10	29	–	–
	11	33	–	IV.1a-b
	12	27	–	–
	13	56	–	IV.3
	14	78	–	–
	15	92	–	II.1
	16	36	–	–
	17	–	–	–
cf. III.7	18	69	–	–
	19	101	–	–

	Cantuar.	Roff.	Wig.Alt.	Belver.
	20a-i	37a-g	–	–
	21	39	–	–
	22a-m	112a-l	{ 4a-c 5a-c	I.10a-c
	23	48, 79	1a-b	I.12a-l
	24	–	–	–
	25	–	–	–
	26a-b	94a-b	–	–
	27	90	–	–
	28.i-iii	95a-b	–	–
	29	96	–	–
cf. II.2	30	52	–	–
	31	97	–	–
cf. I.9	32	77	–	–
	33	65	–	–
cf. II.3	34	74	–	–
	35	68	–	–
	36	41	–	–
	37a-c	111a-c	–	II.4
	38a-c	40a-d	–	–
	39	–	–	–
	40a-h	38a-g	–	–
	41a-e	42a-d	12	I.18a-b.1-vi
	42a-d	46a-d	11	–
	43	–	–	–
	44	–	–	–
	45	73	–	–
cf. I.49	46	100.ii	–	–
	47	44, 61	–	–
	48	62	–	–
cf. I.46	49	100.i	–	–
	50a-b	63	–	–
	51	64	8	I.15
	52a-d	47a-c	–	–
	53	58	–	–
	54	53	–	–
	55	57	–	–
	56	{ 88, 89a-l	–	–
	57	54	–	–
	58	30	–	–
	59a-b	32	–	–
	60	51	–	–
cf. I.2	61	67	–	–
	62	50	–	IV.9

		Cantuar.	Roff.	Wig.Alt.	Belver.
Part II					
	1a-i		123, 81	–	–
cf. I.30	2		52	–	–
cf. I.34	3		74	–	–
	4		–	3	I.9
	5		108.1	–	–
Part III					
	1		(103)	–	–
	2		–	–	–
	3		–	–	I.17
	4		–	–	–
	5		–	–	–
	6.i-v		–	7a-b	I.14a-d
cf. I.18	7		69	–	–
	8		–	–	–
	9		98	–	–
	10		–	–	–
	11		–	–	–
	12		–	–	–
	13		–	–	–
	14		–	–	I.6
	15		–	–	–
	16		–	–	–
	17		–	–	–
	18		–	–	–
	19		117	–	–
	20		–	–	–
	21		–	--	–
	22		84c	–	--

Part IV
Canons of the Third Lateran Council, 1179.

IV

Roffensis: The Rochester Collection
British Museum Royal MS. 10 C. iv, fols. 137v–154

ANALYSIS

28. Idem monachis et canonicis (regularibus per Cantuariensem provinciam constitutis).
Cum deceat nos . . . . . respondere.
J-L 13829: 1159–81.

29. Idem archiepiscopo Cantuariensi et suffraganeis eius. *F.140r.*
Indecorum est admodum . . . . puniemus.
J-L 13820: 1159–81.

30. Idem episcopo Sagiensi.
Insinuatum est auribus nostris . . . formidare.
Not in J-L. Cf. Cantuar. I. 58. 1159–81.

31. Idem Exoniensi et Wintoniensi episcopis.
Significavit nobis D. presbiter . . . impetratis.
J-L 14224: 1164–79. Cf. Claud. 90: Exoniensi et Wigorniensi episcopis.

32. Idem archiepiscopo Cantuariensi et suffraganeis eius.
Cum clerici vestre iurisdictionis . . . reportare.
J-L 13816: 1159–81.

33. Idem eidem et suffraganeis.
Ex crebris querimoniis . . . . compellatis.
J-L 13814: 1159–81.

34. Idem archiepiscopo Cantuariensi et suffraganeis. (*MS.:* archiepiscopo et suffraganeis Cantu')
Ex frequentibus querelis . . . . presumatis.
J-L 13817: 1174–81.

35. Idem abbatibus et fratribus monasteriorum Cisterciensis ordinis, qui sunt in Anglia constituti. *F.140v.*
Relatum est auribus nostris . . . sinistri.
J-L 12412: 1161–75.

36. Idem B(artholomeo) Exoniensi episcopo.
Ex presentium latoris insinuatione . . cohercere.
J-L 13911: 1162–81.

37. Idem episcopo Wintoniensi.
Quamvis simus multiplicitate . . . dampnandus.
    (a) Quamvis simus . . . . potest.
    (b) Porro, si aliquis . . . . puniri.
    (c) Super eo vero, quod a nobis . . debet.
    (d) Quemlibet autem . . . . consuevit.
    (e) Sententiam vero . . . . potestatem.
    (f) Si vero ius patronatus . . . irritanda.
    (g) Ad hec, si persona . . . . dampnandus.
J-L 14152, 14154 and 14156: 21 July 1177.

38. Idem episcopo Luxoviensi. *F.141r.*
In litteris, quas tua nobis . . . . aboletur.
    (a) In litteris, quas tua . . . . functus.

(b) Super videlicet questione . . . restituendus.
(c) Item, si quis rei . . . . diffinire.
(d) Item, cum quis dicit . . . existere.
(e) Ad hec, cum aliquis . . . stare.
(f) Preterea, licet ad personatum . . recipere.
(g) De his sane, qui . . . . aboletur.
J-L 13915, 13921 and 14219: 1162–81. Elsewhere: Exoniensi.

39. Idem episcopo Lundoniensi.
Cum tibi sit de benignitate . . . terminandam.
J-L 13991: 1159–81.

40. Idem archiepiscopo Eboracensi.
Inter ceteras consultationes . . . ordinare.
(a) Inter ceteras . . . . . decernere.
(b) Sane, si a nobis . . . . impediri.
(c) De cetero, cum aliqua causa . . iniquitatem.
(d) Ad hec, cum laici . . . . ordinare.
J-L 13878 and 14346: 1179–81.

41. Idem episcopo Herefordensi. *F.141v.*
Intelleximus ex parte . . . . procedas.
J-L 13950: 1159–81.

42. Idem abbati Ramesiensi.
Sicut Romana ecclesia . . . . ministrare.
(a) I. Sicut Romana . . . . declarare.
II. Sane, quesitum est a nobis . . generali.
(b) Super eo vero, quod interdum . . deferendum.
(c) Si autem infra certum . . . suscepisse.
(d) Preterea, super hoc . . . ministrare.
J-L 12293 and 13874. Cf. Cantuar. I. 41.

43. Idem episcopo Wigorniensi.
Sollicite cures et diligenter . . . differas.
J-L 14139: 1159–81.

44. Idem Wigorniensi episcopo.
Audita querela . . . . . iuramentum.
J-L 14143: 1159–81. Cf. Roff. 61 and Cantuar. I. 47.

45. Idem archiepiscopo (*MS.*: episcopo) Eboracensi. *F.142r.*
In eminenti specula. . . . . conferri.
J-L 14350: 1179–81.

46. Idem Remensi archiepiscopo. *F.142v.*
Cum sacrosancta Romana ecclesia . . credimus.
(a) Cum sacrosancta . . . . excommunicavit.
(b) Ad hoc, si in una causa . . . sit.
(c) Item, si duobus . . . . appellasse.
(d) Denique quod in fine . . . credimus.
J-L 12020: 22 March 1171–2.

47. Herefordensi episcopo.
    Super eo, quod quesitum fuit . . . standi.
       (a) Super eo, quod . . . . venerunt.
       (b) Sane super eo, quod . . . . ordinare.
       (c) Quesisti etiam utrum . . . standi.
    J-L 13946, 13948 and 13949: October 1174–81.

48. Idem Exoniensi episcopo.   *F.143r.*
    Sicut dignum est . . . . . immunis.
    J-L 12180: 31 January 1171–2. Cf. Wig.Altera 1.

49. Idem Siracus(ensi) episcopo.   *F.143v.*
    Cum sint homines in tua . . . . prescriptio.
    J-L 14012: 1159–81.

50. Abbati et monachis Sancte Andree.
    Si de terra, quam habetis . . . . surripiendas.
    J-L 13739: 1159–81.

51. Idem Placentino episcopo.
    Fraternitatis tue nos . . . . iuramentis.
    J-L 14066: 1159–81.

52. (Alexander III Rotrudo Rotomagensi archiepiscopo et abbati
    Gemetrensi.)   *F.144r.*
    Ex certa quorundam relatione . . . parere.
    J-L 14087: 1165–81.

53. Idem G(ilberto) Lundoniensi et R(ogerio) Wigorniensi epis-
    copis.
    Pervenit ad nos ex parte R. . . . imponere.
    J-L 13160. Cf. Cantuar. I. 54: 1164–79.

54. (Alexander III Cantuariensi archiepiscopo et Wigorniensi
    episcopo.)
    Precipimus ut N. ecclesia . . . . amoveri.
    J-L 13825: 1159–81.

55. Idem Cantuariensi archiepiscopo. (*MS.*: arch'e epo.)
    Ex parte venerabilis fratris . . . compellas.
    J-L 14317: 16 July 1174–81.

56. Idem Lundoniensi et Wigorniensi episcopis.
    Pervenit ad nos, quod . . . . persolvant.
    J-L 13821: 1159–81. Cf. Cantuar. I. 13: Cantuariensi archi-
    episcopo et suffraganeis eius.

57. Idem Wigorniensi (episcopo) et abbati Sancti Albani.
    Quia Willelmus, qui . . . . iudicaretur.
    J-L 14140: 1159–81.

58. Idem abbatibus Sancti Albani et Leicestrie. (*MS.*: Leirt.)
    Cum episcopus quidam . . . . restituatis.
    J-L 13729. Cf. Cantuar. I. 53: 1159–81.

59. Idem Dunelmensi (*MS.*: Dunholm'si) episcopo.
Contingit interdum . . . . removeri.
J-L 13868: 1159–81. Cf. Wig. II. 29.

60. Idem Wigorniensi episcopo. *F.144v.*
Causam, que inter Francum . . . procedatis.
J-L 13932: 1159 81.

61. Idem Wigorniensi (episcopo).
Licet nuntius Hugonis . . . . temptetis.
J-L 14143: 1159–81. Cf. Roff. 44.

62. Idem Exoniensi episcopo.
Suggestum est auribus nostris . . . amovere.
J-L 13913: 1162–81.

63. Idem R(icardo) archiepiscopo Cantuariensi et episcopo
Cicestrensi.
Retulit nobis A. . . . . . terminare.
J-L 13824: 1174–81.

64. G(aufrido) Lincolnensi (*MS.*: Lincoll.) archidiacono.
Ad presentiam nostram accedens . . . amoveas.
J-L 13982: c.1173. Cf. Wig.Altera 8.

65. Idem archiepiscopo Cantuariensi.
Cum teneamur singulorum . . . licebit.
J-L 13809: 1159–81.

66. Idem Norwicensi episcopo. *F.145r.*
Significasti nobis . . . . . admittende.
J-L 14027: 1159–81. Cf. J-L 13920 and 14234; Wig. VII. 52.

67. Idem Wigorniensi episcopo.
Causam, que vertitur . . . . suscitare.
J-L 13166: 1164–79.

68. Idem Cantuariensi (archiepiscopo) et eius suffraganeis.
Pervenit ad nos, quod . . . . astringatis.
J-L 13794: 1159–81.

69. Idem episcopo Wigorniensi et abbati de Evesham.
Cum aliquibus adiudicata . . . . corporali.
J-L 14035: 1164–79.

70. Multorum experimenta morborum . . dubitamus.
    (a) Multorum experimenta . . . mandato.
    (b) Quia vero ecclesie per Angliam . . requirantur.
    (c) Preterea, statuimus . . . . suspendatur.
    (d) Sanctorum patrum vestigia . . . exheredare.
    (e) Prava nimis et sanctorum . . . prohibemus.
    (f) Nichilominus et presentis . . . subiciantur.
    (g) Hoc quoque presentis . . . dubitamus.
Theobald's Council, 1151; cf. Mansi, XXI, cols. 749–52.

N

71. R(icardo) archiepiscopo Cantuariensi.   *F.145v.*
    Cum te consulente .   .   .   .   . teneris.
    J-L 13976: 1174–81. Cf. Wig. VII. 35.

72. Wintoniensi episcopo.
    Causam principalem, que inter Jordanum   . mulctari.
    Not in J-L. Cf. Wig. VII. 25, Claustr. 224 and Brug. XL. 13: 1159–81.

73. Idem episcopo Norwicensi.
    Ad aures nostras perlatum   .   .   . revoces.
    Not in J-L. Cf. Cantuar. I. 45 and Wig. IV. 17: Exoniensi epis-
    copo. *1162–81.*

74. Idem archiepiscopo Cantuariensi et suffraganeis eius.   *F.146r.*
    Relatum est auribus nostris   .   .   . incurrant.
    J-L 13823: 1159–81.

75. Idem Wigorniensi et Coventrensi (*MS.:* Covest.) (episcopis).
    Ex litteris, quas nobis   .   .   .   . suadere.
    J-L 14142: 1159–81. Cf. Claud. MS., fol. 215ra: Cantuariensi
    archiepiscopo et Wigorniensi episcopo.

76. Idem archiepiscopo Cantuariensi.
    Ad hoc, in beatorum   .   .   .   . compellas.
    J-L 12448 and 14314: 23 March 1175. Cf. Cantuar. I. 1.

77. Idem Cantuariensi archiepiscopo et eius suffraganeis.   *F.146v.*
    Viris ecclesiasticis .   .   .   .   . extorquere.
    Not in J-L. Cf. Cantuar. I. 9: 1159–81.

78. Eugenius papa (III) Jocel(ino) episcopo Saresberiensi.
    Clerici, qui relicto .   .   .   .   . generari.
    J-L 8959. Cf. Cantuar. I. 14: 26 Nov. 1146.

79. Idem Bathoniensi episcopo.
    Si vero aliquis   .   .   .   .   . iuramentum.
    *J-L 13771: chapter from decretal Sicut dignum, to Bartholomew of
    Exeter, 31 January 1171–2. Cf. Wig. III. 36.*

80. Idem episcopis, archidiaconis et aliis ecclesiarum prelatis per
    Galliam constitutis.
    Parrochianos autem vestros   .   .   . representent.
    J-L 13742: 1159–81. Cf. Wig. IV. 18e: Andrenensi episcopo.

81. Idem Bathoniensi episcopo.   *F.146v.*
    Mulieres vel etiam   .   .   .   . probatur.
    *Inscription uncertain. For variant readings, cf. Wig. VII. 27 and
    Lohmann, loc. cit., p. 131: addressed to Chartres, Exeter, etc. J-L
    13768; cf. J-L 13769 and 13770. 1159–81.*

82. Idem eidem.
    Porro, si aliqui violentas .   .   .   . possunt.
    J-L 14025: 1159–81. Cf. Roff. 85 and 86: abbati de Neuhus.

83. Idem Cantuariensi archiepiscopo.
    Licet iuxta apostolorum   .   .   .   . observari.
    J-L 14315: 1174–81. Cf. Wig. III. 27.

84. Idem Vigiliensi (*MS.*: Vigelen.) episcopo.   *F.147r.*
  Cum Romana ecclesia sit mater .   .   . cogendi.
    (a) Cum Romana ecclesia   .   .   . potes.
    (b) Vir aut mulier   .   .   .   . debet.
    (c) Si vero puella   .   .   . commonendi.
    (d) Sponsam autem alterius   .   . copulare.
    (e) Debitores autem   .   .   . cogendi.
  J-L 14126: 1159–81. Roff. 84c = Cantuar. III. 22. Cf. Wig. IV.
  14 and J-L 14127.

85. Idem abbati de Neuhus.
  Consuluit nos tua .   .   .   . punire.
  Cf. Roff. 82 and 86.

86. Idem eidem.
  Porro, si aliqui violentas .   .   . confessi etc.
  J-L 14025: 1159–81. Cf. Roff. 82 and 85.

87. Idem eidem.
  Nulli autem monachi   .   .   . vitari.
  J-L 13908: 1159–81. Cf. Wig. VII. 52d: Norwicensi episcopo.

88. Idem archiepiscopo Salernitano (MS.: Sal'nita).
  Licet preter solitum   .   .   . remanere.
  Cf. Roff. 89.

89. Idem eidem.
  Verum autem filii .   .   .   . incurrit.
    (a) Verum autem   .   .   . habeat.
    (b) Si vero vir vel mulier   .   . patrocinari.
    (c) De cetero, laicos in accusatione   . admitti.
    (d) Et si clerici .   .   .   . videtur.
    (e) Si vero coram   .   .   . removendi.
    (f) De adulteriis .   .   .   . conterere.
    (g) Porro, si clericus   .   .   . subsecuta.
    (h) In causis vero ecclesiasticis .   . disputari.
    (i) De quarta vero decime   .   . non admittit.
    (k) De presbitero autem   .   . extitisset.
    (l) Presbiterum autem .   .   . incurrit.
  J-L 14091: 1174–6. Cantuar. I. 56a-m = Roff. 88 and 89.

90. Alexander papa III B(artholomeo) Exon(iensi) episcopo.   *F.147v.*
  Significatum est nobis   .   .   . cogendi.
  J-L 13094: 1162–81.

91. Idem decano et capitulo.
  Cum institisset apud nos .   .   . gravamen.
  J-L 13983: 1159–81. Cf. Claud. MS., fol. 196vb: Lemovicens.;
  Wig. I. 6: Lincolnie.

92. Idem Lundoniensi episcopo.   *F.148r.*
  Accepimus, quod plerique .   .   . poteris.
  J-L 14267: 1171–81.

93. Idem Cantuariensi archiepiscopo et suffraganeis.
Sicut ad extirpanda vitia . . . . compellatis.
J-L 13813: 1174–81.

94. Idem (!) Celestinus papa Florentine ecclesie. *F.148r.*
Videtur nobis . . . . . recipiuntur.
(a) Videtur nobis . . . . assumere.
(b) Quod autem parentes . . . recipiuntur.
Uncertain origin; J-K 384, J-L 4920. Cf. Cantuar. I. 26.

95. Exoniensi episcopo.
Super hoc, quod a nobis . . . . coniungant.
(a) Super hoc, quod . . . . servetur.
(b) De peregrinationis . . . . coniungant.
J-L 13903, 13907 and 13916: 1162–81. Cf. Cantuar. I. 28.

96. Idem ad eundem. *F.148v.*
Venit ad audientiam nostram . . . terminare.
J-L 14214: 1162–81.

97. Idem B(artholomeo) Exoniensi episcopo.
Ex presentium latoris . . . . procedas.
J-L 13900: 1162–81.

98. Idem abbati Sancti Albani. (? : Astionensi electo.)
Propositum est nobis . . . . reportare.
J-L 12636; cf. Cantuar. III. 9 and Wig. I. 15: 1159–81.

99. Idem Pictavensi episcopo.
Veniens ad nos P. lator . . . . accipere.
J-L 14058: 1159–81.

100. Idem Norwicensi episcopo.
Querelam R. nobilis . . . . exequatur.
Not in J-L: 1175–81. Cf. Claustr. 320 and Cantuar. I. 49.

101. Idem episcopo Norwicensi. *F.149r*
Rediens ad nos W(illelmus) . . . adherere.
J-L 13902 and 14159: 1176–81.

102. Idem (Exoniensi episcopo).
Pervenit ad nos quod quidam . . . compellat.
J-L 13901: 1162–81. Cf. Wig. I. 4.

103. Idem Bathoniensi episcopo.
Utrum mulier, que . . . . . abstineri.
J-L 13767: 1159–81. Cf. Claustr. 300. 1.

104. Idem Tiburnic(ensi) episcopo.
Casum, quem tuis . . . . imponas.
Not in J-L: hitherto known only in Claustr. 301; 1159–81.

105. Idem Sagiensi episcopo.
Consuluit nos tua fraternitas . . . observari.
J-L 14178: 1159–81. Cf. Claustr. 299; Claud. MS., fol. 207va:
Norwicensi episcopo.

106. Idem (Strigoniensi et Colocensi archiepiscopis). *F.149v.*
    Coniugatus in monasterium . . . occasio.
    J-L 14104: 1159–81. Cf. Wig. I. 10.

107. (Alexander III Treverensi episcopo.)
    Super eo, quod nos . . . . coherceri.
    J-L 14151: 1159–81. Cf. Wig. I. 3 and Claud. MS., fol. 203vb.

108. Idem Lucensi episcopo.
    Consuluit nos tua discretio . . promovendus.
    J-L 14005: 1159–81.

109. Idem Pisano episcopo.
    Quidam intravit monasterium . . . corporis.
    J-L 14061: 1159–81. Cf. Wig. I. 25 and Claud. MS., fol. 207ra.

110. Idem Auctav'ensi episcopo.
    Litteris tue fraternitatis . . . . perseveret.
    J-L 14166: episcopo cuidam vel Exoniensi. 1159–81.

111. Idem abbati Sancti Albani. *F.150r.*
    Quesitum est siquidem . . . . spoliari.
       (a) Quesitum est . . . . prorogare.
       (b) De cetero, si aliquis . . . . removeri.
       (c) Donationes vero . . . . spoliari.
    J-L 12636: 8 April 1173–6. Cf. Belver. II. 4.

112. Idem Wigorniensi episcopo.
    Super eo, quod a nobis . . . . expirare.
       (a) Super eo, quod a nobis . . . sedeatur.
       (b) Si autem adversa . . . . inhibeatur.
       (c) De appellationibus . . . . deferendum.
       (d) Quod si aliquis . . . . iniungenda.
       (e) Verum si appellantes . . . compellas.
       (f) Ceterum, si abbatem . . . iudicandum.
       (g) Verum, cum alicui . . . . habere.
       (h) Meminimus nos ex parte . . . rescindere.
       (i) De monachis autem . . . . respondere.
       (k) Preterea, illi qui episcopo . . . observandum.
       (l) Si lis infra certum . . . . expirare.
    J-L 13162: 1164–79.

113. (Alexander III Wigorniensi episcopo.) *F.150v.*
    Veniens ad apostolice sedis . . . decimas.
    J-L 14137: 1159–81. Cf. Wig. IV. 7.

114. Idem abbati Sancti Petri super Divam. *F.150v.*
    Ad aures nostras pervenisse . . . castiges.
    J-L 13865: 1159–81. Cf. Wig. II. 4.

115. Idem Volterano archiepiscopo et M. abbati de Spongia. *F.151r.*
    Ex litteris vestris . . . . . terminetis.
    J-L 14129: 1159–81. Cf. Wig. VII. 46.

116. Idem decano et clericis Maturiensibus.
Quoniam rationis ordo   .   .   .   . compellat.
J-L 12666: 1159–81.

117. Idem abbati de Rivallis et priori de Bridlington.
Dilecti filii nostri   .   .   .   .   . procedatis.
Not in J-L: 1159–81. Cf. Cantuar. III. 19.

118. Idem Cantuariensi archiepiscopo.
Qua fronte super   .   .   .   .   . sepulture.
  (a) Qua fronte super   .   .   .   . appellandum.
  (b) Super eo vero   .   .   .   . sepulture.
J-L 14312: 1174–81. Cf. Wig. V. 10.

119. Lucius (III) Wigorniensi episcopo.   *F.151v.*
Significavit nobis T.   .   .   .   . vexentur.
Datum Velletr.Nonas Julii.
J-L 14964: 7 July 1182–3. Cf. Claud. MS.,fol. 213rb; Lucius III
B(alduino) Wigorniensi episcopo.

120. Alexander (III) Lundoniensi et Wigorniensi (episcopis).
Significatum est nobis   .   .   .   . spolietis.
Not in J-L: 1159–81. Cf. Wig. VII. 7.

121. Lucius papa (III) Johanni episcopo Norwicensi.
Constitutus apud nos   .   .   .   . satisfactum.
Dat.Rome.
J-L 14963: 1181.

122. Alexander papa III Eboracensi archiepiscopo et Coventrensi
episcopo.
Ex parte N. capellani   .   .   .   . impetrate.
J-L 13890: 1159–81.

123. Idem Carnotensi episcopo.
Sane quia nos in primis   .   .   .   . observari.
J-L 13835: 1176–80. Cf. J-L 13770 and 13768.

124. Idem archiepiscopo Remensi.   *F.152r.*
Super eo, quod abbas Sancti Apollinaris   . admittendam.
J-L 14073: 1159–81.

125. Idem episcopo Lundoniensi.
Si aliquando ordinatio   .   .   .   . evicerit.
J-L 13996: 1159–81. Cf. J-L 13990, 13992 and 14181.

126. Idem Andrensi episcopo.
Super eo vero, quod   .   .   .   . sororem.
J-L 14075: 1159–81.

127. Idem Brixiensi (*MS.*: Brissien.) episcopo.
Si vir ille mulierem illam   .   .   .   . transire.
J-L 13787: 1159–81.

128. Benedictus papa. *F.152r.*
Quo pacto per nuda . . . . monstratis.
J-L 3773: 972–4.

129. Idem episcopo Dunelmensi (*MS.:* Dunholm.).
Suggestum est auribus nostris . . . cognoscas.
J-L 13870: 1159–81.

130. (Alexander III Toletano episcopo.)
Presentium lator P., cum litteris . . separetur.
J-L 14120: 1159–81.

131. Idem monachi(s) de Neublosia. *F.152v.*
Dilecti filii nostri . . . . . extendere.
J-L 14023: 1159–81.

132. Idem abbati et fratribus monasterii de Loregio.
Quando Romana ecclesia . . . . proponunt.
J-L 14004: 1159–81.

133. Augustinus.
Si quis superedificat . . . . fundamentum.
Unidentified chapter.

134. Ambrosius.
Per Abraham levi qui decimas . . . traxit.
Unidentified chapter.

135. Idem Wintoniensi episcopo.
Ad aures nostras pervenit . . . . restitui.
Not in J-L: 1159–81. Cf Claustr. 329 and Chelt. MS., fol. 24v.

136. Idem Wigorniensi episcopo.
Conquerente nobis M. . . . . postponas.
J-L 14138: 1159–81.

137. Idem Tranensi episcopo. *F.153r.*
Continebatur in litteris . . . . separetur.
J-L 14032: 1159–81.

138. Idem Exoniensi episcopo et decano Lincolnensi (*MS.:* Lincoll.) in causa que vertebatur inter canonicos de Giseburne et archiepiscopum (*MS.:* archiepiscopo) Eboracen(sem).
Provideas attentius . . . . investigetis.
J-L 13934: 1159–81.

139. Idem Capitulano episcopo et abbati sancte Lucie et priori Sancte Crucis.
Causam, que inter N. et O. monachos . . terminetis.
J-L 13831: 1159–81.

140. Idem Bituri(c)ensi archiepiscopo.
Significasti nobis quod quidam miles . . debent.
J-L 14107: 1159–81. Cf. Berol. 45: Terraconensi archiepiscopo.

141. Ex concilio Turon(ensi).
Si constitutus in clerico . . . . videatur.
Tours, 1163: Mansi, c.2.

142. Idem Wigorniensi episcopo. *F.153r.*
Querelam monachorum de Acra . . . spoliari.
J-L 13165: 1164–79.

143. Idem Cicestrensi episcopo. *F.153v.*
Ex litteris tue discretionis . . . . possidet.
J-L 13845: 1159–81.

144. Idem Exoniensi episcopo. . . . .
Accepta querimonia P. clerici. . . . imponatis.
J-L 13984: 1159–81. Cf. Claud. MS., fol. 190va: decano Lin-
colnensi et abbati Rivallensi.

145. Lucius papa III Johanni Norwicensi episcopo.
Quesitum est a nobis ex parte tua . . declinare.
J-L 15185: 1181–5.

146. Idem eidem.
Tua fraternitas duxit . . . . videretur.
J-L 14029: 1181–5. Cf. Claud. MS., fol. 212ra: Lucius III
J. Norwicensi episcopo. *J-L has: Alexander III: 1159–81.*

147. Alexander III Panormitano archiepiscopo. *F.154r.*
De illis autem, qui . . . . . consecuta.
J-L 14043: 1159–81.

148. Idem eidem.
Veniens ad presentiam nostram . . . postponas.
J-L 14165: 1159–81.

149. Idem Cassiano abbati.
Ex litteris tuis ad nos directis . . . ignorent.
J-L 13838: 1159–81.

150. Lucius papa III W(alterio) Lincolnensi (*MS.*: Lincoll.) epis-
copo.
Ad aures nostras te significante . . . delegatum.
J-L 14965: 1183–4. Cf. J-L 14966.

151. (Celestinus III Johanni decano Rotomagensi.)
Prudentiam tuam debita . . . . exercebunt.
XV Kal. Julii pontificatus nostri anno tertio.
J-L 17019· 17 June 1193. Cf. Pet. MS. 203, quire I, fol. 2rb.

Comparative Table

COLLATING THE ROCHESTER, CANTERBURY, WORCESTER II AND BELVOIR COLLECTIONS

Roff.	*Cantaur.*	*Wig.Alt.*	*Belver.*
1–26: Canons of the Third Lateran Council, 1179.			
27	I.12	–	–

	Roff.	Cantaur.	Wig.Alt.	Belver.
	28	I.7	–	IV.8
	29	I.10	–	–
	30	I.58	–	–
	31	–	–	–
	32	I.59	–	–
	33	I.11	–	IV.1a-b
	34	I.4	–	–
	35	I.8	–	IV.4
	36	I.16	–	–
	37a-g	I.20a-i	–	–
	38a-g	I.40a-h	–	–
	39	I.21	–	–
	40a-d	I.38a-c	–	–
	41	I.36	–	–
	42a-d	I.41a-e	12	I.18a-b. I-VI
	43	–	–	–
cf. 61	44	I.47	–	–
	45	–	–	–
	46a-d	I.42a-d	11	–
	47a-c	I.52a-d	–	–
cf. 79	48	I.23	1a-b	I.12a-l
	49	–	–	–
	50	I.62	–	IV.9
	51	I.60	–	–
	52	I.30	–	–
		II.2		
	53	I.54	–	–
	54	I.57	–	–
	55	I.3	–	–
	56	I.13	–	IV.3
	57	I.55	–	–
	58	I.53	–	–
	59	–	–	–
	60	–	–	–
cf. 44	61	I.47	–	–
	62	I.48	–	–
	63	I.50a-b	–	–
	64	I.51	8	I.15
	65	I.33	–	–
	66	–	–	–
	67	I.61	–	–
	68	I.35	–	–
	69	I.18; III.7	–	–
	70a-g	–	–	–
	71	–	–	–
	72	–	–	–

	Roff.	Cantaur.	Wig.Alt.	Belver.
	73	I.45	–	–
	74	I.34; II.3	–	–
	75	–	–	–
	76	I.1	–	IV.2a-b
	77	I.9; I.32	–	–
	78	I.14	–	–
cf. 48	79	I.23	1	I.12
	80	–	–	–
cf. 123	81	II.1	–	–
cf. 85–6	82	–	–	–
	83	–	–	–
	84a-e	III.22	–	–
cf. 82	{ 85	–	–	–
	{ 86	–	–	–
	87	–	–	–
	{ 88	I.56a	–	–
	{ 89	I.56b-m	–	–
	90	I.27	–	–
	91	–	–	–
	92	I.15	–	II.1
	93	I.5	–	–
	94a-b	I.26a-b	–	–
	95a-b	I.28.i-iii	–	–
	96	I.29	–	–
	97	I.31	–	–
	98	III.9	–	–
	99	–	–	–
	100	I.49, 46	–	–
	101	I.19	–	–
	102	–	–	–
	103	(III.1)	–	–
	104	–	–	–
	105	–	–	–
	106	–	–	–
	107	–	–	–
	108	II.5	–	–
	109	–	–	–
	110	–	–	–
	111a-b	I.37a-c	–	II.4
	112a-l	I.22a-m	{ 4a-c	I.10a-c
			{ 5a-c	
	113	–	–	–
	114	–	–	–
	115	–	–	–
	116	–	–	–
	117	III.19	–	–

	Roff.	Cantuar.	Wig.Alt.	Belver.
	118a-b	–	–	–
	119	–	–	–
	120	–	–	–
	121	–	–	–
	122	–	–	–
cf. 81	123	II.1a-c	–	–
	124	–	–	–
	125	–	–	–
	126	–	–	–
	127	–	–	–
	128	–	–	–
	129	–	–	–
	130	–	–	–
	131	–	–	IV.7
	132	–	–	–
	133	–	–	–
	134	–	–	–
	135	–	–	–
	136	–	–	–
	137	–	–	–
	138	–	–	–
	139	–	–	–
	140	–	–	–

141: Canon of the Council of Tours, 1163; Mansi, c.2.

	142	–	–	–
	143	–	–	–
	144	–	–	–
	145	–	–	–
	146	–	–	–
	147	–	–	–
	148	–	–	–
	149	–	–	–
	150	–	–	–

J-L 17019:

	151	–	–	–

V

The First Book of the Worcester Collection collated with the Klosterneuburg, 'Cheltenham', Cottonian and Peterhouse Collections

COMPARATIVE TABLE

Claustr.	Wig. I	Chelt. Fols.	Cott. Fols.	Pet. I.
26	1	–	224v	92

Claustr.	Wig. I	Chelt. Fols.	Cott. Fols.	Pet. I.
27	2	–	213v	13
28	3a.1	–	{ 214r	18
–	II	–		–
29	b	–	–	–
30	4	43va	213v	14
31	5	43vb	214r	15
32	6	44ra	–	–
33	7	43ra	212v	9
34	8=47	44rb	218r	46
35	9	44rb	213r	10
36	10	–	218r	45
37	11	43ra	218r	50
38	12	44va	210v	1
39	13	44va	214r	19
40	14a	44vb	{ 220r	57a
41	b	45ra		b
42	15	45ra	222r	66
43	16	45ra	222r	76
44	17a	{ 45rb	{ 218v	51a
45[1]	b			b
II	c			c
46	18	45va	222v	78
47[1]	19a	{ 45vb	{ 224v	93a
II	b			b
48	c			c
49	20	46ra	218v	52
50	21	46ra	219r	53
51	22	46va	217r	39
52	23	46vb	217r	41
53	24	–	217r	40
–	25	–	218r	47
54	26a	–	{ 215v	26a
55	b	–		b
56	27	–	224v	94
57[1]	28a.1	–	{ 210v	3a }
II	II	–		
58	b	–		b
59–65	c–q	46vb		c–o
66	29	47vb	215v	28
67	30	48ra	222r	65
68	31	48ra	222v	77
69	32	48rb	221r	62
70	33	48rb	214v	20a
–	34a	51rb	–	–

Claustr.	Wig. I	Chelt. Fols.	Cott. Fols.	Pet. I.
71 }	b c	{ 48va	214v }	b c
72 = 300.1 73	35 36	{ 48vb	215r }	21a b
310	37	49vb	214v	20a
309	38a-c	49va	210v	2a-b
311	39	50ra	216v	71
312	40	50ra	219r	54
74 75	41a b	{ 49rb	217v }	42a b
313	42	50rb	219v	55
314.1-III	43a-b	50rb	219v	67a-b
315	44	50vb	221r	73
–	45	51ra	224r	88
47.1	46 = 19a	–	224v	93a
34	47 = 8	–	218r	46
–	48	–	–	–
35	49 = 9	–	213r	10

VI

The First Book of the Peterhouse Collection collated with the *Appendix*, Bamberg, Bruges, Leipzig and Cassel Collections and with *Compilatio I*

COMPARATIVE TABLE

Pet. I	Appendix	Bamb.	Brug.	Lips.	Cass.	Comp. I.
1	–	–	–	–	–	–
2	6.18,19	50.16	49.4	59.29	58.18	IV.4.4(6)
3	6.8	50.5	52.5	59.5	58.6	4.3
4	50.41,42	50.35	53.6	59.52–4	58.37	4.7(9)
5	6.22	50.19	49.7	59.32	58.21	4.6(8)
6	6.31	50.28	49.5	59.41	58.29	1.10
7	45.6	50.31	49.27	59.48	58.32	1.12
8	6.26	50.23	–	59.36	58.25	1.9
9	6.28	50.25	49.12	59.38	58.26	17.3
10	6.2	50.2	–	59.2	58.3	1.3
11	–	–	53.15	–	–	17.1
12	–	–	–	–	–	–
13	45.1	–	–	–	–	–
14	45.3	–	–	–	–	–
15	6.13	50.12	49.9	59.23	58.13	7.2
16	50.61	–	–	–	–	–
17	6.5	–	51.3	59.44	–	5.1

Pet. I	Appendix	Bamb.	Brug.	Lips	Cass.	Comp. I.
18	6.10	50.9	53.5	59.20	58.10	2.8
19	12.2	51.2	49.1	60.2	59.2	2.5
20	6.7	50.4	49.6	59.4	58.5	2.6
21	6.29	50.26	49.15	59.39	58.27	2.9
22	6.6	50.6	49.17	59.17	58.7	2.3
23	–	–	–	–	–	–
24	–	–	–	–	–	–
25	12.8	51.7	48.3	60.8	59.7	1.18
26	6.30	50.27	49.30	59.40	58.28	19.2
27	–	–	53.10	–	–	–
28	8.23	50.37	53.4	59.57	58.39	19.3
29	6.32	50.29	53.3	59.46	58.30	14.2
30	–	–	–	–	–	–
31	–	–	–	–	–	–
32	–	–	–	–	–	1.1
33	–	–	–	–	–	–
34	–	–	–	–	–	11.3
35	–	–	–	–	–	–
36	49.10	–	–	–	–	–
37	50.17	–	–	–	–	3.3
38	–	–	–	–	–	–
39	5.8	49.8	52.7	58.8	57.9	III.28.7
40	21.1	16.1	49.3	16.1	26.1	27.8
41	5.10	49.10	–	58.13	57.11	IV. 6.8
42	44.4	50.33	49.21	59.50	58.34	6.7
43	–	–	–	–	–	–
44	–	–	–	–	–	–
45	5.6,7	49.6,7	–	58.6,7	57.7,8	III.28.5,6
46	5.3	49.3	52.8	58.3	57.3	28.4
47	5.2	49.2	52.6	58.2	57.2	28.3
48	–	–	–	–	–	–
49	–	–	–	–	–	–
50	12.5	–	–	–	–	–
51	12.7	51.6	49.22	60.7	59.6	–
52	12.4	51.4	49.18	60.5	59.4	IV.13.3
53	12.3	51.3	49.24	60.3	59.3	–
54	–	50.32	49.20	59.49	58.33	17.2
55	–	–	–	–	–	–
56	–	51.8	43.1	60.9	59.8	–
57	6.15	50.14	49.2	59.27	58.16	13.2
58	–	–	–	–	–	–
59	50.5	–	–	–	–	13.5
60	–	–	–	–	–	–
61	–	–	–	–	–	–
62	6.14	50.13	50.4	59.26	58.14	20.4
63	–	–	–	–	–	–
64	–	–	–	–	–	–
65	45.2	–	–	–	–	–
66	6.1	50.1	49.14	59.1	58.1	7.1
67	–	53.6	27.5	63.4	–	18.4
68	–	–	-	–	–	–

Pet. I.	Appendix	Bamb.	Brug.	Lips.	Cass.	Comp. I.
69	–	–	–	–	–	–
70	8.17	39.13	–	43.17	48.13	II.13.20
71	33.2	53.9	54.1	63.7	62.6	IV.21.2
72	50.46	55.3	–	65.3	64.3	21.1
73	6.11	50.10	53.12	59.21	58.11	II.19.9
74	–	–	–	–	–	–
75	–	–	53.11	–	–	–
76	33.1	53.8	–	63.6	62.5	IV.18.6
77	33.3	53.3	51.3	63.1	62.1	18.1
78	33.5	53.4	51.6	63.2	62.2	18.2
79	8.11	53.5	53.9	63.3	62.3	18.3
80	–	53.7	32.4	63.5	62.4	18.5
81	33.4	–	32.1	–	–	18.7
82	–	–	–	–	–	V.13.4
83	–	–	–	–	–	–
84	50.40	–	–	22.2	–	III.26.25
85	–	–	–	–	–	–
86	–	–	–	–	–	–
87	–	–	53.7	–	–	–
88	–	–	–	–	–	–
89	–	–	–	–	–	–
90	50.28	–	53.8	–	–	IV.16.3
91	50.63	–	50.1	–	58.40	8.3
92	37.2	52.1	50.3	61.1	60.1	8.1
93	37.3	52.2	50.2	61.2	60.2	8.2
94	45.7	–	49.8	–	65.1	9.1
95	–	–	–	–	–	–

VII
The Cambridge, Trinity and Cottonian Collections

COMPARATIVE TABLE

Cantab.	Trin.	Cott. Book and Fol.
–	II.21a	III.244v
–	21b	244v
–	22	V.272v
–	23	III.244r
–	24	247v
–	25	245r
35	26	245r
–	27	243v
–	28a	247v
–	28b	247v
–	29	IV.26or

Cantab.	Trin.	Cott. Book and Fol.
–	III.1a	V.263v
–	1b	263v
13	2	264v
21	3	273v
22	4	II.227r
–	5	III.246r
–	6	IV.261v
–	7	256v
5	8	256v
–	9	V.264v
–	10	II.228r
27	11	V.266v
–	12a	274r
–	12b	274r
–	13a	274r
–	13b	274r
–	14	273v
–	15a	263v
30c; 65Ba	15b	263v
–	16	IV.260r
–	17a.I	V.270r
–	17a.II	270r
–	17b	270r
–	17c	270r
16	18	
–	19	IV.259r
–	20	V.265r
–	21	VI.279v
–	22	V.265r
–	23	266v
–	24	265v
–	25	266v
–	26a	VI.280v
–	26b	280v
63a	IV.1	V.270v
–	2	268r
–	3.I	II.228v
–	3.II	228v
–	4	III.243r
–	5	IV.258r
–	6	III.252r
–	7	VI.276v

PLATES

The following plates will serve to clarify the main phases in the technical development of English primitive decretal collections, and illustrate their wider historical interest. The examples chosen are reproduced from manuscripts now in the British Museum; and all, except the final item, have been selected from collections discussed in the present study.

PLATE I: The Worcester II Collection

Wigorniensis Altera: B.M. Royal MS. 11 B. II, fol. 101r. Vellum; 10⅛ in. × 6⅞ in. Pp. 46 and 69–70, above.

This folio from the Worcester II Collection records the technical style of the most primitive English collectors, who transcribed their decretals in full, with initial and final protocols, inscriptions and dates. In later collections the longer letters were dissected into their component chapters, and these were redistributed to suit a more convenient method of subject classification. The inscription and initial letter of the decretal *Sicut Romana* have been omitted by the rubricator in the example given here. The Worcester II Collection is a member of the primitive 'English' family, and is one of the earliest decretal collections now extant.

PLATE II: The Royal Collection

Regalis: B.M. Royal MS. 15 B. IV, fol. 107v. Vellum; 8 in. × 5⅝ in. Pp.8 1–4.

The opening folio of the Royal Collection reveals alike the professional advantages and the historical disadvantages of its more advanced technical style. This collection is the most juristically mature member of the 'English' family; and, though correctly described as primitive, it incorporates several notable systematic devices: its longer letters are dismembered in some instances, and their component parts distributed to suit a schematic arrangement of topics; the non-juridical matter is drastically abbreviated or excised in places; decretal inscriptions are entirely omitted from some decretals, but accurately retained in others; conventional abbreviations are freely used to indicate where an excision has been made or to avoid the transcription of repetitive common form. The Royal Collection is much less attractive in format than other decretal manuscripts examined in this study.

PLATE III: The Canterbury Collection

Cantuariensis: B.M. Royal MS. 10 B. IV, fol. 55r. Vellum; 10⅞ in. × 7⅛ in. Pp. 48 and 73–6, above.

O

The Canterbury Collection is a further member of the primitive 'English' family. The folio selected in this instance reveals the value of such early collections in providing more accurate historical details for decretals already known from other sources in a less reliable form. Thus, the letter addressed in this transcription to Robert Foliot, bishop of Hereford from 1174, was hitherto dated simply by the pontifical years of Alexander III: 1159–81. But now the much narrower limits of Robert's consecration and the death of Alexander, 1174–81, are fixed by this fresh evidence. In many other details also this example typifies the format and style of the earliest collections.

<h2 style="text-align:center">PLATE IV: The Claudian Collection</h2>

Claudiana: B.M. Cotton MS. Claudius A. iv, fol. 199v. Vellum; 9¼ in. × 6⅝ in. Pp. 84–91.

The Claudian Collection, a representative member of the primitive 'Bridlington' family, is a careful and finely transcribed collection. Its individual decretals and canons are numbered in a single sequence throughout the work; each item is placed under a rubricated summary of the juridically significant matter contained in it; an apparatus of marginal cross-references correlates passages of cognate interest in different parts of the composition; and points of legal interest are sometimes further discussed in brief marginal gloss commentaries. Although the initial letters have been omitted from decretal inscriptions, the Claudian Collection attains a high standard of accuracy in its personal and place-name references. All these features are illustrated in the single folio selected here.

<h2 style="text-align:center">PLATES V and VI: The Worcester Collection</h2>

Wigorniensis: B.M. Royal MS. 10 A. 11, fols. 14r and 63v. Vellum; 9 in. × 5¾ in. Pp. 49–51, 95–8 and 110–15.

Plate V records the typical features of the Worcester Collection, one of the earliest members of the primitive 'Worcester' family. The collection is devised in seven books on a subject-matter basis; the separate decretals are numbered in sequence within these parts; and each book begins on a fresh folio-recto. The professional advantages of this style of composition are clear enough when compared with that of the 'English' and 'Bridlington' families. The example chosen here is the opening folio of Book II. One of the final folios of the volume containing the Worcester Collection is reproduced in Plate VI. The decretals transcribed on this folio were not part of the original scheme of composition, but are later rescripts acquired independently and added to the manuscript already containing the earlier work. They provide significant evidence concerning the provenance both of the Worcester Collection itself and of the completed manuscript volume in which it is the principal part.

stras. indulget biennium. nisi forte iudex
a quo appellatum fuerit secundum locorum 7
prouinciar distanciam. restituat temporis
ratis tempus fuerit moderatus. infra quod si
is q appellauit causam appellationis non
fuerit psecut tenebit sentencia. si p senten
ciam appellauit. 7 a causa sua cecidisse iu
detur. 7 nec amplius super eodem negocio audie
tur appellans. Si uero absq omni grauami
ne. 7 ante litis ingressu fuerit appellatu
huiusmodi audietur appellans. cum sacri
canones passim appellare pmittunt. Si
uero an sentencia appellauit n cogetur
illi stare iudicio a quo noscit appellasse.
Si autem in agro uel alias an cause ingres
sum fuerit appellatu n solent dici appel
lationes. si ad causam uocationes. preter
ea si rapto sit. ut alias uiolent detrimor
aliene rei tsi q appellat huiusmodi appel
lato facta iniudicio apud ecclasticas pso
nas solet audiri nisi forte manifestus
rapto uel fornicator existit. sicut ille q
absentem. 7 n requisitum apls excommuni
cauit. Ad h si in una ca aliquis appellauit
7 pendente appellatione aliquod crimen
committat. uel pri commisisse dicat. ut
in 7 accuset uel conueniat de alia re
de q n fuerit appellatu. nec illa contin
gat ad audiencia iudicis a q malio q
negocio appellauit. eum potest si uo
luerit tanq suspectu uitare. Alioqn
debebit stare iudicio illi a quo appellatu
z. maxime si iudex suus ordinarius ex
stitit. Item si duobz cora suo iudice litigan

tibz. alt ad uiam. alt ad sui iudicis au
dienciam sup eodem negocio appella
uerit. 7 ille q ad suum iudice appella
uit ad diem appellationis ueniens ad
eum se appellasse pponit eo tacito qd
aduersarius ei ad audienciam Roma
ni pontificis appellasset. si legittime ci
tatus neq uenerit. neq alique mise
rit responsale. Aut n alias parere con
tempserit. 7 in eum excommunicatoi
siuam tulerit. tenebit utiq excommu
nicationis siam p contumacia quousq
cognouerit iudex eu ad audienciam
Romani pontificis appellasse. Denique
qd in fine questionu tuar queris si acui
li iudice an iudicium ut p ad nram
audienciam fuerit appellatu an hu
iuscemodi appellatio teneat. tenerit ei
dem in his qui nre sunt spiali iuris
dictioni subiecti. In aliis u 7 si de consu
etudine eccle teneat secundum iuris rigore
tene n credim. Dat. Tusculi. xi. kl. Aprilis.

icut Romana
eccla omnium ecclar disponente
deo mater 7 magistra. ita etiam no
q eidem eccle licet immiti supne dispo
sitionis prudencia psidem p ut nobis
dns ministrat consultacionibz respon
dere cogimur singulor. 7 que uident
dubia apostolice circuspectionis pru
dencia declarare. Sane questrm za nob
ex parte tua utris si aliqn ca insali
qs delegatis iudicibz absq remedio ap
pellationis committit. 7 alia pars

I. THE WORCESTER II COLLECTION
B.M. Royal MS. 11 B.II, fol. 101r.

II. THE ROYAL COLLECTION

B.M. Royal MS. 15 B.iv, fol. 107v.

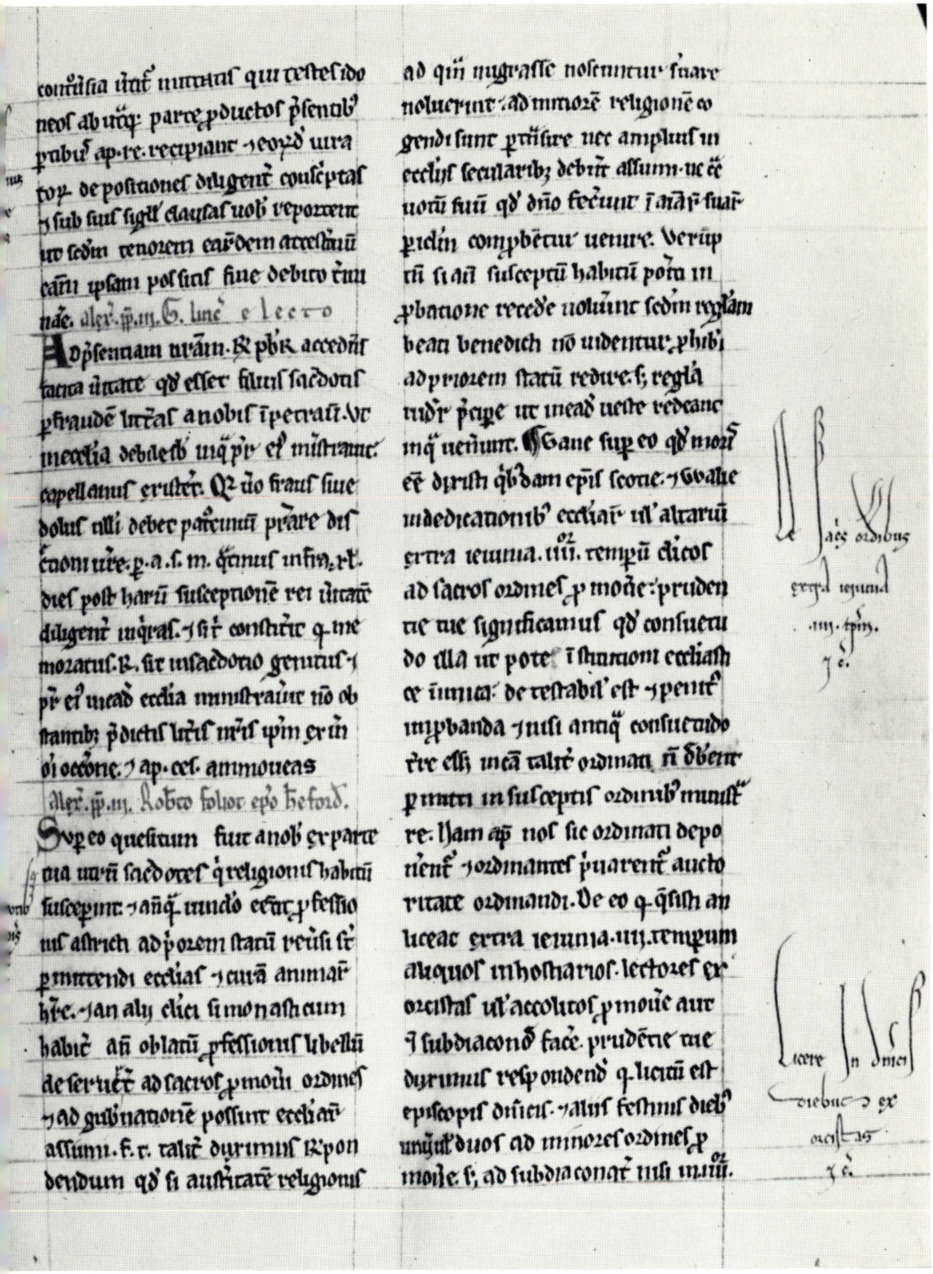

III. THE CANTERBURY COLLECTION

B.M. Royal MS. 10 B.iv, fol. 55r.

IV. THE CLAUDIAN COLLECTION
B.M. Cotton MS. Claudius A.iv, fol. 199v.

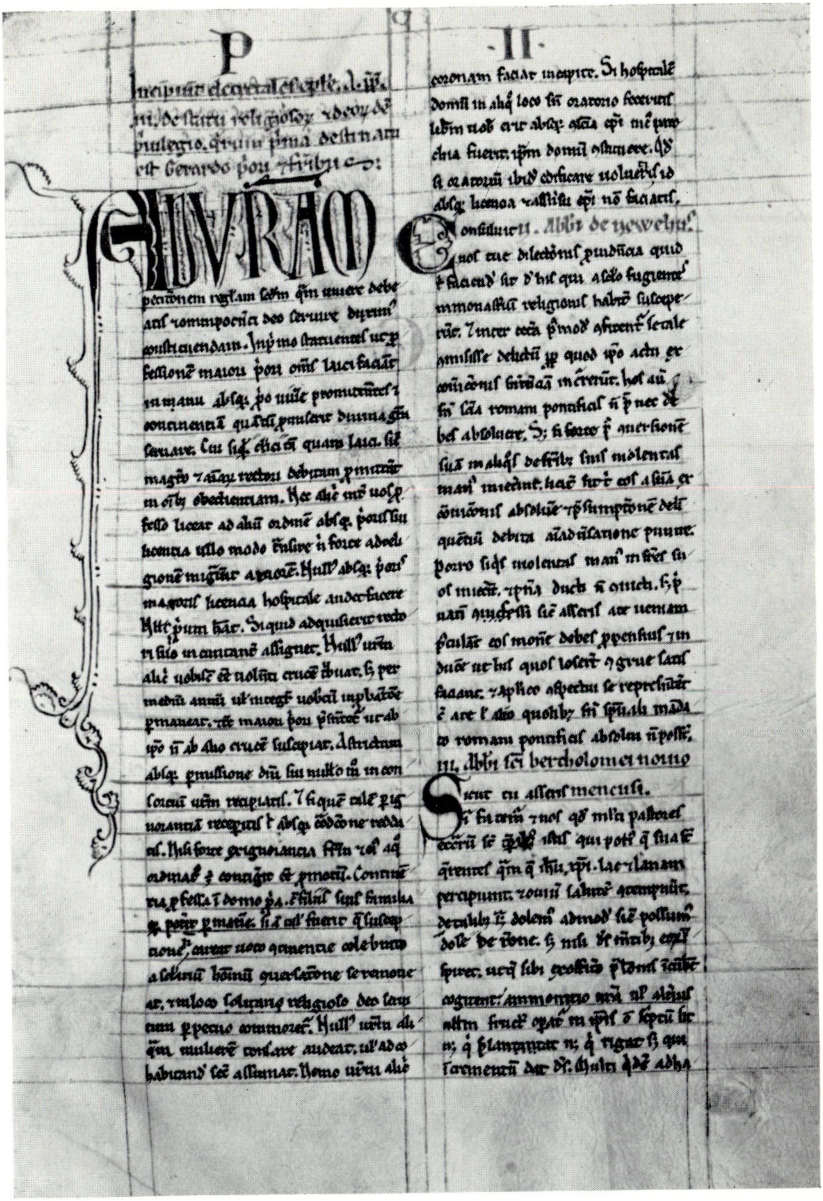

V. THE WORCESTER COLLECTION
B.M. Royal MS. 10 A.II, fol. 14r.

MVSEVM
BRITAN
NICVM

VI. THE WORCESTER COLLECTION
B.M. Royal MS. 10 A.ii, fol. 63v.

VIII. THE 'FRANKFURT' COLLECTION
B.M. Egerton MS. 2901, fol. 3v.

PLATE VII: The 'Cheltenham' Collection

Cheltenhamensis: B.M. Egerton MS. 2819, fol. 86v. Vellum; 10 in. × 7⅛ in. Pp. 98–103.

The 'Cheltenham' Collection is a large and beautifully transcribed work, recording a distinct line of technical development within the 'Worcester' family. Occasional groups of rubricated titles reveal a measure of juristic skill in the arrangement of its subject-matter. A two-fold dependence on the Bamberg-Leipzig group of continental systematic collections and an early member of the primitive 'Worcester' family is fully discussed in the chapters above. Plate VII provides a typical instance of the grouping of rubricated titles, and also reveals the extent of marginal glossing characteristic of this work.

PLATE VIII: The 'Frankfurt' Collection

Francofurtana: B.M. Egerton MS. 2901, fol. 3v. Vellum; 9½ in. × 6¼ in.

This final example is of outstanding interest in recording the growth and elaboration of a decretal collection in the hands of professional canonists. It is a typical folio from a systematic collection, in which both English and continental sources are intermingled. The layers of composition are patent in the very appearance of the manuscript, and in the different hands of the main transcription and the marginal additions: the latter include both glossatorial commentary and further decretals inserted by a later, characteristically English, hand. The growth of the collectors' professional skill is obvious if this example is compared with the extract from the Worcester II Collection provided in Plate I. The 'Frankfurt' Collection has not yet been fully discussed or analysed; nor is it examined in the present study. It is preserved in three manuscripts, including the Egerton MS. 2901, now in the British Museum but belonging at an earlier date to St Maximin in Trier. For details of the 'Frankfurt' manuscripts, see Holtzmann and Kemp, *op. cit.,* p. xiv.

LIST OF WORKS CITED

I. MANUSCRIPTS

CAMBRIDGE: Caius College MS. 28 (17).
Caius College MS. 283 (676).
Pembroke College MS. 72
Peterhouse MSS. 114, 180, 193 and 203.
St John's College MS. 148 (F.11).
Trinity College MS. R.9.17.
Trinity College MS. R.14.9.

DURHAM: Library of the Cathedral Chapter MS. C. III. 1.

LINCOLN: Library of the Cathedral Chapter MS. 121.

LONDON: BRITISH MUSEUM:
Additional MS. 18369.
Additional MS. 24659.
Arundel MS. 490.
Cotton MS. Claudius A. IV.
Cotton MS. Vitellius E. XIII.
Egerton MS. 2819.
Egerton MS. 2901.
Royal MS. 9 E. VII.
Royal MS. 10 A. II.
Royal MS. 10 A. III.
Royal MS. 10 B. IV.
Royal MS. 10 C. IV.
Royal MS. 11 B. II.
Royal MS. 15 B. IV.

LONDON: LAMBETH PALACE:
Lambeth Palace MS. 411.

OXFORD: Bodley MS. 357.
Bodley MS. e. Mus. 249.
Bodley MS. Laud Misc. 527.
Bodley MS. Tanner 8.

KLOSTERNEUBURG:
Klosterneuburg Stiftsbibliothek MS. XXXII. 19.

2. PRINTED SOURCES

A. *Decretal Collections*

Note: The abbreviation an. indicates where a collection has been analysed, without a complete edition of the text.

ABRINCENSIS: an., H. Singer, 'Neue Beiträge über die Dekretalensammlungen vor und nach Bernhard von Pavia', *Sitz.KA.Wien*, CLXXI (1913), pp. 355–400.

ALANUS: an., R. von Heckel, 'Die Dekretalensammlungen des Gilbertus und Alanus', *ZRG., Kan.Abt.*, XXIX (1940).

APPENDIX CONCILII LATERANENSIS: ed., P. Laurens in P. Crabbe, *Concilia omnia tam generalia quam particularia*, II, Cologne (2nd ed., 1551), pp. 386–944.

AUREAEVALLENSIS: an., W. Holtzmann, 'Beiträge zu den Dekretalensammlungen des Zwölften Jahrhunderts', *ZRG., Kan.Abt.*, XVI (1927), pp. 77–115.

BAMBERGENSIS: an., E. Friedberg, *Canonessammlungen*, pp. 84–115.

—. an., W. Deeters, *Die Bambergensisgruppe der Dekretalensammlungen des 12. Jahrhunderts*, Doctoral dissertation: Bonn (1956).

BEROLINENSIS: an., J. Juncker, 'Die Collectio Berolinensis', *ZRG., Kan. Abt.*, XIII (1924), pp. 284–426.

BRUGENSIS: an., E. Friedberg, *Canonessammlungen*, pp. 136–70.

CANTABRIGIENSIS: an., E. Friedberg, *Canonessammlungen*, pp. 5–21.

CASSELANA: an., E. Friedberg, *Canonessammlungen*, pp. 130–6.

CLAUSTRONEOBURGENSIS: ed., F. Schönsteiner, 'Die Collectio Claustroneoburgensis', *Jahrbuch des Stiftes Klosterneuburg*, II (1909), pp. 1–154.

COMPILATIO PRIMA, SECUNDA, etc: an., E. Friedberg, *Quinque Compilationes Antiquae necnon Compilatio Lipsiensis*, Leipzig (1882).

DECRETALES GREGORII IX: ed., E. Friedberg, *Corpus Iuris Canonici*, II, Leipzig (1881).

DERTUSENSIS: an., W. Holtzmann, 'Beiträge zu den Dekretalensammlungen des Zwölften Jahrhunderts', *ZRG., Kan.Abt.*, XVI (1927), pp. 39–77.

EBERBACENSIS: an., W. Holtzmann, 'Die Collectio Eberbacensis', *ZRG., Kan.Abt.*, XVII (1928), pp. 548–55.

GILBERTUS: an., R. von Heckel; see ALANUS, above.

LIPSIENSIS: an., E. Friedberg, *Canonessammlungen*, pp. 115–30; *idem*, *Quinque Compilationes Antiquae necnon Compilatio Lipsiensis*.

PARISIENSIS I: an., E. Friedberg, *Canonessammlungen*, pp. 45–63.

PARISIENSIS II: an., E. Friedberg, *Canonessammlungen*, pp. 21–45.

ST. JOHN'S COLLECTION: an., C. Duggan, 'English Canonists and the Appendix Concilii Lateranensis; with an analysis of the St. John's College, Cambridge, MS. 148', *Traditio*, XVII (1962).

SANGERMANENSIS: an., H. Singer, 'Neue Beiträge über die Dekretalensammlungen vor und nach Bernhard von Pavia', *Sitz.KA.Wien*, CLXXI (1913), pp. 68–354.

P

TANNER: an., W. Holtzmann, 'Die Dekretalensammlungen des 12. Jahrhunderts: 1. Die Sammlung *Tanner*', *Festschrift zur Feier des 200 jährigen Bestehens der Akademie der Wissenschaften in Göttingen, Phil.-Hist.Kl.* (1951), pp. 83–145.

TRINITATIS: an., C. Duggan, 'The Trinity Collection of Decretals and the Early Worcester Family', *Traditio*, XVII, New York (1961), pp. 506–26.

WIGORNIENSIS: an., H. Lohmann, 'Die Collectio Wigorniensis', *ZRG., Kan.Abt.*, XXII (1933), pp. 36–187.

Note: See also C. R. Cheney and W. Holtzmann in List 3, below.

B. *Other Printed Sources*

DECRETUM GRATIANI: ed., E. Friedberg, *Corpus Iuris Canonici*, I, Leipzig (1879).

HOSTIENSIS: *Henrici a Segusio Cardinalis Hostiensis Aurea Summa*, Venice (1605).

ITALIA PONTIFICIA: supplements by W. Holtzmann, 'Kanonistische Ergänzungen zur Italia Pontificia', *Quellen und Forschungen aus italienischen Archiven und Bibliotheken*, XXXVII (1957), pp. 55–102; and XXXVIII (1958), pp. 67–175.

IVO of CHARTRES: 'Ivonis Carnotensis Episcopi Opera Omnia', *Pat.Lat.*, CLXI, cols. 9–1344.

PAPSTURKUNDEN IN ENGLAND: ed., W. Holtzmann, 'Papsturkunden in England', *Abhandlungen*, 3 Vols. (1930, 1935 and 1953).

PAPSTURKUNDEN IN SPANIEN: ed., P. Kehr, 'Papsturkunden in Spanien', *Abhandlungen*, 2 Vols.: I Katalanien (1926); II. Navarre und Aragon (1928).

PAUCAPALEA: ed., J. F. von Schulte, *Die Summa des Paucapalea über das Decretum Gratiani*, Giessen (1890).

PSEUDO-ISIDORE: ed., P. Hinschius, *Decretales Pseudo-isidorianae et Capitula Angilramni*, Leipzig (1863).

REGESTA PONTIFICUM ROMANORUM: ed., P. Jaffé, *Regesta Pontificum Romanorum*, 2 Vols. (2nd ed., G. Wattenbach, S. Löwenfeld, F. Kaltenbruner and P. Ewald, 1885 and 1888).

ROLANDUS: ed., F. Thaner, *Die Summa Magistri Rolandi nachmals Papstes Alexander III*, Innsbruck (1874).

RUFINUS: ed., H. Singer, *Die Summa Decretorum des Magister Rufinus*, Paderborn (1902).

SANCTA CONCILIA: ed., J. D. Mansi, *Sanctorum Conciliorum nova et amplissima collectio*, Florence (1759–98).

SIMON of BISIGNANO: J. Juncker, 'Die Summa des Simon von Bisignano und seine Glossen', *ZRG., Kan.Abt.*, XV (1926), pp. 326–500.

—. T. P. McLaughlin, 'The Extravagantes in the Summa of Simon of Bisignano', *Mediaeval Studies*, XX, Toronto (1958), pp. 167–76.

STEPHEN of TOURNAI: ed., J. F. von Schulte, *Die Summa des Stephanus Tornacensis über das Decretum Gratiani*, Giessen (1891).

3. Select List of Articles and Secondary Works

BABUT, E. CH, *La plus ancienne décrétale*, Paris (1904).

BARRACLOUGH, G., review of KUTTNER, S., *Repertorium der Kanonistik*, in *EHR.*, LIII (1938), pp. 492–5.

BOEHMER, H., *Die Fälschungen Erzbischof Lanfranks von Canterbury*, Leipzig (1902).

BOUARD, A., *Manuel de diplomatique française et pontificale*, II, Paris (1948–9).

BOULET-SAUTEL, M., 'Les Paleae empruntées au droit romain dans quelques manuscrits du Décret de Gratien conservés en France', *Studia Gratiana*, I, Bologna (1953), pp. 147–58.

BRESSLAU, H., *Handbuch der Urkundenlehre für Deutschland und Italien*, 2 Vols., Leipzig (1912 and 1931).

BROOKE, C. N. L., 'Canons of English Church Councils in the Early Decretal Collections', *Traditio*, XIII, New York (1957), pp. 471–80.

BROOKE, Z. N., 'The Effect of Becket's Murder on Papal Authority in England', *CHJ*, II (1928), pp. 213–28.

—. *The English Church and the Papacy from the Conquest to the Reign of John*, Cambridge (1931).

CARLYLE, R. W., and A. J., *A History of Medieval Political Theory in the West*, London and Edinburgh (3rd ed., 1930–6).

CASPAR, E., *Geschichte des Papsttums*, 2 Vols., Tübingen (1930 and 1933).

CHENEY, C. R., *English Bishops' Chanceries, 1100–1250*, Manchester (1950).

—. 'Legislation in the Medieval English Church', *EHR*, L (1935), pp. 193–224 and 385–417.

—. 'Decretals of Innocent III in Paris, B.N. MS. Lat. 3922A', *Traditio*, XI (1955), pp. 149–62.

—. *From Becket to Langton: English Church Government, 1170–1213*, Manchester (1956).

—. 'Three Decretal Collections before Compilatio IV: Pragensis, Palatina I, and Abrincensis II,' *Traditio*, XV (1959), pp. 464–83.

CHENEY, M. (see also HALL, M. G.), 'The Compromise of Avranches of 1172 and the Spread of Canon Law in England', *EHR*, LVI (1941), pp. 177–97.

DUGGAN, C., *Twelfth Century Decretal Collections and their Importance in English History*. Unpublished Ph.D. thesis in the University of Cambridge, 2 Vols. (1954).

—. 'The Trinity Collection of Decretals and the Early Worcester Family', *Traditio*, XVII (1961), pp. 506–26.

—. 'English Canonists and the *Appendix Concilii Lateranensis*; with an Analysis of the St. John's College, Cambridge, MS. 148', *Traditio*, XVII (1962).

FEINE, H. E., *Kirchliche Rechtsgeschichte*, Weimar (1950).

—. 'Gliederung und Aufbau des Decretum Gratiani', *Studia Gratiana*, I (1953), pp. 353–70.

FORCHIELLI, J. and STICKLER, A. M., edd., *Studia Gratiana post octava Decreti saecularia auctore consilio commemorationi Gratianae instruendae edita*, Bonn/Bologna: Institutum Gratianum (1953–proceeding).

FOURNIER, P., 'Yves de Chartres et le droit canonique', *Revue des questions historiques*, LXIII, Paris (1898), pp. 51–98 and 384–405.

—. 'Un tournant de l'histoire du droit', *NRHD*, LXI, Paris (1917), pp. 128–180.

FOURNIER, P. and LE BRAS, G., *Histoire des collections canoniques en Occident depuis les Fausses Décrétales jusqu'au Décret de Gratien*, 2 Vols., Paris (1931–2).

FOREVILLE, R., *L'Église et la Royauté en Angleterre sous Henri II Plantagenet, 1154–89*, Paris (1943).

FOREVILLE, R. and ROUSSET, J., *Du premier Concile du Latran à l'avènement d'Innocent III, 1123–98*, II, Paris (1953): A. Fliche and V. Martin, edd., *Histoire de l'Église depuis les origines jusqu'à nos jours*, IX, ii.

GHELLINCK, J. de, *Le mouvement théologique du XIIe siècle*, Bruges and Paris (2nd ed., 1948).

GIRY, A., *Manuel de diplomatique*, 2 Vols., Paris (1925).

HALL, M. G. (See also CHENEY, M.), *Roger Bishop of Worcester, 1164–79*, unpublished B.Litt. thesis in the University of Oxford (1940).

HAMPE, K., 'Reise nach England', *Neues Archiv*, XXII (1897), pp. 225–86 and 337–415.

HOLTZMANN, W., 'Papst Alexander III und Ungarn', *Ungarische Jahrbücher*, VI (1926), pp. 397–426.

—. 'Krone und Kirche in Norwegen im 12. Jahrhundert', *Deutsches Archiv*, II (1938), pp. 341–400.

—. 'Die Register Papst Alexanders III. in den Händen der Kanonisten', *Quellen und Forschungen aus italienischen Archiven und Bibliotheken*, XXX (1940), pp. 13–87.

—. 'Über eine Ausgabe der päpstlichen Dekretalen des 12. Jahrhunderts', *Nachrichten* (1945), pp. 15–36.

—. 'Die Dekretalen Gregors VIII', *Festschrift für Leo Santifaller: Mitteilungen*, LVIII (1950), pp. 113–24.

—. 'Die Benutzung Gratians in der päpstlichen Kanzlei im 12. Jahrhundert', *Studia Gratiana*, I (1953), pp. 323–50.

—. Review of KUTTNER, S., and RATHBONE, E., *Anglo-Norman Canonists*, in *ZRG., Kan.Abt.*, XXXIX (1953), pp. 465–9.

—. 'La collection "Seguntina" et les décrétales de Clément III et de Célestin III', *Revue d'histoire ecclésiastique*, L (1955).

HOLTZMANN, W., and KEMP, E. W., *Papal Decretals relating to the Diocese of Lincoln in the Twelfth Century*: Lincoln Record Society, XLVII (1954).

HOVE, A. van, *Prolegomena ad Codicem Iuris Canonici*, Malines and Rome (2nd ed., 1945).

—. 'Quae Gratianus contulerit methodo scientiae canonicae', *Apollinaris*, XXI, Vatican City (1948), pp. 12–24.

JUNCKER, J., 'Summen und Glossen', *ZRG., Kan.Abt.*, XIV (1925), pp. 384–478.

KLEWITZ, H. W., 'Kanzleischule und Hofkapelle', *Deutsches Archiv*, IV (1940–1), pp. 224–8.

KNOWLES, D., *Archbishop Thomas Becket: A Character Study* (British Academy Raleigh Lecture, 1949).

—. *The Episcopal Colleagues of Archbishop Thomas Becket*, Cambridge (1951).

KURTSCHEID, B., *Historia Iuris Canonici*, Rome (1951).

KUTTNER, S., 'Zur Frage der theologischen Vorlage Gratians', *ZRG.*, *Kan.Abt.*, XXIII (1934), pp. 243–68.

—. 'Repertorium der Kanonistik, 1140–1234', *Studi e Testi*, LXXI, Vatican City (1937).

—. 'Bernardus Compostellanus Antiquus', *Traditio*, I (1943), pp. 277–340.

—. 'Liber Canonicus. A note on Dictatus Papae c.17', *Studi Gregoriani*, II, Rome (1947), pp. 387–401.

—. 'Notes on a Projected Corpus of Twelfth-Century Decretal Letters', *Traditio*, VI (1948), pp. 345–51.

—. 'De Gratiani opere noviter edendo', *Apollinaris*, XXI (1948), pp. 118–128.

—. 'The Scientific Investigation of Medieval Canon Law: the Need and Opportunity', *Speculum*, XXIV, Cambridge/Mass. (1949), pp. 493–501.

—. 'Graziano: L'Uomo e l'Opera', *Studia Gratiana*, I (1953), pp. 17–29.

—. 'Some Considerations on the Role of Secular Law and Institutions in the History of Canon Law', *Scritti di Sociologia e Politica in Onore di Luigi Sturzo*, II, Bologna (1953), pp. 1–15.

—. 'New Studies on the Roman Law in Gratian's Decretum', *Seminar* (Annual Extraordinary Number of *The Jurist*), XI, Washington (1953), pp. 12–50.

KUTTNER, S., and RATHBONE, E., 'Anglo-Norman Canonists of the Twelfth Century: An Introductory Study', *Traditio*, VII (1951), pp. 279–358.

LE BRAS, G., 'Alger de Liége et Gratien', *Revue des sciences philosophiques et théologiques*, XX (1931), pp. 5–26.

MAITLAND, F. W., *Roman Canon Law in the Church of England*, London (1898).

—. Introduction to translation of O. Gierke, *Political Theories of the Middle Ages*, Cambridge (1900; 1938 imp.).

MOREY, A., *Bartholomew of Exeter*, Cambridge (1937).

—. 'Canonist Evidence in the Case of St. William of York', *CHJ*, X (1952), pp. 352–3.

NAZ, R., ed., *Dictionnaire de droit canonique*, Paris (1935-proceeding).

PEITZ, P. W., 'Dionysius Exiguus als Kanonist', *Schweizer Rundschau*, II (1945–6).

PEITZ, P. W. and EBERS, G., 'Gratian und Dionysius Exiguus', *Studia Gratiana*, I (1953), pp. 51–82.

PLÖCHL, W. M., *Geschichte des Kirchenrechts*, I, Vienna (1954).

PLUCKNETT, T. F. T., 'Maitland's View of Law and History', *LQR*, LXVII (1951), pp. 179–94.

—. *A Concise History of the Common Law*, London (4th ed., 1948).

POOLE, R. L., *Lectures on the History of the Papal Chancery to the time of Innocent III*, Cambridge (1915).

RASHDALL, H., *The Universities of Europe in the Middle Ages*, 3 Vols, revised and edd., F. M. Powicke and A. B. Emden, Oxford (1936).

RATHBONE, E., *The Influence of Bishops and Members of Cathedral Bodies in the Intellectual Life of England, 1066–1216,* unpublished Ph.D. thesis in the University of London (1935).

RATHBONE, E., 'John of Cornwall', *Recherches de théologie ancienne et médiévale,* XVII (1950), pp. 46–60.
(See also KUTTNER, S., and RATHBONE, E., above.)

RE, N. del, *La curia Romana: lineamenti storico-giuridici,* Rome (1952).

SAGMÜLLER, J. B., *Zur Geschichte des päpstlichen Gesetzgebungsrechts,* Rottenburg (1937).

SALTMAN, A., *Theobald Archbishop of Canterbury,* Athlone Press: University of London Historical Studies, 2 (1956).

SANTIFALLER, L., 'Beschreibstoffe im Mittelalter', *Mitteilungen* LXI (1953).

SCHULTE, J. F. von, *Die Geschichte der Quellen und Literatur des canonischen Rechts,* 3 Vols., Stuttgart (1875–7).

SECKEL, E., 'Ueber drei Canonessammlungen des ausgehenden 12. Jahrhunderts', *Neues Archiv,* XXV (1900), pp. 523–5 and 529–31.

STICKLER, A., *Historia Fontium Iuris Canonici,* I, Turin (1950).

THANER, F., 'Ueber Entstehung und Bedeutung der Formel: *Salva sedis apostolicae auctoritate* in den päpstlichen Privilegien', *Sitz.KA.Wien,* LXXI (1872), pp. 807–51.

THORNE, S. E., 'Le droit canonique en Angleterre', *RHD.,* 4th Series, XIII (1934), pp. 499–513.

ULLMANN, W., *Medieval Papalism,* London (1949).

—. 'A Scottish Charter and its Place in Medieval Canon Law', *The Juridical Review,* LXI (1949), pp. 225–41.

—. 'A Forgotten Dispute at Bridlington Priory in its Canonistic Setting', *Yorkshire Archaeological Journal,* XXXVII (1951), pp. 456–73.

—. 'Cardinal Humbert and the Ecclesia Romana', *Studi Gregoriani,* IV (1952), pp. 111–27.

—. 'The Medieval Interpretation of Frederick I's Authentic *Habita*', *Estratto dagli Studi in memoria di Paolo Koschaker: L'Europa e il Diritto Romano,* I, Milan (1953), pp. 101–36.

—. 'The Paleae in Cambridge Manuscripts of the Decretum', *Studia Gratiana,* I (1953), pp. 161–216.

VETULANI, A., 'Gratien et le droit romain', *RHD.,* 4th Series, XXIV (1946–7), pp. 11–48).

—. 'L'Origine des collections primitives de décrétales à la fin du XIIe siècle' *Congrès de Droit Canonique Médiéval,* Louvain (1959), pp. 64–72.

—. 'Le Décret de Gratien et les premiers Décrétistes à la lumière d'une source nouvelle', *Studia Gratiana,* VII (1959).

REGISTER OF DECRETALS CITED

I. Alphabetical List of Decretal Incipits in Appendices I–IV

The following list includes decretals and decretal chapters in the Worcester
II, Belvoir, Canterbury and Rochester Collections, analysed in Appendices
I–IV, above. Conciliar canons are not included. For brevity, the four
collections are identified by their initial letters only.

Abbas Sancti Edmundi: C. III.13.
Accepimus quod plerique: C. I.15; R. 92. Cf. Universalis ecclesie.
Accepta querimonia: R. 144.
Ad audientiam nostram: B. II.3.
Ad audientiam nostram: B. II.7.
Ad aures nostras: W. 6a; B. I.13.1.
Ad aures nostras: C. I.45; R. 73.
Ad aures nostras: R. 114.
Ad aures nostras: R. 135.
Ad aures nostras: R. 150.
Ad hec, cum aliquis: C. I.40e; R. 38e.
Ad hec, cum contingat: C. I.52d.
Ad hec, cum laici: C. I.38c; R. 40d.
Ad hec, de sacerdote: W. 7b; B. I.14.iv.
Ad hec, quia sunt: C. I.59b.
Ad hec, si in una: C. I.42b; R. 46b.
Ad hec, si persona: C. I.20i; R. 37g.
Ad hoc, in beatorum: B. IV.2a; C. I.1a; R. 76.
Ad hoc, si in una: C. I.42b; R. 46b. Cf. Ad hec, si in una.
Ad presentiam nostram: W. 8; B. I.15; C. I.51; R. 64.
Archidiaconis de: C. I.2.
Audita querela: R. 44. Cf. Licet nuntius.
Audivimus quod: B. IV.6.

Casum, quem: R. 104.
Causam principalem: R. 72.
Causam, que inter: R. 60.
Causam, que inter: R. 139.
Causam, que vertitur: C. I.61; R. 67.
Cautum siquidem: W. 10b.; B. I.11b. Cf. Sed pie recordationis.
Ceterum, cum aliquam: W. 4c; B. I.10e; C. I.22l.
Ceterum, si abbatem: W. 5c; B. I.10m; C. I.22f; R. 112f.
Ceterum, si aliquis: C. I.20e.

Clerici, qui: C. I.14; R. 78.
Clericos autem: B. I.12f. Cf. Sicut dignum.
Commisse nobis: B. IV.5.
Communi vita: W. 10c.III; B. I.11c.III.
Coniugatus in: R. 106.
Conquerente nobis: R. 136.
Constitutus apud nos: R. 121.
Consultationibus singulorum: B. II.4a. Cf. Quesitum est siquidem; and
    Singulorum.
Consuluit nos: C. II.5; R. 108.
Consuluit nos: R. 85.
Consuluit nos: R. 105.
Continebatur in litteris: R. 137.
Contingit interdum: R. 59.
Cum aliquibus: C. I.18; R. 69. Cf. Scripsimus.
Cum clerici: C. I.59a; R. 32.
Cum deceat nos: B. IV.8; C. I.7; R. 28.
Cum episcopus: C. I.53; R. 58.
Cum ex defectu: C. I.6.
Cum H. de Dive: C. III.18.
Cum institisset: R. 91.
Cum nos tibi: W. 9; B. I.16.
Cum olim E.: C. III.16.
Cum Romana: R. 84a. Cf. Cum sancta Romana.
Cum sacrosancta (a): W. 11; C. I.42a; R. 46a.
Cum sacrosancta (b): C. II.1a.
Cum sancta Romana: C. III.22. Cf. Cum Romana
Cum Simon clericus: C. I.17.
Cum sint homines: R. 49.
Cum te consulente: R. 71.
Cum teneamur: C. I.33; R. 65.
Cum tibi sit: C. I.21; R. 39.
Cum vos plerumque: C. I.12; R. 27.
Cura pastorali: C. III.5.

De adulteriis: C. I.56g; R. 89f.
De appellationibus: W. 4b; B. I.10i; C. I.22c; R. 112c.
Debitores autem: R. 84e.
De cetero, cum aliqua: C. I.38b; R. 40c.
De cetero, laicos: C. I.56d; R. 89c.
De cetero, si aliquis: B. II.4b; C. I.37b; R. 111b.
Decimas a populo: W. 10c.II; B. I.11c.II.
Decrevit sacer iste: W. 10c.IV; B. I.11c.IV.
De his autem: C. II.1e.
De his sane, qui: C. I.40g.; R. 38g.
De illis autem, qui: R. 147.
De illis, qui: C. III.1.

De monachis: W. 4d; B. I.10b; R. 112i. Cf. Nemo monachos.
Denique quod in fine: C. I.42d; R. 46d. Cf. Cum sacrosancta (a).
De peregrinatione: R. 95b. Cf. Super hoc, quod.
De presbitero autem: C. I.56l; R. 89k.
De quarta vero: C. I.56k; R. 89i.
De sacerdotibus: W. 3b; B. I.9b.III.
De testibus: C. II.1b.
Dilecti filii nostri: B. IV.7; R. 131.
Dilecti filii nostri: C. III.4.
Dilecti filii nostri: C. III.19; R. 117.
Donationes vero: B. II.4c; C. I.37c; R. 111c.

Ea que honestatis: C. III.2.
Eos vero, qui: B. I.12d. Cf. Sicut dignum.
Et si clerici: C. I.56e; R. 89d.
Ex certa quorundam: C. I.30; C. II.2; R. 52.
Ex crebris querimoniis: B. IV.1; C. I.11; R. 33.
Ex frequentibus querelis: C. I.4; R. 34.
Ex insinuatione: C. III.11.
Ex litteris, quas: R. 75.
Ex litteris tue: R. 143.
Ex litteris tuis: R. 149.
Ex litteris vestris: R. 115.
Ex parte N.: R. 122.
Ex parte venerabilis: C. I.3; R. 55.
Ex presentium latoris: C. I.16; R. 36.
Ex presentium latoris: C. I.31; R. 97.
Ex tenore litterarum: C. III.6. Cf. Personas ecclesiarum.

Fraternitatem tuam: W. 10a; B. I.11a.
Fraternitatis tue: C. I.60; R. 51.

Gaudendum est: B. II.8.

Helias iste: C. III.12.

Illas vero terras: W. 6b; B. I.13.II.
Illi quoque non: B. I.12c. Cf. Sicut dignum.
Illi vero, qui: B. I.12b. Cf. Sicut dignum.
Illi vero, qui: B. I.12e. Cf. Sicut dignum.
Illis etiam: B. I.10c. Cf. Meminimus nos.
Illud etiam: B. III.13.
In causis vero: C. I.56i; R. 89h.
Indecorum est: C. I.10; R. 29.
In eminenti: R. 45.
In litteris, quas: C. I.40a; R. 38a.
Insinuatum est: C. I.58; R. 30.

Intelleximus ex parte: C. I.36; R. 41.
Inter cetera, sollicitudinis: W. 2; B. I.9a.
Inter ceteras: C. I.38a; R. 40a.
Item, cum quis: C. I.40d; R. 38d.
Item, quia quesitum: C. II.1f.
Item, si duobus: C. I.42c; R. 46c.
Item, si quis rei: C. I.40c; R. 38c.

Lator presentium R.: C. I.24.
Licet iuxta: R. 83.
Licet nuntius: C. I.47; R. 61. Cf. Audita querela.
Licet preter: C. I.56a; R. 88.
Litteras tue: C. III.21.
Litteris tue: R. 110.

Meminimus fraternitati: C. I.43.
Meminimus nos: W. 5a; B. I.10a; C. I.22h; R. 112h.
Monachi vero: B. I.12h. Cf. Sicut dignum.
Mulieres vel etiam: R. 81. Cf. Cum sacrosancta (b).

Nemo monachos: C. I.22i. Cf. De monachis.
Nosti sicut vir: C. III.8.
Novum exactionis: W. 10c.vi; B. I.11c.vi.
Nulli autem: R. 87.

Officialis pro: B. I.12k. Cf. Sicut dignum.

Parrochianos autem: R. 80.
Personas ecclesiarum: W. 7a; B. I.14.1.
Pervenit ad nos ex parte: C. I.54; R. 53.
Pervenit ad nos quod: B. IV.3; C. I.13; R. 56.
Pervenit ad nos quod: C. I.35; R. 68.
Pervenit ad nos quod: C. I.39.
Pervenit ad nos quod: R. 102.
Porro, si aliqui: R. 82; R. 86.
Porro, si aliquis C. I.20b; R. 37b.
Porro, si clericus: C. I.56h; R. 89g.
Precipimus ut N.: C. I.57; R. 54.
Presbiterum autem: C. I.56m; R. 89l.
Presentium etiam: W. 3a; B. I.9b.ii; C. II.4.
Presentium lator P.: R. 130.
Preterea, de his: B. IV.2b; C. I.1b.
Preterea, illi: B. I.10d; C. I.22k; R. 112k. Cf. Meminimus nos.
Preterea, licet: C. I.40f; R. 38f.
Preterea, super hoc: C. I.41d; R. 42d.
Propositum est: R. 98. Cf. Singulorum.
Provideas attentius: R. 138.
Prudentiam tuam: R. 151.

Qua fronte: R. 118a.
Quamvis simus: C. I.20a; R. 37a.
Quando Romana: R. 132.
Quemlibet autem: C. I.20g; R. 37d.
Querelam A.: C. III.10.
Querelam monachorum: R. 142.
Querelam R.: C. I.49; R. 100.
Quesisti etiam: C. I.52c; R. 47c.
Quesitum est a nobis: R. 145.
Quesitum est siquidem: C. I.37a; R. 111a. Cf. Consultationibus.
Questioni vero: C. II.1c.
Quia vero sollicitudini: C. I.50b.
Quia Willelmus: C. I.55; R. 57.
Quidam intravit: R. 109.
Quod autem parentes: C. I.26b; R. 94b.
Quod quia indignum: B. I.9b.1. Cf. Inter cetera.
Quod si aliquis: W. 5b; C. I.22d; R. 112d.
Quod si aliquis: B. I.14.11. Cf. Personas ecclesiarum.
Quod si clerici: C. I.23b.
Quod si questio: C. I.20d.
Quoniam quesitum: B. II.5.
Quoniam rationis: R. 116.
Quotiens aliqui: C. III.17.

Rediens ad nos: C. I.19; R. 101.
Redolet Anglia: B. II.9.
Relatum est auribus: B. IV.4; C. I.8; R. 35.
Relatum est auribus: C. I.34; C. II.3; R. 74.
Retulit nobis: C. I.50a; R. 63.
Robertus de Ber: B. I.17; C. III.3.

Sabbato vero: C. II.1i.
Sane laborum: W. 10c.1; B. I.11c.1.
Sane, quesitum est: R. 42a.11. Cf. Sicut Romana.
Sane, quia nos: R. 123. Cf. Cum sacrosancta (b).
Sane, si a nobis: R. 40b. Cf. Inter ceteras.
Sane, si his exequendis: C. I.46.
Sane, super eo: C. I.52b; R. 47b.
Scripsimus vobis: C. III.7. Cf. Cum aliquibus.
Scripta vero: W. 5e; B. I.100.
Sed pie recordationis: W. 10b; B. I.11b. Cf. Cautum siquidem.
Sententiam vero: C. I.20h; R. 37e.
Si aliquando ordinatio: R. 125.
Si aliquis parrochianorum: B. I.10k. Cf. Meminimus nos.
Si autem adversa: B. I.10h; C. I.22b; R. 112b. Cf. Meminimus nos.
Si autem id: B. I.10l. Cf. Meminimus nos.
Si autem infra: C. I.41c; R. 42c. Cf. Sicut Romana.

Si autem lis: B. I.10f. Cf. Meminimus nos.
Si clericum vero: B. I.12l. Cf. Sicut dignum.
Sicut ad extirpanda: C. I.5; R. 93.
Sicut dignum: W. 1a; B. I.12a; C. I.23a; R. 48.
Sicut ex tuarum: C. III.20.
Sicut Romana ecclesia: W. 12; B. I.18; C. I.41a; R. 42a.1.
Si de terra: B. IV.9; C. I.62; R. 50.
Significasti nobis: R. 66.
Significasti nobis: R. 140.
Significatum est: B. II.6.
Significatum est: C. I.27; R. 90.
Significatum est: R. 120.
Significavit nobis D.: R. 31.
Significavit nobis T.: R. 119.
Si lis infra: C. I.22m.; R. 112l. Cf. Meminimus nos.
Singulorum consultationibus: C. III.9. Cf. Consultationibus.
Si quis sacerdos: B. III.1–2.
Si vero aliquis: B. I.12i; C. I.23b; R. 79. Cf. Sicut dignum.
Si vero aliquis: C. I.41e. Cf. Preterea, super.
Si vero coram: C. I.56f; R. 89e.
Si vero in secundis: C. I.20f.
Si vero ius: R. 37f. Cf. Quamvis simus.
Si vero puella: R. 84c. Cf. Cum sancta Romana.
Si vero vir: C. I.56c; R. 89b.
Si vir ille: R. 127.
Sollicite cures: R. 43.
Sponsam autem: R. 84d.
Statuimus ut monasteria: W. 10c.v; B. I.11c.iii.
Statuimus ut, si super: W. 10c.vii; B. I.11c.vii.
Subdiaconos autem: C. II.1h.
Suggestum est auribus: C. I.48; R. 62.
Suggestum est auribus: R. 129.
Suggestum est quod: C. III.15.
Super eo autem quod: C. II.1d.
Super eo quesitum: C. I.52a; R. 47a. Cf. Super eo quod quesitum.
Super eo quod: W. 4a; B. I.10g; C. I.22a; R. 112a.
Super eo quod abbas: R. 124.
Super eo quod nos: R. 107.
Super eo quod quesitum: R. 47a. Cf. Super eo quesitum.
Super eo vero: W. 1b; B. I.12g; C. I.41b; R. 42b.
Super eo vero: C. I.20c; R. 37c.
Super eo vero: R. 118b.
Super eo vero: R. 126.
Super hoc quod: C. I.28.i–iii; R. 95a.
Super videlicet: C. I.40b; R. 38b.

Terminum vero: C. II.1g.

Tua fraternitas: R. 146.

Universalis ecclesie: B. II.1. Cf. Accepimus quod.
Utrum autem filii: C. I.56b.
Utrum mulier: R. 103. Cf. De illis, qui.

Veniens ad apostolice: B. II.2. Letter of papal vicar.
Veniens ad apostolice: R. 113.
Veniens ad nos P.: R. 99.
Veniens ad nos R.: C. I.44.
Veniens ad presentiam: R. 148.
Veniens P. lator: C. I.25.
Venit ad audientiam: C. I.29; R. 96.
Verum autem: R. 89a.
Verum, cum alicui: W. 5d; B. I.10n; C. I.22g; R. 112g.
Verum, si appellantes: C. I.22e; R. 112e. Cf. Meminimus no.
Verum, si coram te: B. I.14.III. Cf. Personas.
Videtur nobis: C. I.26a; R. 94a.
Vir aut mulier: R. 84b.
Viris ecclesiasticis: C. I.9; C. I.32; R. 77.

II. Numerical List of Decretals in Appendices I–IV

The following list includes decretals and decretal chapters in the Worcester II, Belvoir, Canterbury and Rochester Collections, analysed in Appendices I–IV, above, and identified by their reference numbers in P. Jaffé, ed., *Regesta Pontificum Romanorum*. It is followed by details of items included in the four collections, but not listed in the *Regesta*, or not yet identified, together with a list of conciliar canons and other miscellaneous chapters.

384: C. I.26; R. 94. Cf. 4920.
3773: R. 128.
4920: C. I.26; R. 94. Cf. 384.
8959: C. I.14; R. 78.
9657: C. III.17.
11398: B. II.3.
11660: B. IV.5.
12020: W. 11; C. I.42; R. 46.
12180: W. 1; B. I.12; C. I.23; R. 48. Cf. 13771.
12201: B. II.8.
12203–4: B. II.9.
12252: B. III.13.

12253: W. 7; B. I.14; C. III.6. Cf. 14146.
12254–5: W. 2–3; B. I.9; B. III.1–2; C. II.4.
12293: W. 12; B. I.18; C. I.41; R. 42.
12412: B. IV.4; C. I.8; R. 35.
12448: B. IV.2; C. I.1.; R. 76. Cf. 14314.
12636: B. II.4; C. I.37; C. III.9; R. 98; R. 111.
12666: R. 116.
12753: C. III.8.

13094: C. I.27; R. 90.
13160: C. I.54; R. 53.
13162: W. 4–5; B. I.10; C. I.22; R. 112.
13163: W. 6; B. I.13. Cf. 14132.
13164: W. 9; B. I.16.
13165: R. 142.
13166: C. I.2; C. I.61; R. 67.
13583: B. II.5.
13729: C. I.53; R. 58.
13739: B. IV. 9; C. I.62; R. 50.
13742: R. 80.
13767: C. III.1; R. 103.
13768–70: C. II.1; cf. R. 81. Cf. 13835.
13771: W. 1; B. I.12; C. I.23; R. 79. Cf. 12180.
13787: R. 127.
13794: C. I.35; R. 68.
13809: C. I.33; R. 65.
13813: C. I.5; R. 93.
13814: B. IV.1; C. I.11; R. 33.
13816: C. I.59; R. 32.
13817: C. I.4; R. 34.
13820: C. I.10; R. 29.
13821: B. IV.3; C. I.13; R. 56.
13822: C. I.12; R. 27.
13823: C. I.34; C. II.3; R. 74.
13824: C. I.50; R. 63.
13825: C. I.57; R. 54.
13829: B. IV.8; C. I.7; R. 28.
13831: R. 139.
13835: C. II.1; R. 123. Cf. 13768–70.
13838: R. 149.
13845: R. 143.
13865: R. 114.
13868: R. 59.
13873: W. 10; B. I.11.
13870: R. 129.
13874: R. 42.
13878: C. I.38; R. 40. Cf. 14346.
13890: R. 122.
13893: C. III.5.
13900: C. I.31; R. 97.
13901: R. 102.
13902: C. I.19; R. 101. Cf. 14159.

13903: C. I.28; R. 95. Cf. 13907 and 13916.
13904: C. I.27.
13907: C. I.28; R. 95. Cf. 13903 and 13916.
13908: R. 87.
13911: C. I.16; R. 36.
13913: C. I.48; R. 62.
13915: C. I.40; R. 38. Cf. 13921 and 14219.
13916: C. I.28; R. 95. Cf. 13903 and 13907.
13917: C. I.43.
13920: cf. 14027.
13921: C. I.40; R. 38. Cf. 13915 and 14219.
13924: C. I.17.
13930: B. I.17; C. III.3. Cf. 14228.
13932: R. 60.
13934: R. 138.
13946: C. I.52; R. 47. Cf. 13948–9.
13947: C. III.21.
13948–9: C. I.52; R. 47. Cf. 13946.
13950: C. I.36; R. 41.
13976: R. 71.
13978: B. IV.6.
13982: W. 8; B. I.15; C. I.51; R. 64.
13983: R. 91.
13984: R. 144.
13988: C. I.25.
13990: cf. R. 125. Cf. 13992, 13996 and 14181.
13991: C. I.21; R. 39.
13992⎤ cf. R. 125. Cf. 13990 and
13996⎦ 14181.
14004: R. 132.
14005: C. II.5; R. 108.
14012: R. 49.
14023: B. IV.7; R. 131.
14025: R. 82; R. 85–6.
14027: R. 66. Cf. 13920 and 14234.
14029: R. 146.
14032: R. 137.
14035: C. I.18; C. III.7; R. 69.
14043: R. 147.
14058: R. 99.
14061: R. 109.

14066: C. I.60; R. 51.
14073: R. 124.
14075: R. 126.
14085: C. III.4.
14087: C. I.30; C. II.2; R 52.
14091: C. I.56; R. 88–9.
14097: C. III.15.
14104: R. 106.
14107: R. 140.
14120: R. 130.
14126: C. III.22; R. 84.
14129: R. 115.
14131: C. III.13.
14132: W. 6; B. I.13. Cf. 13163.
14137: R. 113.
14138: R. 136.
14139: R. 43.
14140: C. I.55; R. 57.
14142: R. 75.
14143: C. I.47; R. 44; R. 61.
14146: W. 7; B. I.14; C. III.6. Cf. 12253.
14151: R. 107.
14152 ⎫
14154 ⎬ C. I.20; R. 37.
14156 ⎭
14159: C. I.19; R. 101. Cf. 13902.
14165: R. 148.
14166: R. 110.

14178: R. 105.
14181: cf. R. 125. Cf. 13990, 13992 and 13996.
14214: C. I.29; R. 96.
14215: C. I.44.
14218: C. I.24.
14219: C. I.40; R. 38. Cf. 13915 and 13921.
14222: B. II.6
14223: B. II.7.
14224: R. 31.
14228: B. I.17; C. III.3. Cf. 13930.
14234: cf. R. 66. Cf. 13920 and 14027.
14267: B. II.1; C. I.15; R. 92.
14312: R. 118.
14313: C. I.39.
14314: B. IV.2; C. I.1; R. 76. Cf. 12448.
14315: R. 83.
14317: C. I.3; R. 55.
14346: C. I.38; R. 40. Cf. 13878.
14350: R. 45.
14963: R. 121.
14964: R. 119.
14965: R. 150.
15171: C. III.2.
15185: R. 145.
17019: R. 151.

Decretals or decretal chapters not listed in the *Regesta*, or not yet identified:

Canterbury Collection:

I. 6, 9 and 32, 45, 46, 49 and 58.
III. 10, 11, 12, 16, 18, 19 and 20.

Rochester Collection:

30, 72, 73, 77, 100, 104, 117, 120 and 135.

Conciliar canons:

Theobald's Council, 1151: R. 70.
Council of Tours, 1163: B. I.1–8; C. III.4; R. 141.
Council of Westminster, 1175: B. III.1–20.
Third Lateran Council, 1179: C. IV; R. 1–26.
See also B. III.21: 'Ex concilio Spanensi.'

The Belvoir Collection also includes one letter from the papal vicar, Walter of Albano: B. II.2; and the Rochester Collection includes two patristic texts: R. 133, Augustine; and R. 124, Ambrose.

Concordance with Holtzmann's Analyses[1]

The following tables collate the system of numeration adopted in this volume for the Belvoir, Canterbury and Rochester Collections with that hitherto used by Professor Holtzmann, whose numbers are placed under the heading WH in the columns below.

Belver.

	WH
Part I	
1–18	1–18
Part II	
1–9	19–27
Part III	
Proemium	28
1–3	29–31
4–5	32
6–21	33–48
Part IV	
1–9	49–57

Cantuar.

Part I	Part I
1–58	1–58a
59	58b–c
60–2	59–61
Part II	
1–5	62–6
Part III	Part II
1–22	1–22
Part IV	
Lateran canons	23cc.1–25

Roff.

1–132	1–132a
133	132b
134	132c
135–51	133–49

[1] I am indebted to Professor Holtzmann for his kindness in letting me print this concordance. His recent article, 'Zu den Dekretalen bei Simon von Bisignano', *Traditio*, xviii (1962), pp. 450–9, appeared too late for use in this study, but his discussion of the St. Florian Collection (*ibid.*, pp. 451–2) supports the brief reference to that collection on p. 131, above.

Index

This index does not include the major themes or topics which recur throughout the volume, such as canon law, the Papacy, decretals, decretal collections and so forth. The decretal items in the Appendices are also omitted, being listed separately in alphabetical and numerical registers, pp. 203-11.